The Match of My Life

The Match of My Life

BOB HOLMES

The Kingswood Press

First published in Great Britain in 1991
Reprinted 1992
by The Kingswood Press
Michelin House, 81 Fulham Road, London SW3 6RB

Copyright © 1991 ARMS

A CIP catalogue record for this book
is available from the British Library
ISBN 0 413 66260 8

Phototypeset by Deltatype Ltd, Ellesmere Port
Printed in Great Britain
by Clays Ltd, St. Ives plc

Contents

Acknowledgements

In the writing of this book I have been assisted by a great number of organisations and individuals, among whom the *Daily Star* must receive a special acknowledgement for their help and consideration in all respects. Singular mention must also be made of Jim Hossack and John Maddocks, above all others.

Thanks are also due to the *Evening Standard*; and to Steve Acteson, Steve Andresier, Geoff Bennett, John Carroll, John Cullen, John Dee, Bob Denman, John Docherty, John Evans, Keith Farnsworth, Jim Gorman, Duncan Hamilton, Bob Higgins, Doug Jackson, Mike King, Willie Kings, Joe Lancaster, Tony Pritchett and Roger Wash. Thanks and apologies alike to Malcolm Allison, Ron Atkinson, Terry Butcher, Jimmy Hill, Denis Howell, Jimmy Johnstone, Wilf Mannion, Steve Perryman, Martin Peters, Alan Robinson and Joe Royle, all of whom contributed to the project but whose matches could not be squeezed in for reasons of time and space.

The publishers would like to thank the following for their kind permission to reproduce quotes and extracts: Grafton Books, from *No Half Measures* by Graeme Souness; Viking, from *Billy* by Billy Bingham; Mainstream Publishing, from *The Only Game* by Roddy Forsyth; and BBC Books, from *The Great Derbies* by Archie McPherson. Also the following for their kind permission to reproduce these photographs: the Press Association (1, 3, 7, 9, 11, 13, 14, 15, 25, 31, 36); Express Newspapers (2, 4, 6, 8, 10, 16, 17, 19–24, 26, 28, 29, 30, 33, 34, 35, 37–41); Colorsport (cover, of George Best, Emlyn Hughes, Bobby Moore and Denis Law, 5, 12, 18); Sport & General (27); *Daily Mirror* (32); and Tommy Hindley (42).

Preface

by Bob Holmes

Perhaps the best way to introduce this collection of memorabilia is to make a confession. It is part of football folklore that fans often wonder whether the report they read in the paper was written by someone who had attended a different game to the one they saw. Well, of the fifty-five matches in this book, the 'reporter' did not attend more than a dozen, and one or two of those were seen from the terraces, the touchline, and as a 3-year-old on his Dad's shoulders.

So do not expect precise accounts; traditional match reports have a life span of no more than twenty-four hours anyway, so attempts to rehash the details a decade or two later would certainly be doomed to failure. No, this is a collection of essays describing some of British football's finest moments as seen through the occasionally rheumy eyes of the men who made them. In many cases, their recollections were less than comprehensive and their memory sold them the odd dummy, but always there was an essence of what went on, an essence which, with the aid of books, cuttings, videos, club historians and hindsight, has enabled me to stitch together the following accounts. Some of the players to whom I spoke may be surprised that our snatched conversations as they hurried off to take training have been sprinkled on to such a broad canvas. I just hope you appreciate the end product, and thank you for your time and trouble.

Most of the great British players are here, and many of the great matches; if there are gaps, it is because we could not reach either the players or the background material in time. Nevertheless, it has been a great privilege to chat to the legends of our national pastime and to be linked with such a worthy cause as Football against MS – a match that football is honoured to play a small part in winning.

Foreword

by Sir Stanley Matthews

No football fan will be able to put this book down. It is a wholehearted celebration of the great moments in the game, vividly recalled by the men who made them and colourfully related in a way that will make you think you were there, even if the match took place before you were born.

For old-timers like myself, a feast of memories will come flooding back from days gone by, while youngsters will remember every kick of recent matches involving their current heroes. Grandchildren will have a great chance to check whether those tales their grandad told them were a little bit exaggerated, while dads will be able to relive their youth by poring over the game's last golden age in the late 1960s.

But whether you start with Ivor Allchurch and end with Alex Young, or dip in and out to discover George Best running rings around Benfica, Gordon Banks saving from Pele, Geoff Hurst's hat-trick in 1966, Pat Jennings defying the Spaniards in Spain and Jim Baxter gaining sweet revenge over the 'auld enemy' at Wembley, you are in for a great read.

The biographical bits help introduce the older players to the younger reader and come up with the occasional gem – Baxter being bought for £2 – 10 – 0, for instance. It is a world-class team of fifty players, but the stories of managers, commentators and a referee help give a wider perspective.

Too often in the last few years, those of us in football have had to remind ourselves what a great game we enjoy;

this book helps us to do just that. It is an honour to be asked to kick off a publication that is part of such a worthy cause, and I wish it every success. If the author was not at all of the matches, it could only have been because they were sold out – which is what this book will be very soon, I am sure.

Ivor Allchurch

Wales 2 Hungary 1
World Cup finals, Pool 3 play-off, Solna, Sweden, 17 June
1958

Born 16 October 1929. Joined Swansea straight from school and turned down many offers from bigger clubs before signing for Newcastle United in 1958 for £28,000. Idolised on Tyneside but League and Cup honours eluded him before he returned to Swansea via Cardiff City and retired in 1967. Played 68 times for Wales and scored 251 League goals. Still turned out at 50 – for Pontardawe in the Second Division of the Welsh League. A true gentleman of the game, he was never booked in his career and was awarded the MBE for services to soccer.

Just as Rugby Union once boasted a fly-half 'factory' in South Wales, soccer, too, possessed an élite production line. West of the rugby heartlands and overlooking the Bristol Channel, it was out on a bit of a limb, but the finished products were such that for a brief spell in the late 1950s the secondary schools of Swansea ensured that soccer, and not rugger, was THE game in Wales.

Indeed, but for a moment's hesitation in the Wales defence and a late goal from the 17-year-old Pele – his first in the World Cup – soccer may have become a much bigger part of the fabric of Welsh society. Brazil's 1–0 quarter-final win in Sweden in 1958, however, ended the fairy tale, and Wales have not been back to the final stages since. But the memory of the Principality's finest footballing hours remain undimmed for the legendary likes of Ivor Allchurch.

'I think it was the greatest side Wales has ever had,' says the famous inside forward. 'We had tremendous players, great team-work, terrific enthusiasm . . . it was all there. And we gave Brazil one of their hardest games. Who knows what might have happened if we'd hung on in there? As it was, the 2–1 win over Hungary was probably my greatest memory – not least because I scored with a thirty-five-yard volley! So it wasn't a bad performance for us to beat the mighty Magyars and lose to perhaps the greatest of the Brazilian sides. But it must be said,' adds Allchurch with the modesty that was his hallmark, 'the Hungarians were not quite what they were.'

The Hungarian uprising had decimated the magical side that had twice destroyed England in 1953–54, but the remnants were deemed strong enough to deal with Wales – even though they drew 1–1 when the two countries met in their pool in the finals. But since that fighting performance, when the great John Charles had headed a memorable equaliser, Wales had gone off the boil and were themselves held to draws by Mexico and Sweden. Hungary, still capable of the slick pass and devastating thrust, were overwhelming favourites to reach the last eight – so much so that only 2,832 people turned up to watch in Solna's Rasunda Stadium.

'The Swedes did not seem to rate us that highly,' says Allchurch. 'When we played them, they had already qualified and rested some of their best players. We got the point we wanted but had 'keeper Jack Kelsey to thank for a marvellous display.'

Perhaps the hosts remembered how Wales had scraped into the final stages thanks to politics and the luck of the draw. Having finished as runners-up to Czechoslovakia in their qualifying group, Wales were in fact eliminated. But when Israel 'won' the Asia–Africa group after their opponents, Turkey, Egypt, Sudan and Indonesia, had all withdrawn, FIFA decreed that no country apart from the hosts and the holders could reach the final stages without playing a match. A draw was then held between the runners-up from all the groups and Wales were fortunate enough to be pulled out of the hat to meet Israel in a two-leg play-off. Comfortably winning both matches by 2–0, Wales thus ensured that all four home countries reached the World Cup finals for the first time. Relishing a second chance against the Hungarians, Wales were out to make their own indelible mark on the competition.

With only the goal-keeper Groscis, defender Bozsik and the legendary Hidegkuti, who was 38 and later dropped, left of the 1954 runners-up, Hungary resorted to rough-house tactics to upset the Welshmen and John Charles in particular. Only released by Juventus at the last minute, Charles had made a massive impact in Sweden, having already established himself elsewhere on the continent as one of the giants of the game. His header in the earlier pool match ensured that he would be even more closely marked in the play-off and, with some lenient refereeing from a Soviet official, the 'Gentle Giant' was subjected to some savage treatment. But while the Hungarians had done their homework on Charles, they neglected the other Swansea-reared stars and were particularly surprised by the class of Allchurch and the Spurs wingers Terry Medwin and Cliff Jones.

'They never expected us to play like we did,' says the inside forward, whose own coruscating skills, wondrous body-swerve and sharp shooting had made the Vetch Field a magnet for scouts from all the top clubs in Division One. Billy McCandless, his old manager, once described him as, 'One of the truly greats . . . when he cares to take his jacket off.' However, Allchurch, whose brother Len also played for Wales, was a home-loving man and even turned down a move to Stan Cullis's Wolves. 'I didn't like the area,' he explained to incredulous reporters. 'Anyway, we have a great bunch of lads down here, and I think we can bring First Division football to Swansea.'

Thanks to injuries and an inevitable exodus, the Swans

failed to achieve it in the 1950s but the Golden Boy was determined to make the most of a rare chance to shine on the world stage – even if the ground was almost empty. To the delight of a global audience, Allchurch, of the golden locks and quicksilver skills, revealed his full repertoire to unhinge one of the tournament favourites. Hungary had taken the lead through the brilliant Tichy after 33 minutes but were on the receiving end of one of the goals of the tournament ten minutes into the second half.

'It was one of the best I ever scored,' says Allchurch. 'A volley from about thirty-five yards is the sort you always remember wherever you score them but, when it brings you level in a World Cup play-off, it's a bit special. I don't think I ever scored a more important one in my career. If that was the outstanding moment for me, the match was memorable, too, for the spirit in the side. Nobody fancied us but ourselves. And we refused to lie down. We had a lot of class, too, and when they started getting rough, we knew we had worried them. It was a sure sign.

'Their 'keeper, the great Grosics, had a bit of a nightmare, too, and when he made a mess of a clearance, Terry Medwin nipped in to score the winner. I'll never forget the feeling among the team. There was no way we were going to lose it after that despite what the Hungarians threw at us, and it was quite a lot.' Sipos was eventually sent off for a foul on Hewitt, and Wales had made it to the quarter-finals.

England and Scotland had gone out, but Ireland had also made it to the last eight where the giants of the game were lying in wait. Brazil stood in Wales's path and, after another gallant display without the injured Charles, the dragon eventually bowed to the Black Pearl – Pele. But it had been a wonderful tournament for Wales and for Allchurch. The Swansea star, who was soon to join Newcastle, had finally taken his jacket off.

Wales: Kelsey, Williams, Hopkins, Sullivan, M. Charles, Bowen, Medwin, Hewitt, J. Charles, Allchurch, Jones.

Scorers: Allchurch, Medwin.

Hungary: Groscis, Matrai, Sarosi, Bozsik, Sipos, Kotasz, Budai, Bencsis, Tichy, Bundzsak, Fenyvesi.

Scorer: Tichy.

Ossie Ardiles

Argentina 3 Holland 1 (aet)
World Cup final, Buenos Aires, 25 June 1978

Born August 3 1952 in Cordoba. Rose from Red Star boys team to Huracan and Argentine national side for whom he won 56 caps. A cultured midfielder who, along with Ricky Villa, broke the mould of British transfers when he joined Spurs just after helping his country to win the 1978 World Cup. A tiny figure but a towering talent, he became a great favourite at White Hart Lane. Took a 'sabbatical' during the Falklands War and joined Paris St Germain. Returned to Tottenham for the twilight of his career before going into management at Swindon and then Newcastle.

According to a famous line from Chas and Dave, whose 1981 Spurs Cup final song reached the Top Ten, 'Ossie's going to Wembley, his knees have gone all trembly.' Three years earlier, a less worldly-wise Ossie found himself playing in the World Cup final on home soil. The knees? 'Oh, no problem,' he smiles. 'But one ankle was twisted and the stomach full of butterflies.'

The tension surrounding the 1978 final in Buenos Aires was unbearable for armchair neutrals in Hemel Hempstead, so just what it must have been like for a member of the home team to have to spend the last half-hour plus extra-time on a tormented bench next to a chain-smoking manager is impossible to comprehend. But that is only half the story.

Ardiles is a sensitive man, an intellectual even, who was at an impressionable age when Argentina were promised the eleventh World Cup as long ago as 1966. The boy Ardiles knew then he would be in his prime in 1978 and, although too modest to admit it, had a place on football's premier stage at the back of his mind ever since. But the ruling *junta* had put the dream in jeopardy; for a nation that had not come close to capturing the ultimate prize since losing to neighbours Uruguay in the 1930 final, it was a chance that could not be missed. 'Losing the right to stage the finals was something that could not be allowed to happen,' was a view shared by Ardiles and every other Argentinian, aspiring player or not.

The generals did their best to blow it, however, their behaviour arousing fears among even apolitical footballers as to the host nation's ability to stage the event. There was open talk of a boycott – Johan Cruyff declined to attend – and the president of the Argentine World Cup organising committee was assassinated by guerrillas. Fortunately, sanity prevailed, the left-wing Mononeros group declaring that football was 'OK' as it was 'a working-class sport', and the generals deciding not to risk any further wrath among the populace. The World Cup was therefore deemed a bigger issue than the disappearance of thousands of political opponents.

After all that, Argentina's footballers did not deserve the toughest group in the competition, but France, Italy and Hungary were not their only problems; many of their stars were playing in Europe and were somewhat estranged. For that reason, manager Cesar Menotti decided not to use them, with one exception. Mario Kempes had made no impact as a 19-year-old in the 1974 finals but had learned much playing in the Spanish League for Valencia. Menotti saw the powerful Kempes as the ideal executioner who could capitalise on the quick brain of a diminutive, almost dainty, midfielder from Huracan. His name was Osvaldo Ardiles.

The combination dealt effectively with both Hungary and France with the aid of some rough-house tactics and controversial refereeing, but the lightweight Ardiles was getting the brunt of the retaliation for his own team-mates' rugged approach. In a 0–1 defeat by Italy, Ossie was left holding his face after a clash with Italian hatchet-man Benetti but he recovered to supply the pass for Kempes's clinching goal against Poland in the second phase. But a 0–0 draw with Brazil, who had beaten Peru 3–0, left his ankle only loosely tethered, and he hobbled off after half an hour. The result had not appeared disastrous until those bitter South American rivals boosted their goal tally to six with a 3–1 win over Poland.

Having insisted – much to the understandable chagrin of Brazil – that their remaining match kicked off after their neighbours', Argentina knew exactly what they had to do to reach the World Cup final: score at least four times and win by three clear goals. All Ardiles had to do was declare himself fit, but he could not. But six goals, with a couple from Kempes, were more than enough against a 'keeper, Quiroga, who was born in Argentina. The cynics had a field day, with one Brazilian claiming: 'If Brazil had beaten Poland 50–0, Argentina would have won 52–0!'

None of that, however, worried the 77,260 who squashed into the Estadio Antonio Liberti 'Monumental' in Buenos Aires for the final, like corned beef in a can of Fray Bentos. Not until it took seven minutes for their heroes to take the field. Psychology ruled, it seemed, which was tough on countries as diverse as South Africa and China, who were paying through the satellite nose for the privilege of watching it live. But the delay was meant to be even tougher on the orange-shirted Dutchmen who were left watching the tunnel anxiously during their kick-in. When this gross act of gamesmanship was finally ended, the hosts were greeted with the now-obligatory ticker-tape reception but immediately took exception to the light and perfectly acceptable plaster cast being worn by René van der Kerkhof.

It was ten more minutes before a kick-off could be negotiated. Even then the whistle was blown by Signor Sergio Gonella, a late replacement for Israel's Abraham

Klein whom the hosts did not want because of Holland's political ties with Israel. Amid all these shenanigans, Ardiles was an agonised observer, concerned only with being ready for the match of his life. He made it. Just.

'It cost us a bit to settle into it,' he admits, as Holland, denied by West Germany four years earlier, were determined not to let this one slip. Without Cruyff and without their customary self-control, they played it tough from the outset. The delay had done little for their tempers, and four players – two from each side – were booked.

'I had been very doubtful,' says Ardiles, 'and was soon suffering.' But the pain suddenly disappeared in the 38th minute. Ardiles combined with Leopoldo Luqué to send Kempes through for the opener. 'I played a small part in it,' is all he acknowledges. 'Actually, I don't remember much about the game.' He remembers being substituted on the hour, his ankle giving way at 1–0, and he remembers Holland 'applying a lot of pressure in the second half.' He also remembers 'conversations with Johan Neeskens which were not exactly friendly. He was marking me and could speak Spanish and Italian. We talked a lot,' he chuckles.

Gradually, the Dutch began to weave their traditional masterpieces but were already rueing a miss by Rensenbrink just before the break. It was the best chance of a match which was simultaneously within their grasp and beyond their reach. But Argentina were worried by the amount of Dutch possession. 'The tension on that bench was unbelievable,' says Ardiles. Menotti's outpourings rivalled those of a small chimney. An equaliser duly arrived from the substitute Dick Nanninga, who headed in a cross from René van der Kerkhof with just seven minutes left on the clock and Ardiles almost at the end of his tether. 'I couldn't bear to look at times, but the crowd lifted me – they were tremendous, the atmosphere electric.'

Rensenbrink, immortality beckoning, somehow

contrived to hit the post from five yards with as many seconds remaining, and Holland were never the same in extra-time. Kempes hared around as if on skates to the Dutchmen's clogs and, when he slid past three men to lash a rebound past the valiant Jongbloed, he effectively decided the issue. It was his sixth goal of an outstanding tournament. There was still time for Kempes to scythe through the despairing Dutch once more to let in Bertoni for the clincher. Delirium on the field, bedlam in the stands but, Ardiles insists, 'on the bench the overwhelming feeling was relief. Relief for the ordeal we had gone through.' But he leapt to his feet with the rest of them. He just did not expect to land at White Hart Lane.

Argentina: Fillol, Olguin, Galvan, Passarella, Tarantini, Ardiles, Gallego, Kempes, Bertoni, Luqué, Ortiz.

Subs: Larrosa (Ardiles), Houseman (Ortiz).

Scorers: Kempes 2, Bertoni.

Holland: Jongbloed, Jansen, Brandts, Krol, Poortvliet, Haan, W. van der Kerkhof, Neeskens, R. van der Kerkhof, Rep, Rensenbrink.

Subs: Suurbier (Jansen), Nanninga (Rep).

Scorer: Nanninga.

Jimmy Armfield

Everton 4 Liverpool 4 (aet)
FA Cup fifth round replay, Goodison Park, 20 February
1991

*Born 21 September 1935. Played for Lancashire Schools at both
soccer and rugby before signing amateur forms for Blackpool in
1951. Originally a right-winger, he found himself in the shadow
of Stanley Matthews and so switched to right-back on turning
professional in 1954. Played a club record 568 League games,
won nine Under-23 caps and made 43 appearances for England,
captaining his country 15 times. Voted best full-back in the
world during the 1962 World Cup in Chile. Managed Bolton
Wanderers and Leeds United during the 1970s but now works as
a broadcaster and reporter.*

'It was like a boxer against a fighter; Liverpool had the
class but Everton kept getting up off the floor. Four times
Liverpool had them down for counts of nine, but never
ten, and each time Everton got up to fight on. It was a
classic. I have not seen a better game for a long, long time.'
So said Jimmy Armfield whose inter-round summaries
between the live commentary of Alan Green and Mike
Ingham will long be remembered by Radio Five listeners.
'If I was picking a match I had played in,' said the former
England full-back and captain, 'I would probably go for
the time England beat Scotland 9–3 at Wembley because
that doesn't happen every day. But, as a broadcaster, I
have to go for this one. I'll never forget it.'
   The teams had drawn 0–0 at Anfield on the previous
Sunday and, inevitably, it was a game tinged with
controversy. Everton appeared to be denied a penalty
when Pat Nevin was tripped by Gary Ablett; the Blues

protested long and hard, but to no avail. Kenny Dalglish later referred to the incident as 'the goal-kick' and 'the derby tackle'. At the other end, Neville Southall had to make a tremendous save from Jan Molby. It had not been the greatest derby or Cup-tie, but it set the scene perfectly for the replay.

Liverpool still led the table by 2 points from Arsenal, while Everton, in belated response to Howard Kendall's return, had eased away from the lower reaches. With not a lot to play for in the League apart from pride, they did not want to lose to their neighbours. But then they never do. Goodison was packed for the occasion and already resounding to that unique Merseyside derby din which the incessant rain could not dilute. Dalglish, perhaps bowing to the growing clamour for the return of Peter Beardsley, had restored the England man and left David Speedie on the bench. Kendall brought left-back Andy Hinchcliffe back after injury, but left out midfielder Stuart McCall, with Mike Newell playing alongside Graeme Sharp up front.

Everton soon reminded Ian Rush of the respect in which they hold players who have almost a goal-a-game record against them with two rugged challenges. The fans were left wondering what sort of game they were witnessing with two electrifying end-to-end exchanges. 'Invariably, these derby games are tight, low-scoring affairs,' says Armfield, 'but this one felt different.' Beardsley, justifying his recall and his manager's request to find the target, had a long-range shot parried by Southall who then brilliantly blocked Rush's lightning strike on the rebound. Everton stormed down the field only to be beaten back again, and the nearest the home side came to scoring was when Nevin's left-foot shot was held by a diving Bruce Grobbelaar near the post. Then Barnes hit the side-netting.

After 32 minutes Everton skipper Kevin Ratcliffe allowed Rush to whip past him and then round Southall before unleashing a shot that was brilliantly cleared off the line by the fast-retreating Hinchcliffe. The ball fell to Beardsley who lashed it home. With Barnes now finding space and looking dangerous, further Liverpool goals seemed likely. Southall once had to come out as a sweeper and then fashioned a fabulous reflex save from Barnes, only to find that the winger had been ruled off-side. It was already pulsating stuff, and the Goodison crowd sensed that the Blues were in there battling. But Liverpool deserved their half-time lead.

'Even at 1–0, there was a special buzz to this one,' says Armfield. 'But no one could have imagined what was to come.' It took Everton only two minutes to get back, and the tone was set. Hinchcliffe sent a long, teasing cross into the heart of the Liverpool defence and Sharp, rising between two defenders, got in a powerful header from close range. Grobbelaar, groping desperately, got both hands to it but was unable to prevent it going in. It was Sharp's first for nine matches and only his seventh of the season. Everton were grateful, Liverpool unperturbed. Both teams upped the pace.

Everton should have taken the lead when Nevin, after a jinking run, cut inside and, when Ablett and Nicol got in each other's way, seized upon the loose ball only to put a lob over the bar with Grobbelaar stranded. Newell then volleyed wide, and it was left to Beardsley of all people to show where the net was. Left out for weeks because of his lack of goals, the former Newcastle star produced a strike of the highest quality – and out of nothing. Gaining possession in the middle of the Everton half, he cut inside, circumnavigated three defenders and then let fly with a rasping, rising drive that just curled beyond Southall's outstretched fingers. It was a goal fit to grace any Cup final.

But Everton would not be denied and were level almost immediately, although they had Steve Nicol to thank for it. After a towering punt from Southall had reached the edge of the Liverpool box, the defender, apparently oblivious to

Grobbelaar's presence alongside, tapped the ball back towards his own line and a grateful, gleeful Sharp ran it home. 'It was a perfect illustration of the fighter and boxer,' says Armfield. 'Liverpool took the first half, but Everton were stronger in the second and deserve credit for the way they put their opponents under pressure and forced them into two errors.'

Barnes had seen little of the ball in the early part of the second half but still looked capable of snatching it for the champions. Liverpool had possibly reckoned without Everton's tenacity and found it difficult to create clear-cut openings. But did they need to, with Barnes and Rush? Molby centred and Rush, predator extraordinary, put a glancing header past Southall for his 24th goal against Everton, most of them against his Welsh colleague who, during that time, had been just about the hardest to beat in the business. 'Surely that must be it. Everton won't come back from this,' Armfield said in the commentary box. It sounded like a reasonable assumption.

But in a last, despairing gamble, Kendall sent Tony Cottee on for Nevin. Somehow, you felt, it was only a gesture. Liverpool do not allow teams to come from behind twice, let alone three times. But with Liverpool fans whistling and Evertonians assuming their resigned looks, McCall clipped on a McDonald pass and the fresh poacher's legs of Cottee reached it between Ablett's desperate lunge and Grobbelaar's frantic grasp. It was his first touch. Three-all! Kendall & Co. were off the bench, Goodison was in uproar. There was a minute left.

Like the great heavyweight encounters, the moment one contestant landed a blow, the other stormed back straight away, and this was now in the Ali-Frazier league. No sooner had Everton delivered than Liverpool were on the attack once more and, after Southall had twice saved brilliantly, Barnes curled in a twenty-yard shot from a wide angle that was sheer perfection. It had to be: it beat Southall. Barnes had a chance to make it five, and

Liverpool were still playing superb football. 'They were the boxers, the stylists, and Everton the hungrier fighters,' says Armfield. 'By this stage it could have been very difficult from a commentary point of view as you run the risk of repeating yourself, but what I heard from my colleagues was top-class. It was an exhilarating evening all round.'

Stuart McCall, the Everton substitute who knows what it is like to score twice in a Cup final (1989) and be on the losing side, drove narrowly over. But Liverpool were very much on top again and still playing scintillating stuff. The odds were now very much that McCall would lose again tonight. 'At 4–3, I remember looking from the commentary position at the home fans seated in the stand,' says Armfield. 'Their appearance was as if there had been a death in the family. You could tell that, after a great battle, they felt it was finally curtains for their team.'

But then Liverpool gave the ball away, Jan Molby's back-pass being allowed to slip through by Glenn Hysen, although it did not possess the legs to reach Grobbelaar. To gasps from the scarcely believing crowd, Cottee nipped through and stuck it home between Grobbelaar's legs. 'The change in the Everton fans' reactions at 4–4 was incredible,' says Armfield. 'They were instantly transformed, standing on their feet and chairs, and had gone from agony to ecstasy. It was quite a moving moment. Prior to that they were so emotionally drained; I really don't think they could take any more.'

Neither could the players. That was the last of the scoring for the night, but even more drama was to follow when Dalglish resigned two days later, before the replay, which Everton won. 'Perhaps that was the final straw,' suggests Armfield. 'There is only so much a man can take.' Everton and Liverpool had handed out quite a lot that night.

Everton: Southall, Atteveld, Hinchcliffe, Ratcliffe, Watson, Keown, Nevin, McDonald, Sharp, Newell, Ebbrell.

Subs: McCall (Atteveld), Cottee (Nevin).

Scorers: Sharp 2, Cottee 2.

Liverpool: Grobbelaar, Hysen, Burrows, Nicol, Molby, Ablett, Beardsley, Staunton, Rush, Barnes, Venison.

Scorers: Beardsley 2, Rush, Barnes.

Gordon Banks

Brazil 1 England 0
World Cup finals, Group 3 match, Guadalajara, 7 June 1970

Born 30 December 1937. First showed a safe pair of hands as a coalbagger and played football only on Sundays in the Sheffield area where he grew up. Signed for Chesterfield at 18 but had to wait until after his National Service before making it into the first team. It was not long before Leicester City came for him and, displaying agility, economy and courage, he built himself into a legend. Won two FA Cup runners-up medals but made up for a paucity of domestic honours by clutching the greatest prize of all, a World Cup-winners' medal with England in 1966. In his 73 appearances for his country he was to become recognised as the greatest goal-keeper in the world. After 293 League games for Leicester, he joined Stoke City for £50,000 in 1967 and went on to earn a League Cup-winners' medal. Football of the Year in 1972, but his career was curtailed by a car smash in which he lost the sight of one eye.

Seldom has one save been surrounded by so much publicity and subjected to such analysis as Gordon Banks's breathtaking stop from Pele when England met Brazil in a group match at Guadalajara's magnificent Jalisco Stadium in 1970. A world-wide audience of hundreds of millions were witness to that unbelievable moment which confirmed Banks as the finest exponent of his lonesome art on the planet. It was, however, only one of many such interventions in a brilliant career. 'That got all the fuss because it was on TV,' he says. 'And because it was against Pele.'

It says it all about this modest man whose eschewing of the flamboyant, even as an aspiring teenager, did little to get him noticed. He was only spectacular when he had to be, and if diving across the width of the goal like Evel Knievel, arching your back like Olga Korbut and reaching for the ball like a man groping for a window ledge when slipping from a skyscraper can all be accomplished without 'fuss', why make one? That seemed to be the big Yorkshireman's philosophy.

The aforementioned is roughly what he did to prevent Brazil taking a 1–0 lead in the first half and, grudgingly, Banks eventually acknowledges the significance: 'Well, it stopped them going in front,' he says, 'at a time when our heads might have dropped.' When pressed, he will go as far as to say, 'It was one of my better ones.' Pele was a little more explicit: 'The best I've ever seen,' he said, as if some supernatural force had prevented his opening the scoring. Since then, only a well-worn video tape has convinced him that it was not a 'gol'.

That word is what the great man, half the Brazilian team, half the ground, half of Brazil were screaming a split-second after his powerful forehead had made perfect contact with the ball. If ever a header appeared to have 'gol' written all over it, that was it. 'I could not believe he got to it,' said Pele, 'or that he pushed it over. It was the biggest shock I have ever had on the field.' Bobby Moore was also amazed, having mentally prepared himself to fish the ball out of the net. It not only meant that this classic confrontation between the champions of 1966 and the favourites for 1970 continued locked at 0–0 but it meant that the whole competition was still wide open.

England had gone to Mexico with what was generally regarded as a slightly better side than that which won the Cup in 1966, while Brazil, so cruelly kicked out of the previous tournament, were determined to restore their reputation in the sunshine of Latin America. Pele was at his peak and, as if that was not enough to guarantee a terrific assault on the trophy, they had the genius of

Jairzinho on the wing, and those other sublime talents, Carlos Alberto, Clodoaldo, Tostao, Gerson and Rivelino in their most devastating line-up since Pele had first appeared in 1958. Could England, who could not compare in individual skills but had perhaps greater cohesion and all-round solidity, match this wonderful side?

Says Banks: 'We felt we could. I think we were a tiny bit better than in 1966 and we realised that they were the best team around on pure talent. But we had prepared very thoroughly, having been acclimatising for three weeks. This was particularly important for a 'keeper as the ball travelled a lot faster through the thin air and also bounced higher off the harder ground. To get used to this, I would ask Alf [Ramsey] to keep our hardest shooters behind after training to give me some practice in these conditions. I also got used to wearing gloves. It might have looked like Steve Davis wearing boxing gloves to play snooker, but they worked, and gave me the confidence I needed out there. Although we hadn't started brilliantly we were all pretty confident, and the game soon developed into the pattern we had expected – slow, slow build-ups but with quick bursts around the penalty area. It kicked off at noon, and the temperature was 98 degrees.'

Brazil, who had hammered Czechoslovakia 4–1 four days earlier, took the initiative, but England, playing their best football of the tournament in spite of having had a sleepless night deliberately caused by hundreds of Mexican fans staging a night-long carnival outside their hotel, held them at bay. Moore, whose own build-up to the competition had been even more rudely interrupted by the infamous stolen jewellery charge on a pre-World Cup tour in Bogota, was magnificent in defence and in prompting England's own increasingly confident attacks. Banks was as safe as ever behind him.

'It was going exactly how we felt it would,' says the 'keeper. 'We were containing them and gradually exerting our own pressure. But you could never relax for a moment.

Players of that calibre are always capable of producing something unexpected.

'The save incident started when Carlos Alberto bent a fantastic pass around Terry Cooper with the outside of his foot and into the path of Jairzinho who cut Terry out of the picture with a terrific bit of pace. Bobby Moore had to leave Tostao, and I went to the near post in case of a shot. This all left Pele, coming in at the far post, on his own. Jairzinho centred perfectly for Pele, and my biggest job was getting across the goal in time. I had both the confidence and the agility – I always felt I had a decent spring in my body – to go for it and I got across all right. But then when I had arrived, Pele, like the great player he was, headed it down, so I still had to anticipate the bounce.' All this, of course, took about half a second.

'With the ball travelling so quickly through the air and off the ground, there was even less time than you usually get in such situations. But as Pele thought he'd scored, I somehow managed to reach it and push it over. I didn't think it was that special until I saw it on TV afterwards. But I suppose I should have realised it was a good 'un by the look of disbelief on Pele's face.'

As it turned out, the save was irrelevant, Jairzinho finally piercing England's splendid rearguard to win the match when he cut in from the right in the 59th minute. As he unleashed a real rocket from close range, not even Banks could get near it. Unbowed, England largely controlled the game after that and should have levelled when Jeff Astle missed a sitter with almost his first touch after coming on for Francis Lee. Alan Ball hit the bar, 'but the feeling was,' says Banks, 'that it would not matter. England and Brazil seemed destined to meet again. Or so everyone thought. We were a bit disappointed to lose 'home' advantage and have to travel to meet West Germany, but that was overridden by the feeling that we had played very well and could play even better next time. Little did we know.

'As for the save, people would come up to me years later and say the one they had just seen me make was as good, if not better, than the one against Pele.' And the England team's reaction? 'The lads just told me I should have held it . . .'

Brazil: Felix, Carlos Alberto, Brito, Piazza, Everaldo, Clodoaldo, Cesar, Jairzinho, Tostao, Pele, Rivelino.

Sub: Roberto (Tostao).

Scorer: Jairzinho.

England: Banks, Wright, Cooper, Mullery, Labone, Moore, Lee, Ball, R. Charlton, Hurst, Peters.

Subs: Astle (Lee), Bell (Charlton).

Jim Baxter

England 2 Scotland 3
Wembley, 15 April 1967

Born 29 September 1939. Raised in a miner's row in Hill O'Beath, Baxter's career began with Sunday football, and he joined Crossgates Primrose for the princely sum of two pounds and ten shillings before his talent was unearthed by Raith Rovers in 1957. Rangers soon spotted his potential and paid £12,000 for him in 1960. A peerless left-half and sometime inside forward, 'Slim Jim' earned just one Scottish Under-23 cap and played 34 times for the senior side. Won all his club honours with Rangers, including three League Championships, three Scottish Cups and four Scottish League Cups in a glorious five-year spell. Eventually his dislike of training and penchant for the good life was his undoing; 'I don't want to be a millionaire,' he was fond of saying, 'I just want to live like one.' He spent an unsuccessful twilight south of the border, first at Sunderland and then at Nottingham Forest before returning to Ibrox on a free transfer.

By his own admission, he couldn't tackle a fish supper, had no pace and displayed a lofty disdain for hurrying back into defence to cover opposing forwards. One felt that such mundane matters were beneath his dignity while, in life in general, he showed a similarly lofty disdain for hurrying, even when living in the fast lane. But once in possession of the ball, Jim Baxter could not only make it talk, he would have it reciting Rabbie Burns.

In the light blue of Rangers and the dark blue of Scotland, Baxter's left foot composed countless lyrical lines and unforgettable verses. Among those that entered folklore was his game against Partick Thistle at Firhill in

1963, when he said, 'Everything I tried came off', and he had tried EVERYTHING. On the continental stage there was Vienna in 1964, when Rangers beat Rapid 2–0, and Wembley in 1963, when he scored twice against the 'auld enemy'. There was also having what he called 'the hex on Celtic' during a five-year period, 'when I honestly felt they were never likely to beat us'. But it was the 1967 defeat of England that contained the most significant and arrogant phrases he ever scripted. 'Let's take the piss oot o' them,' he had said before the kick-off. After being run ragged for 90 minutes, England's previously all-conquering and unbeaten 1966 World Cup-winners were never quite the same.

'They were world champions and full of themselves; you'd better believe that,' he says. 'And if you remember it was a makeshift Scottish side. But things went for us, and we were so much on top it was unbelievable. People said we should have gone and done 'em 9–3 like they had done us in 1961. But I said, "It's no good bothering about that." I just wanted to bring 'em down a peg or two. I think we did that.'

To Scots, the annual clash with the 'auld enemy' had always meant much more than it did to Sassenachs, and it meant more to win at Wembley than it did to win at Hampden. But not since Bannockburn had it meant as much to beat the English as it did in 1967. One Scottish scribe wrote beforehand: 'The confrontation between England and Scotland has taken a strange twist. It is regarded in Scotland as not so much a football match, but more a means of retribution.' A fresh element had indeed been added to the ancient rivalry, and that was England's victory in the World Cup. Beaten only once in thirty matches, Bobby Moore's team were the game's undisputed kings – apart from in Scotland. Although the Scots had failed to qualify for the 1966 World Cup, the tartan army took the view that if the Dark Blues defeated the world champions on their own midden, Scotland were the rightful successors to the crown. Simple.

'We were laughing at them,' recalls Baxter, 'especially at Alan Ball. Billy Bremner said we should call him Jimmy

Clitheroe after the wee comic with short trousers and squeaky voice, and we ran him daft. And him the hero of the World Cup! I was nutmegging him and he was going potty. After a while they were scared to come at us, scared to try to take the ball from us. And they were supposed to be world champions.'

Memorable and incident-packed it was, but there were lengthy passages of indifferent play illuminated only by Baxter's swagger and strut, his taunting and his keepie-uppie on the edge of his own penalty area. Scottish fans loved it, yet English fans did not hate it as much as they might. Like Celtic supporters enduring an Old Firm humiliation, they sensed that at the end of the day, for Jim, it was only a game. 'Celtic fans never despised me the way they did some Rangers players,' he once said. 'They knew that I couldn't care less about religion and also that I was using skill to beat Celtic. The same with England; if I had been born south of the border, I would have done the same to Scotland. Simple as that.'

In the game itself, England lost the services of Jack Charlton after 15 minutes following a desperate slide-tackle on Bobby Lennox. The big defender had treatment on the touchline for 13 minutes before returning to play heroically on the wing. Moore went to centre-half and Martin Peters dropped back from midfield, but with the much-vaunted strike force of Geoff Hurst and Jimmy Greaves not getting a look in, England were not playing like the champions of Britain, let alone the world. Ball was reddening and Baxter was beginning to purr.

The Rangers maestro set up the first goal after 28 minutes with a pass to Willie Wallace, whose shot was pounced upon by Denis Law. Baxter then took total command. With the veteran débutant Ronnie Simpson assuredly exorcising the ghost of previous Scottish 'keepers in rare England raids, 'Slim Jim' felt he could afford a little indulgence, and his passing assumed the air of elegant brush-strokes. With his team-mates now feeling that he would find them if they jumped into the crowd, and Bremner and Law firing on all cylinders, Scotland teased and tormented Alf Ramsey's superbly drilled and normally cohesive side. The tartan hordes were in heaven.

The only dissenting voice was that of Law, who had been on the golf course the day of England's 1966 triumph and who said: 'I had always wanted to give England a right good thrashing, and this was the only chance. But Baxter wanted to tip it about and all that stuff. Not a bad effort, though.'

Only Gordon Banks and the magnificent Bobby Charlton kept England in the game as Baxter did his stuff, but when Tommy Gemmell's lob was missed by Nobby Stiles, Lennox sent the rampant Lions into ecstasy by making it 2–0 with ten minutes to go. That wounded giraffe, Jack Charlton, had now moved to centre-forward and bravely headed England back into it, but débutant Jim McCalliog made sure with a third at the near post. In a frantic finale, Hurst finally scored at the death but for England, who had commendably kept battling, it was too little, too late. For Scotland, no victory has ever been so sweet.

Not only was it a drubbing of the 'auld enemy', it captured the British championship and a lead in the qualification race for the European Championship the following season. In a return to the heritage, it had been wrought in the traditional Scottish style, too, as noted by Geoffrey Green, who wrote in *The Times*: 'Old graces were aired.' One felt that Baxter would have appreciated that more than a glut of goals. He had played like a millionaire.

England: Banks, Cohen, Wilson, Stiles, J. Charlton, Moore, Ball, Greaves, R. Charlton, Hurst, Peters.

Scorers: J. Charlton, Hurst.

Scotland: Simpson, Gemmell, McCreadie, Greig, McKinnon, Bremner, McCalliog, Law, Wallace, Baxter, Lennox.

Scorers: Law, Lennox, McCalliog.

Colin Bell

Manchester City 4 Newcastle United 0
First Division, Maine Road, 26 December 1977

Born 26 February 1946. Played for East Durham Boys and Horden Colliery Welfare before moving to Bury where he scored 25 goals in 100 games between 1963 and 1965. Manchester City paid a then club record fee of £45,000 for him to become the legs, lungs and brains of their great side of the late 1960s and early 1970s. Nicknamed 'Nijinsky' after the racehorse, Bell won medals for the League Championship, FA Cup and European Cup-Winners' Cup in the heady days of Joe Mercer and Malcolm Allison. Made his England début in 1968 and, after a slow start, established himself as the midfield hub of the national side, earning 48 caps. A model professional, his career was cut short by a knee injury when in his prime: a sad end for a player who could probably have played until he was 40.

'When I used to watch Colin Bell at Bury,' says Malcolm Allison, 'I was aware that other clubs were after him. We wanted to buy him but were waiting for the money to come through. So, when in earshot of the other coaches and scouts, I would say things like: "He can't play, he's no good in the air, he has a hopeless left foot . . ." Until we had the money. Then we bought him.'

A glance at the honours list shows what an outstanding investment Bell proved, but even that fails lamentably to convey the impact he made at Maine Road. A less ebullient character than either Lee or Summerbee, he nevertheless endeared himself to the City faithful in a manner that he had not dreamed of. It was not until his come-back game against Newcastle on Boxing Day 1977, after two years out with a complex knee injury, that he appreciated just how much. By then Bell had won most of the major honours the game has to offer but it is neither a Cup final nor an England international that he remembers most. As he says, 'It was an ordinary League game, and I came on as a sub for the second half, hardly touching the ball. But the reception I got was fantastic.'

Bell had had to take some stick in his career as bewildered defenders resorted to desperate lunges and rough-house methods in their increasingly frantic efforts to stop him. Whenever this happened, City fans would leap to their feet in fury at the treatment of their idol. Only twice (in 1966–67 and 1974–75) did Bell complete a full League programme for City. Yet the challenge that dispatched him to the rehabilitation room for the best part of two years was at worst clumsy and perpetrated by a player whose tool bag was devoid of hatchets.

City were at home to United in a League Cup local derby on 12 November 1975, and Bell had embarked upon one of his characteristic runs toward the United penalty area after picking up a pass from Dennis Tueart. United's Martin Buchan was the defender charged with cutting him off. He raced across, and Bell saw him coming. 'I had three options,' he says. 'I could shoot. But the pitch was too uneven, and I was too far out. I could carry on. I decided against. I thought I should check and drag the ball back inside him as he ran past me at speed. But it didn't work as my studs were buried in the pitch, and Buchan caught me. I knew it was bad.'

At first the commentator said: 'He's fallen over the ball.' But then he realised it was serious when a stretcher was called. But no one knew the magnitude until much later. Being 'out for a month' seemed bad enough, but that was before the full extent of the damage was known. Both an artery and a blood vessel had burst, but after a come-back against Leeds in April, clotted blood from the original injury caused a cartilage to splinter. 'That injury was the start of the end of my career,' Bell says. 'But I don't believe it was done on purpose.'

Bell tried everything to get back: receiving extensive treatment, working out in the gym, running mile after mile. 'I flogged myself to death,' he says. 'But my knee was like a rusty joint; it needed lots of exercises just to get it going.' City seemed to suffer in sympathy with him, and the club's patience was a mark of how much he was revered at Maine Road. Said chairman Peter Swales: 'I consider Colin Bell to be one of the best players of all time and the most finely-tuned athlete I've ever seen. He's irreplaceable.'

Bell eventually returned in the reserves in the 1976–77 season and won a Central League medal, but it was the big time he craved. Countless come-back dates were mentioned, but each one passed with some further set-back. Undaunted, Bell carried on, and City waited for him. Eventually, acting manager Tony Book named him as substitute for the Newcastle game. 'The plan was,' says Book, 'to give him a 20-minute run at the end, but an injury to Paul Power forced my hand and he came on for the second half.'

'Word got around,' says Bell, 'that I was likely to come on and I could hear the crowd roaring when I came into the tunnel. I've never heard anything like it. I had a lump in my throat before I'd even got half-way through the tunnel. It just went on and on, both sets of supporters giving me a standing ovation that never seemed to end. It was a very personal thing, but I'd never expected anything like that. I was stunned and floated six inches above the pitch. I was just overwhelmed.' So were Newcastle as an inspired City suddenly responded to the crowd and to the presence of one of their elder statesmen. Summerbee and Lee had gone, but the sight of the lean, pale figure with the penguin flap of the arms as he delivered a thunderbolt of a shot or a telling pass, had the desired effect. Tueart knocked in a hat-trick and Brian Kidd the other to send the crowd home euphoric.

Bell was to make a further sixteen League appearances

that season and played seventeen times in the following campaign. But, slowly and reluctantly, City fans began to realise that it was not the same Colin Bell. With the knee weakening, Bell was told that a further knock could render him a permanent cripple and, however grudgingly, he had to bow to the inevitable. He announced his retirement from football in August 1979. 'I could have played for another four or five years,' he says. 'But at least I had to be thankful I wasn't in my early 20s when it happened. Then I would have been really upset.'

Swales said: 'No words can express the debt which Manchester City and England owe to Colin Bell.' Mike Summerbee declared: 'I'm only sad we never saw his true ability. He could be in the box one second and then back defending the next, before you could say "Jack Robinson".' Franny Lee added: 'He was the most complete inside forward you'd ever see, coming from deep positions and making everything so easy.' Not bad for a player whose left foot was hopeless and who couldn't head the ball.

Manchester City: Corrigan, Clements, Donachie, Booth, Watson, Power, Barnes, Owen, Kidd, Hartford, Tueart.

Sub: Bell (Power).

Scorers: Tueart 3, Kidd.

Newcastle United: Carr, Nattrass, Barker, Cassidy, Bird, Blackley, Martin, Burns, Cannell, Tommy Craig, Robinson.

Sub: Gorry (Blackley).

George Best

Benfica 1 Manchester United 5
European Cup quarter-final, second leg, Lisbon, 9 March
1966

*Born 22 May 1946. A scrawny kid from the streets of East Belfast,
Best was considered 'too frail' for Northern Ireland schoolboy
honours. But, playing for Cregagh Boys Club, he impressed
Manchester United's scout Bob Bishop enough to be packed off
to Old Trafford. Best blossomed into not just a genius on the
field, but a cult figure of the 1960s: an outside-right who
competed for headlines and idolatry at the top of the same
frenzied league as The Beatles. His emergence, along with
Denis Law and Bobby Charlton, completed Matt Busby's
rebuilding after the Munich air disaster and brought another
golden age to Old Trafford. United won the League in 1965, the
trio's first full season together, and 1967, with the crowning
glory of the European Cup following in 1968. It was then that
Best was voted Player of the Year and European Footballer of
the Year. Yet his demise was premature and tragic, taking him
to Hibernian, Dunstable, Stockport, Fulham and Los Angeles
Aztecs. At 26, Best opened a Manchester night club called Slack
Alice. He came back briefly to football, but it was not the same.
Altogether, he played for eleven seasons in the First Division,
scoring 178 goals in 466 games – longer than many people think,
but still not long enough.*

'He had ice in his veins, warmth in his heart and timing
and balance in his feet,' said Danny Blanchflower.
Geoffrey Green called him, 'A living James Dean, a rebel
with a cause.' Never has a footballer made a greater
impact on British life than George Best. It was the
swinging sixties, the age of Beatlemania, and Best was a

man of his time. 'I was christened El Beatle by the Portuguese press after the win over Benfica in Lisbon,' says Best. 'I already had the haircut, of course, and regard that match as my breakthrough into the really big time. Although winning the European Cup two years later has to be my most important game for the club, the Lisbon game was the match of my life.

'When I arrived at Old Trafford in 1961, there was an eerie feel to the place as it was only three years after Munich. There was still a great sense of loss and, although it's sad to say it, Munich made a lot more people attach themselves to the team. It became a mission to be the first English club to win the European Cup.' Matt Busby, who had bravely set out to do just that after his beloved 'Babes' had been destroyed, bought in expensive stars such as Denis Law and Paddy Crerand to add to survivors such as Bill Foulkes and Bobby Charlton. The new side was taking shape, but Busby could hardly believe his luck – or his ears – about reports coming out of the youth team.

There was a spindly Irish kid who could sell such a good dummy, it was said, that defenders did not merely go the wrong way, they had to queue at the turnstiles to get back into the ground. After a handful of reserve team games, Busby tossed him into League action against West Brom and a tough-tackling full-back called Graham Williams. It was 14 September 1963, and Best was aged 17 years and 4 months. His verdict? 'Easy.'

With Law and Charlton proving the perfect partners, Best's genius blossomed, and United won the League in 1965 to return to the European Cup. After strolling through two rounds against Helsinki HJK and ASK Vorwaerts, the Red Devils found themselves playing the Eagles of Benfica in the quarter-final. What *The Times* called 'a necklace of events' in a momentous first leg at Old Trafford left United with a slender 3–2 lead. 'Benfica had not been beaten at home in Europe for nineteen games,' recalls Best, 'and in front of a full house in the Stadium of Light, we were not given much of a chance.' But, *The Times* said, 'Tomorrow is tomorrow.'

For Busby it might also have been yesterday, and he warned his players to 'keep it tight' for the first 20 minutes. The venerable manager had bitter memories of another night in Lisbon in 1964, when United had squandered a 4–1 lead from the home leg to lose 0–5 to Sporting. Busby, renowned for his composure, ranted and raged at his players for that performance. With Munich on his mind, he did not want another surrender. He did not get one.

'It was the noisiest crowd I've ever heard, 96,000 of them, and the atmosphere sent the blood coursing through my veins,' remembers Best. 'It seemed to add power to my muscles, my imagination and my brain. Sir Matt used to say that I must have had cotton wool in my ears during his team talk. He felt our best chance was to protect our lead and not to give away an early goal. We didn't: we were 3–0 up after 14 minutes!'

Rockets lit the Lisbon night as Benfica's Eusebio was presented with a statuette before the kick-off to mark his nomination as European Footballer of the Year. The ground was shimmering in anticipation; the Eagles had twice won the European Cup and in nineteen contests at home had scored 78 goals against 14. As Best admits: 'We weren't expected to win.' But when the 19-year-old winger rose brilliantly to head home a Tony Dunne free-kick in the sixth minute, United were two goals to the good on aggregate, and the Stadium of Light was immediately dimmed. Six minutes later, and the place might have been in total darkness but for the sheer iridescence of Best's second goal. Receiving a header from David Herd just inside the Portuguese half, Best simply scorched past two defenders as if they were wax effigies and finished with a low shot into the far corner. Two minutes later, after marvellous work by Law, Best slipped the ball to John Connelly for the third.

'It was like writing your own script,' says Best, 'and I

was lucky enough to get two. We played football that was close to perfection that night. We were celebrating at half-time, and Sir Matt had to remind us there was still another half. They did score but it was an unlucky own goal, and we got two more through Paddy Crerand and Bobby Charlton. The Benfica fans had never seen their team so humiliated, and I could just do no wrong. In fact, we had two goals disallowed, and one of them was probably my best of the lot. So I was a wee bit disappointed not to have had a hat-trick.'

The critics were raving: Matthews, Garrincha, Finney, Eusebio were all mentioned, but even they would have paled that night in comparison with the kid from East Belfast. With Best threading his way at will through one of Europe's most formidable defences, United had produced what was adjudged the finest performance by a British side on a foreign field. The accolades poured in: one Spanish observer even compared the Reds to Real Madrid at their finest, while another judge said: 'Congratulations. Tonight we are seeing the first British champions of Europe.' Alas for Busby's team, it was not to be that season. With Best injured, they went down to Partizan Belgrade in the semi-final. But, as Law remembers, 'Sir Matt called the night in Lisbon our finest hour, and I think that sums it up.'

Best, described by his landlady as 'puny and petrified' when he arrived in Manchester as a 15-year-old, had shone like a beacon in the Stadium of Light. Puny he was still, but inside his scrawny frame was the heart of a lion. 'Of all the compliments I have been paid,' he says, 'the ones that pleased me most are the ones about my bravery.' No wonder Sir Matt says: 'We had our problems with the wee fellah, but I prefer to remember his genius.'

Benfica: Costa Pereira, Cavem, Germano, Cruz, Pinto, Coluna, Augusto, Silva, Eusebio, Torres, Jose Augusto.

Scorer: Brennan (og)

Manchester United: Gregg, Brennan, Dunne, Crerand, Foulkes, Stiles, Best, Law, Charlton, Herd, Connelly.

Scorers: Best 2, Connelly, Crerand, Charlton.

Billy Bingham

Luton Town 2 Norwich City 1
FA Cup semi-final replay, St Andrews, 18 March 1959

*Born 5 August 1931. A high-scoring centre-forward who
grabbed two goals on his début for Northern Ireland schoolboys
against Eire, he won nine youth caps with Glentoran where, at
5ft 6in, he was considered too light for the No.9 jersey. After
playing for the Irish League, he moved to Sunderland for £8,000
in October 1950. Became a favourite with the crowd during his
eight years at Roker and won his first full cap in 1951. As part of a
Northern Ireland side which included such talents as Danny
Blanchflower and Peter McParland, he reached the last eight of
the 1958 World Cup. Surprisingly, Sunderland then sold him to
Luton Town for £15,000, and he scored in every round of their FA
Cup run that season, except the final which they lost to
Nottingham Forest. In 1960 he joined Everton where he scored
28 goals in 96 games before moving to Port Vale where a broken
leg ended his career at 32. For his country he scored 10 goals in
56 games. Eighteen months later he became manager at
Southport and part-time boss of Northern Ireland, twice taking
his country to the World Cup finals (1982 and 1986) after having
a spell in charge of Greece. Also managed Plymouth, Linfield,
Everton, Mansfield and the Greek side PAOK.*

When wingers were recently said to be as obsolete as
Spitfires in football's modern warfare, Billy Bingham took
it as a compliment. For the Irishman, above all exponents
of his mercurial art, exhibited many characteristics
associated with the old flying machine: speed, courage,
manoeuvrability and a great strike rate. It is for the last
quality that Bingham picks the match of his playing life, a
performance that would have had him billed as a Tornado
today.

'Scoring the winning goal in a FA Cup semi-final replay has to be my most treasured memory as a player,' he says. 'Northern Ireland beating Spain in the 1982 World Cup would get it for me as a manager, but the Luton-Norwich match was special as it got us to Wembley. I had been wondering if I'd ever get there, apart from internationals, as the FA Cup final was, of course, the only other way to do it in those days.'

Bingham was particularly pleased to be passing under the twin towers with an unfashionable club like Luton after having been inexplicably unloaded by 'Bank of England' Sunderland at the start of the season. Only that summer, Bingham had helped Northern Ireland to the quarter-finals of the World Cup in Sweden and felt that he was 'at the peak of my playing career'. But his peak was not apparently high enough for demanding new Roker boss Alan Brown and, after being dropped and encountering a difference of opinion, Bingham was glad to leave for the humbler, but still ambitious confines of Kenilworth Road. 'Luton had a good side then with several internationals,' he recalls, 'and they had been after me for some time.'

With England's Ron Baynham in goal, Scotland's Gordon Turner, George Cummins of the Republic of Ireland, and the most celebrated Lutonian of them all, Syd Owen, all in the side, Bingham in no way felt that he had left the Bank of England for the Co-op savings counter. Indeed, Luton were looking to build on their creditable eighth place in the 1957–58 season, and the newcomer received the following welcome from the local *Telegraph*: 'Town have borne in mind the crying need for directness on the wings, and Bingham is just the type to supply it on the right.'

Those words seemed prophetic when Luton raced to the top of the League after two months. But, after manager Dally Duncan departed in October, they began to slide, and the FA Cup was all they had to play for. 'We had the sort of team that could put together a decent run – nice balance and a good rapport among the players – and I felt that I was at my best both athletically and as a goal-scorer.' With two goals in a 5–1 win over Leeds, another in a 1–1 draw with Leicester and one more in a 5–2 crushing of Ipswich, Bingham had propelled Luton into the sixth round, and he had scored in every one. Perhaps nobody would have mentioned Stan Mortensen's record of six Cup goals in a campaign had Luton not been drawn away to Blackpool, but Bingham remained in hot pursuit with a goal in a 1–1 draw.

'While we were having our run,' he recalls, 'Norwich, who were in the Third Division, were having theirs and we met in the semi-finals. It was the first time either club had been that far, and their giant-killing performances had been such that many people made them favourites. They gave us a good game, too, but we ended up drawing 1–1 and went to St Andrews for the replay.'

Donald Saunders wrote of the first match in the *Daily Telegraph*: 'There is little doubt that Bingham's Irish magic all but caused Norwich City's historic Cup run to splutter tamely to its end before half-time. During those first, comparatively quiet 45 minutes, Bingham seemed the most dangerous winger in British football. No one . . . could control the fleet-footed, quick-thinking little Irishman as he danced down the wing and curled the ball menacingly into the penalty area with ever-increasing frequency.' But he had not scored.

With Norwich having the better of the first half in the replay, Luton's hopes of reaching Wembley looked bleak. Seconds before the break they looked to be losing interest, but a miraculous clearance off the line by full-back Brendan McNally from Jimmy Hill's header sent them to the dressing-room mightily relieved to be level. Bingham, who had teased and tormented Norwich full-back Ron Ashman throughout, appeared the only hope of piercing the otherwise sound Canaries rearguard. 'I had a pretty good game up until then,' Bingham remembers, 'but the goal came a bit out of the blue. In fact, I was taken by surprise by Bob Morton's back-heel. I flashed at the ball and it went into the top corner of the net. For a moment I thought it was over the top.'

Norwich, as befitted their battling tradition, rallied and strove desperately to become the first Third Division club to reach a Cup final. They appeared to have saved the game when Errol Crossan's drive looked a goal all the way, but was somehow blocked. Luton, with Bingham still prominent, finally remembered that they were a First Division outfit and began to knock the ball around sweetly. 'We played a bit after the goal,' says Bingham, 'but they kept coming right till the end.' Indeed, after the dangerous Crossan had once again caused havoc on the right and crossed to Brennan, Norwich again looked about to level, but the outside-left could get no power behind his shot with only Baynham to beat.

'When the whistle went,' says Bingham, 'there were tremendous scenes and great emotion. Our supporters had been a bit quiet at times but they made up for it then and actually chaired me off the field. Yes, winning a semi and thinking of Wembley is wonderful. I was even given a straw hat and put it on at the end. I had never worn a boater before in my life. Great scenes, great jubilation; marvellous.'

It must have been – even the undemonstrative Syd Owen danced a jig – and Bingham had equalled Mortensen's record of scoring in every round. Sadly for him and Luton, he was not able to add to it in the final, Nottingham Forest winning 2–1. So Bingham swelled the ranks of those who have enjoyed a semi-final more than a final. But he did gain consolation: the way he played in his two and a half years at Luton caught the eye sufficiently for Everton to sign him, and at Goodison he won a League champions' medal. Bingy could not be grounded for long; just like a Spitfire.

Luton Town: Baynham, McNally, Hawkes, Groves, Owen, Pacey, Bingham, Brown, Morton, Cummins, Gregory.

Scorer: Bingham.

Norwich City: Kennon, Thurlow, Ashman, McCrohan, Butler, Crowe, Crossan, Allcock, Bly, Hill, Brennan.

Tony Book

Newcastle United 3 Manchester City 4
First Division, St James's Park, 11 May 1968

Born 4 April 1935. First played inside forward with Peasedown St John in the Western League. Was converted to full-back by his RMS at Aldershot, but was rejected by Ted Drake after a trial at Chelsea. Became a part-time professional at Frome Town so that he could keep his job as a bricklayer, but was released to Bath City where he spent eight seasons in the Southern League, winning one Championship medal. Followed Bath coach Malcolm Allison to Plymouth Argyle at the start of the 1964–65 season – at the age of 28 – and then, unbelievably, to Maine Road. Having overcome an inferiority complex about being a non-League player at Home Park, Book was then worried about his age – he was 31 when he joined City. Joe Mercer told him: 'Age doesn't worry me. I didn't really start playing until I went to Arsenal. I was 31.'

You can always tell a Manchester City fan. His fingernails are chewed to the knuckle, his heart is in his mouth and his eyes are down, scouring the pavement for banana skins – and that is in the close-season. During the actual campaign, he can be reduced to an even sorrier state. Only a City fan would stop at the club shop and ask for Valium to help him through a home match with Luton; only a City fan would want the referee's whistle confirmed in writing; and only a City fan would settle for a 4–3 win when 4–0 up after 15 minutes. Not all of this insecurity can be blamed on living in the daunting shadow of Old Trafford, although that may have contributed to the club's habit of snatching defeat not from victory's jaws, but its larynx. All of which is essential to understanding why Tony Book's most indelible memory of the Championship decider at Newcastle in 1968 was: 'Our fans'.

Manchester United's transformation from Second Division side to international institution under Matt Busby was, of course, a major factor, especially as his great European Cup-winning team was being given the finishing touches in 1965. When George Best was jinking on to the scene to form that legendary triumvirate with Denis Law and Bobby Charlton, City played Swindon at home before just 8,015 bereft and bewildered souls. The contrast with the cauldron that was Old Trafford could hardly have been more stark. As the full-house notices went up and United's famous home reverberated in acclaim of that trio's collective genius, City were suffering emptiness, despair and even (whisper it quietly) the possible oblivion of Division Three. But that was before Joe Mercer and 'Big Mal' Allison effected a dramatic turnaround.

Now, on the final day of the 1967–68 season, City and United were level atop the First Division. By a strange fixture quirk, the vibrant, rejuvenated City were away to Newcastle while United entertained lowly Sunderland, who had just done enough to avoid relegation. City had a better goal average, but no one was expecting anything from Old Trafford but a United win, least of all the City fans who descended on Tyneside in their tens of thousands.

'We went there feeling that we had to win the match to win the title,' recalls Book. 'We couldn't approach it in any other way. The build-up was pretty tense, and fans were already going up in droves on the Friday. There was something about them that I'll never forget. No bunch of fans anywhere could have wanted their team to win as much as they wanted us to beat Newcastle and pip United. It was incredible.'

But the fans were not the only ones who thought they were dreaming. The first time Book, who had despaired of being asked to play League football, had an inkling that his luck was about to change was when Allison, who had left Bath for Plymouth, climbed up the scaffolding at a building site on which Book was working. 'That's how he reintroduced himself,' Book remembers, 'and I was on my way to the League. Plymouth and then City.' Even places like the plush Five Bridges Hotel in Gateshead, where the team stayed before the Newcastle match, must have seemed like another universe to Book, who had been considered a mere journeyman full-back in the lower leagues until discovered by Allison. But even his rise was more plausible for most of the fans than seeing City tilt for the Championship, and they were determined to make the most of it.

At St James's Park, the Leazes End is akin to the Kop at Anfield, a place where the die-hard Magpie fans go and where no away supporter dares to trespass. By midday on that fateful Saturday, no Newcastle fan could get near it: the Leazes End was already in City hands. 'I think there was over 20,000 fans there,' says Book, 'and they'd cheered us all the way from the hotel to the ground. It gave us a great boost.' That morning the Pennines had been straddled with sky-blue favours and now Tyneside was awash with them, the team coach journey to St James's Park taking 45 minutes instead of the customary ten. When the players came out to a tremendous Mancunian roar, the City fans had already spilled over the walls and were lining the pitch. Book still shudders at the sense of anticipation: 'We knew it was down to us, but the fans were doing everything they could to help.'

It was the kind of occasion when a narrow 1–0 win would still have been recalled fondly decades later, even if it had been a forgettable game. But what the teams served was unforgettable, Newcastle responding to the atmosphere and making City fight for every yard. Each burst from Francis Lee, every run from Mike Summerbee had to be prised out of the home defence. City fans did not enjoy that first tension-racked 13 minutes, but they did enjoy Summerbee's opening goal. Typically, however, a lead was to be a fleeting luxury as Bryan 'Pop' Robson equalised almost immediately. 'The first of many anxious moments,' admits Book, and he was perhaps the calmest player on the City side.

It was unrelenting. Lee sallied, Summerbee buzzed, Bell foraged, Book steadied and then, 25 unbearable minutes later, Neil Young let fly, lashing in a low drive with that lethal left foot. Once again, however, ecstasy was short-lived, Jackie Sinclair scorching home a second equaliser. Inspired by that brilliant strike, Newcastle were playing out of their skins, and City were relieved to reach the dressing-room at 2–2.

'We didn't need a half-time rollicking,' says Book, 'and we didn't get one. Mal just told us to play like champions. He knew how tense we were, but we also had confidence and, deep down, all the lads felt we would win. We had been playing so well up to then, and I think that we carried that confidence on to the field in the second half.' At last displaying the form that had seen them rise to take the top spot from United, City purred into action. Led by Bell, who forgot about a heavily-strapped ankle, they tore at the Newcastle goal which fell a third time when Young crashed in his second. It was the perfect start to the second half, but it would get better.

Fifteen minutes later, and less than half an hour from the promised land of victory, Bell was again the provider. This time it was Lee, whose joy at rifling in what he thought was the clincher was not confined to the field as the irrepressible striker joined the crowd near the Newcastle corner flag. The City fans were almost on the pitch, but it was not yet over. With Newcastle still battling, and conflicting news coming on the trannies from Old Trafford, John McNamee went up to head a third for the home team. City entered a nerve-jangling spell which even they were not equipped to handle. All those banana skins; all those snatched defeats; surely not now . . . 'It was the best feeling I've ever experienced on a football field,' says Book, 'when that whistle went. But it seemed to be a long time in coming.'

When City fans are jubilant there is about them an animation, a release from a yoke, a joy that is beyond the mere winning of a game. They leap and jump about, rather like Evertonians who have suffered similarly in the shadow of more celebrated red neighbours. On this occasion City fans did not wait for the paper or the documentation. Best of all, they did not have to wait for United, for United had lost. The victory had not really been necessary, but Book and his men were not going to worry about that. 'All the way back to Manchester,' he remembers, 'the City fans were hooting and cheering our coach. It was a great journey.'

Newcastle United: McFaul, Craig, Clark, Moncur, McNamee, Iley, Sinclair, Scott, Davies, B. Robson, T. Robson.

Scorers: B. Robson, Sinclair, McNamee.

Manchester City: Mulhearne, Book, Pardoe, Doyle, Heslop, Oakes, Lee, Bell, Summerbee, Young, Coleman.

Scorers: Summerbee, Young 2, Lee.

Raich Carter

Sunderland 5 Arsenal 4
First Division, Roker Park 28 December 1935

*Born 21 December 1913. A schoolboy international, he signed
for Sunderland in 1931 after being told to 'go home and grow up'
at a trial with Leicester City. A slight figure then, he grew in
stature to become an influential, all-round inside forward who
scored 216 goals in over 450 League matches. After the war he
joined Derby County after being stationed at nearby Lough-
borough and won a FA Cup-winners' medal within three
months at the Baseball Ground, enjoying a fruitful partnership
with Peter Doherty in possibly the best Rams team of all time.
Thanks mainly to the untimely outbreak of war, he won only 13
official caps for England – a shoddy reward for a supreme
talent.*

Arsenal were THE side of the 1930s, and in 1935 the
Gunners collected their third successive League title. At
the end of the season, they had the decency to invite
runners-up Sunderland, among others, to a celebration
dinner at the Holborn Restaurant in London. For Raich
Carter, a Wearside kid who had once ventured as far as
Leicester and been told he was too short, it was a salutary
experience looking up at the giants of the game.

'I had shot up a few inches by then,' remembers Carter,
'but I couldn't help but revere the likes of Alex James and
Cliff Bastin who were receiving their medals. But as I did
so, I decided I wanted some of that for myself.

'We had a great team the following year: players such as
Bobby Gurney and a brilliant left-winger in Jimmy
Connor. I had a good season, too, and, sure enough, we
took the title from Arsenal, while Derby County were

runners-up. It was the first time Sunderland had won it since the year I was born. Of course, they had won it a few times before that, and there was a great tradition on Wearside. But Arsenal were considered to be the best club side in the world in those days, and I always enjoyed playing against them – even at Highbury. Our encounters were always very competitive.

'But some of their great names had gone, including James and David Jack, and we began the season very well. We had had a good run at Christmas and, by the time Arsenal came to visit us, we had opened up a bit of a gap at the top of the League. So the stage was well and truly set. Arsenal were Arsenal and a crowd of 59,250 at Roker suggests that people were interested.' Arsenal knew that they had to win to peg back the rampant Wearsiders, whereas a home victory would leave the reigning champions with much to do to retain their title. Neither club had, of course, ever been out of the First Division, so it really was a clash of titans.

'There was naturally great tension before the game,' Carter remembers, 'even though it had come close to being called off through thick fog. But, when that began to disperse, the crowds flocked and packed Roker to the rafters. It was a marvellous atmosphere, and everybody sensed it was to be our most important game of the season.'

Carter approached the fixture as if his life depended on it, running all over the park, commanding the midfield and setting up a series of assaults that not even Arsenal's much-vaunted defence, Male and Hapgood included, could cope with. Right-winger Dickie Davis went close twice and had the *Blaydon Races* reverberating around the great ground with a goal after just seven minutes. With the Gunners wondering what had hit them, Davis crossed in the 18th minute for the unmarked Patsy Gallacher to head past Moss. Two-nil, and Arsenal knew that their Championship was going to take some keeping.

However, nine minutes later Arsenal were back in the match and the title race thanks to a penalty that to this day Carter does not understand. 'Nothing wrong with the decision,' he is quick to point out, 'but it was as if our wing-half Sandy McNab had suddenly decided to take up rugby. He caught the ball in his own penalty area for no apparent reason, and Cliff Bastin converted the kick.' That inexplicable act seemed to galvanise Sunderland, and Carter took total charge, scoring twice before half-time to send the crowd into raptures. There was an element of luck about his first, a hard drive which Moss appeared to let under his body in the 35th minute, while the second was another spot-kick.

Just before the break, it was an Arsenal defender's turn to experience a rash moment, centre-half Herbie Roberts fouling Gallacher and then up-ending Davis in the same clumsy incident. Carter made no mistake from the spot, and delirium broke out all over Wearside. 'It looked all over,' he says. 'The match, certainly, and even the Championship according to some optimists. But Arsenal were far too good a side to be written off just like that, and we should have known it.'

The Londoners came out with renewed vigour in the second half, but it took an injury to Gallacher to turn the game. The inside-left remained on the field but swapped places with Jimmy Connor, reducing the effectiveness of both. Arsenal, sensing that their time had come and with Ted Drake leading a powerful line with new relish, narrowed the deficit, Drake himself rifling home just three minutes into the half. As the first real signs of unease crept through the Roker ramparts, another international, left-winger Pat Beasley, raced down the flank to centre for Bowden to make it 4–3 after just 53 minutes. 'We did not really think that anybody would beat us all season,' says Carter, 'but when a side comes back from the dead like that, it's very worrying. The only thing we had to do was to regain our composure and keep going. But at 4–3 we were in a spot of bother.

'But Jimmy Connor, who was a wonderful player and had taken Roker by storm when he arrived in 1930, decided to do something about it and set off on a crossfield run from the half-way line. He beat a couple of men before playing a quick one-two with me and then, about twenty-five yards out, lashed in a tremendous shot that brought the house down.' The Wearsiders felt that they were home now and revelled once more in a marvellous exhibition of attacking football. But Arsenal, showing the true mettle of champions, were still not done, and Bowden got a deflection off Ray Clarke with 15 minutes to go to make the home side sweat for their victory.

'We were not going to let it go from there,' says Carter, who had scored 24 goals before Christmas, 'and the confidence we had built up throughout the first half of the season sustained us. It was possibly the most important quarter of an hour we played. It took some doing, but when the incentive is a 7-point lead at the top of the table you don't mind having your backs to the wall. What's more, Arsenal slipped to fourth and never really threatened us again. Derby were second and that's how it finished.

'But that was some match. The only others to compare with it were beating Birmingham 7–2 at Easter and a 4–6 Cup defeat by Everton. No wonder the local paper wrote of "a riot of goal-scoring". But we just worked for each other and didn't care who scored as long as we won. As for me, the paper always remarked about my ability to run all over the place.' A pity that chap from Leicester couldn't have read it for he might just have thought that his little trialist had grown up.

Sunderland: Thorpe, Morrison, Hall, Thomson, Clarke, McNab, Davis, Carter, Gurney, Gallacher, Connor.

Scorers: Carter 2 (1 pen), Connor, Gallacher, Davis.

Arsenal: Moss, Male, Hapgood, Crayston, Roberts, Copping, Rogers, Bowden, Drake, Bastin, Beasley.

Scorers: Bastin, Drake, Bowden.

Bobby Charlton

Manchester United v Sunderland
FA Cup sixth round, March 1964 (Three games).

Born 11 October 1937. Son of a miner and a nephew of the great Jackie Milburn. With elder brother Jack already on Leeds United's books, Bobby joined Manchester United and the Busby Babes, where he had to fight for a first-team place after featuring in three of United's five FA Youth Cup triumphs in the 1950s. Scored twice on his League début in October 1956 but did not establish himself until the following season during which he survived the Munich air disaster. His emergence from the wreckage encouraged Matt Busby to rebuild the team. He was the complete modern footballer, possessing an appetite for hard work, a marvellous pass, surging power and a cannonball shot that were to inspire a generation of footballers world-wide. Won every honour in the game: with United, he won the FA Cup, League Championship twice and European Cup; during a 106-cap England career, he won the World Cup. Scored a record 49 goals for England and was Footballer of the Year in 1966. Holds both the OBE and CBE for his services to the sport. Retired in 1973 after a club record of 604 appearances and 199 goals.

If a writer can remotely resemble a player, Geoffrey Green of *The Times* was probably the closest thing the press box had in style to Bobby Charlton. Among many eulogies, this is one he wrote of him: 'Bobby Charlton: the dashing leader of the line on a white charger, releasing rockets from the edge of the area that go home like a clap of thunder and lift the opposing net as if a gale had struck it.' Here is another: 'His thinning fair hair streaming in the wind, he moved like a ship in full sail.' Another: 'His flowing movements when surging into attack suggested a

hidden poetic line: the ceaseless support for each colleague on the field, while himself rotating as the midfield
hub of the wheel, reflected a selfless loyalty to a cause; his
high standard of behaviour on stage still remains an
example and a reproach to others in a game of violence,
and as such remains a mirror of deeper values.'

After that sort of introduction, one match would simply
not be enough for Bobby Charlton. Not the FA Cup final,
not the European Cup final, not even the World Cup final.
So when he chooses a whole series of games, it seems
entirely appropriate. But against Sunderland? It must have
been quite a saga. 'I've never known such emotion,' he
remembers. 'For sheer excitement, incident, drama,
tension, coming back from the dead . . . you name it, those
games had everything. There were about twice as many
people watching as the official figures. There were also as
many outside the ground who couldn't get in; I'll never
forget them.'

United, the Cup holders, had been drawn at home for
this sixth-round clash with Sunderland, who had the tie
seemingly sewn up after an hour. 'They were 3–1 up and
the *Blaydon Races* was ringing round Old Trafford,'
Charlton recalls. Indeed, Sunderland had played superbly, thoroughly deserving their lead and apparent passage
into the semi-finals. After George Mulhall had put them
ahead in the 41st minute, Johnny Crossan added two more
in the 50th and 59th minutes; a Charlie Hurley own goal in
between was the only comfort for an out-of-sorts United.
There were only five minutes remaining when Denis Law,
who had had a game to forget, got in a header which
seemed to pulverise 'keeper Jimmy Montgomery. The ball
was belted out for a corner by a harassed defence, and
Charlton put United back in the match with a header.

Two minutes later and with the *Races* suddenly
swamped by the Mancunian roar, Hurley made another
mistake and headed straight to George Best. Then only 17,
the Irishman displayed an old head to pick his spot

between the desperate legs of retreating defenders. None of the 61,000 people present could believe it, but the holders were still in.

The official attendance for the replay was 46,727, but most judges who knew their Roker reckoned that over 70,000 were inside the famous ground. 'There were thousands and thousands locked outside,' says Charlton. 'Getting to the ground in the team coach was an unbelievable experience.' Sunderland, once the 'Bank of England' team but for so long underachievers and now in the Second Division, sensed that they could win the Cup this year and set about United once again. Playing scintillating football in what was a 'madhouse of emotion', they took the lead two minutes before half-time when centre-forward Nick Sharkey scored with a spectacular scissors-kick. The ground erupted, and thousands poured on to the pitch. 'People were just going beserk,' recalls Charlton. 'I've never known a home crowd so excited.'

After 62 minutes Law, who had not really figured in the tie so far, suddenly showed just why he could never be ignored. When Montgomery took a divot with a goal-kick and sent the ball straight to him, Law strode forward with renewed purpose and slammed it past the helpless 'keeper. Relief for Manchester, despair for Sunderland, and extra-time. No sooner had it begun than Maurice Setters put a Mulhall centre into his own net. The *Blaydon Races* were now at full gallop. There were only two minutes remaining when, for the second successive match, Charlton was the saviour, nodding home a David Herd centre. After three and a half hours, it was off to Huddersfield on the Monday night. For the players – United's embroiled in Europe and the League Championship race, Sunderland's bidding for promotion – it was the last thing they needed; for the fans, it could not come soon enough.

'It took some getting to,' says Charlton, 'as the crowds were just everywhere. Sunderland were a good side near the top of the Second Division, and they were getting carried away with it all.' Desmond Hackett wrote in the *Daily Express*: 'It was a match to cherish; one that will add to the rich tapestry of the game.'

The irrepressible Sunderland forwards once again came surging towards the United goal and, with some illustrious United names struggling to get a grip, the underdogs took their now-customary lead through Sharkey two minutes into the second half. But with Best showing great character and maturity, Charlton demonstrating his class in every touch, and Crerand beginning to orchestrate matters in midfield, Law finally raced through for a typically thrilling leveller. Moments later, amid delirium from the Manchester faithful, United were ahead for the first time in the tie, Chisnall forcing his way through to fire powerfully home. The floodgates were now open and, with fans cascading down the terraces for a better view, Law scored from the spot after Hurley had up-ended Herd. Now a more commanding figure on his old stamping ground, Law had at last found his form and made it four with only half an hour left. It was not enough for the United faithful who had simply undergone too much to believe three goals were a safe enough cushion. They demanded another; they got it.

Herd scored but was also involved in an ugly skirmish with the bitterly disappointed Hurley. Charlton – too modest to mention it – strode the three ties like a colossus, that thinning thatch of his blowing this way and that as he ran his legs off, spraying the ball all over three parks. Hackett said: 'I shall never forget the passion of that night, when the roaring voices of Sunderland, rejoicing over their lead, suddenly trailed off into a sad lament. Manchester United looked not only Cup-winners but world-beaters.' But were they? 'It took too much out of us,' acknowledges Charlton, 'and we lost the semi-final.' World beaters? Well, Charlton always was.

Second Replay: Manchester United 5 Sunderland 1.

Manchester United: Gaskell, Brennan, Dunne, Crerand, Foulkes, Setters, D. Herd, Chisnall, Charlton, Law, Best.

Scorers: Law 3 (1 pen), Chisnall, Herd.

Sunderland: Montgomery, Irwin, Ashurst, Harvey, Hurley, Elliott, Usher, G. Herd, Sharkey, Crossan, Mulhall.

Scorer: Sharkey.

Results of previous games: Manchester United 3 Sunderland 3 (at Old Trafford); Sunderland 2 Manchester United 2 (aet, at Roker Park).

Stan Cullis

Wolverhampton Wanderers 3 Honved 2,
Molineux, 13 December 1954

*Born 25 October 1915. Ferociously effective centre-half who
played over 300 times for Wolves from 1935 to 1947. Earned 12
full caps for England plus 20 appearances in wartime and
Victory internationals. Managed Wolves from 1948 to 1964. One
of very few men to have had outstanding careers as both player
and manager with same club. Managed Birmingham City from
1965 to 1970.*

All that glistered in British football in 1954 were the old
gold shirts of Wolverhampton Wanderers. The previous,
Coronation year had seen Everest scaled and cricket's
Ashes regained, but at the winter game, which was all that
really mattered to millions, England had been humbled
3–6 by Hungary at Wembley. Six months on, the nation's
football pride had still not recovered when the Magyars
won the return in Budapest 7–1. Salvation came from an
unlikely source: the misty flicker of the new floodlights at
Molineux. Compared to the searchlight shafts of today,
their benign gaze was like that of a Victorian street lamp
but it was sufficient to ignite the touch-paper of revival.
That and the high-voltage management style of a certain
Stanley Cullis.

'Those lights were something special,' recalls Cullis. 'It
was as if an electric fuse went all the way round the
ground. The atmosphere was unique, and the crowd and
the players responded.' Cullis's own fuse was much
shorter, but did as much from the dressing-room. No club
in England turned it on like Wolves did in the mid-1950s:

they were not merely the first with new-fangled illumina-
tions, but they were the pioneers of both the long-ball style
and a series of unforgettable friendlies against foreign
opposition. All of which they won. 'Of course, there were
people who said the friendlies would be a flop,' says
Cullis. 'But we invited the finest continental teams: Real
Madrid, Moscow Spartak and Dynamo. But Honved is the
match I remember most as there was an element of
revenge about it. After all, Honved were the Hungarian
champions and had six of the national team which had
beaten England. The build-up had been perfect. A month
before we had won 4–0 against Spartak, which was
acclaimed England's greatest post-war soccer victory. I
said then that that was the proudest day of my life, as we
had struck such a great blow for English football. You
know, I did not even bring on a substitute when Eddie
Stuart was injured; I was determined to play the game the
good old British way. But the Honved night was even
better.'

Adding to the occasion was a live telecast to the nation,
the cameras whirling just as the second half got underway
and Wolves got into their stride. But the armchair fans had
missed a display of artistry at which the 54,998 who
squeezed into Molineux could only gasp. Honved took
the field throwing flowers to the massed ranks, and the
distinctive gabled roof of the Molineux Street stand
quivered in anticipation. Wolves stood atop the First
Division, undisputed masters of England and voracious
hunters of the long-ball game. Honved, with Puskas,
Kovacs, Kocsis and Czibor, were the unpronounceable
princes of the short pass.

'I have never known an atmosphere like it,' says Cullis.
'It was quite extraordinary.' So was the football. Spring-
ing like gazelles over the Molineux mud, the Hungarians
were soon displaying the ball skills of conjurors. When
these were allied to a slickness of pass that had the crowd
open-mouthed and the Wolves defence frequently ajar, a

repeat of England's drubbings looked likely. After just 14 minutes of Magyar mastery, it looked a certainty. In the 11th minute Ron Flowers handled a cross from the left and Kocsis rose majestically to ram home a Puskas free-kick. Three minutes later, after a couple of bold Wolves counter-attacks, Bert 'The Cat' Williams was again bending disconsolately into the back of his own net and, once again, he had had little or no chance. Koscis this time carved up the committed Wolves defence with a superb through-ball for the dashing Machos to run on to and slot firmly home.

Molineux's misery was only tempered by a sense that this was something very, very special, a kind of football not seen in the ground before or since. The crowd watched transfixed. The television people did the same when they might well have pulled the plug – what kind of humiliation was this to set before the watching nation? Cullis himself might have blown a fuse, but didn't. The pitch was cutting up, the Magyars were losing their razor's edge and, as the first half wore on, Wolves were turning the tide. The crowd could hardly wait for the second half to start.

'Contrary to what was said in many papers,' claims Cullis, 'I did not explode at half-time and there were no shenanigans. In fact, all I told them was to carry on as they were and the goals would come. Even if they didn't, I would be quite satisfied.' He did not have to wait long. Four minutes into the second half, Johnny Hancocks was bundled over by Kovacs and Welsh referee Mervyn Griffiths awarded a penalty. The 5ft 4in Hancocks used his size 2 boot to hammer it past 'keeper Farago's left hand. The gabled roof swayed as the roar swelled. Honved, too, began to creak, and the old gold shirts were now ablaze.

Urged on by skipper Billy Wright, eager to erase the personal anguish of England's defeats, Wolves were rampant now. Peter Broadbent assumed control of midfield and found a few gaps. Hancocks almost bent the bar with a free-kick, Dennis Wilshaw had a fierce drive tipped past the post, and Flowers, too, was forcing Farago into frantic action. Roared on by 55,000 Black Country throats, Wolves could sense Honved's resolve weakening as the pitch sapped their strength and blunted their skills. The scent of a famous victory in their nostrils, the English leaders went for the kill.

Long balls continued to pound the Hungarian lines, foraging wingers snapped at the retreating full-backs' heels and every loose ball was voraciously gobbled and hoisted toward an overworked Farago. Amid unbearable tension and with just 14 minutes remaining, Wilshaw escaped the clutches of Bozsik and Lorant to send a pin-point lob for Swinbourne to head home.

Two minutes later, full-back Bill Shorthouse got in on the act, winning possession on the left, swapping passes with Smith and slipping a ball in towards Wilshaw whose centre was hooked in by Swinbourne on the volley. Delirium broke out in a few million homes as well as Molineux, and although Honved, their reputation as world champions on the line, were not yet done, Wolves held on.

The *Daily Mirror* wrote of the match: 'It had everything – furious speed, blinding skill, pounding power, superlative goal-keeping, and something more.' England's reputation was restored, and a glorious new chapter was embossed in old gold. On an incandescent night, that iron man, Cullis, was, well, satisfied.

Wolverhampton Wanderers: Williams, Stuart, Shorthouse, Slater, Wright, Flowers, Hancocks, Broadbent, Swinbourne, Wilshaw, Smith.

Scorers: Hancocks (pen), Swinbourne 2.

Honved: Farago, Palicsko, Kovacs, Bozsik, Lorant, Banyai, Budai, Kocsis, Machos, Puskas, Czibor.

Sub: Tichy (Machos).

Scorers: Kocsis, Machos.

Derek Dooley

Sheffield Wednesday 6 Notts. County 0
Second Division, Hillsborough, 3 November 1951

*Son of a Sheffield steelworker, he joined Wednesday in 1947
after a brief spell as an amateur at Lincoln City. Dooley's
League career lasted only fifteen months but he had scored 63
goals in 59 games when he collided with Preston 'keeper George
Thompson at Deepdale and broke his right leg. Gangrene set in
and, tragically, surgeons had to amputate the leg to save his life.
So ended the brief but brilliant career of a man who was rated
an England centre-forward of the future; he was 23. Dooley had
helped Wednesday win promotion from the Second Division in
1951–52 and eventually became manager at Hillsborough and
later chief executive at rivals Sheffield United.*

Derek Dooley was 6ft 3in tall, wore size 12 boots and had
hair the colour of the nearby blast furnaces. With his
distinctive name and awkward style, he knew that the
difference between being a headline-writer's dream and
the butt of terrace humour was about two goals a game.
'You were dropped if you didn't score,' he remembers.
And he was – straight into the third team.

It was an age of more precisely defined roles: full-backs
defended, wingers stayed wide and centre-forwards were
supposed to deliver goals by the bucket-load. Among
those who supplied regular shipments were Tommy
Lawton, Nat Lofthouse and Len Shackleton. The livewire
young leader at Hillsborough dreamed of doing likewise
at the top level but had already found that Second Division
defences were not as obliging as the juniors and reserves.

'I had always wanted to be a hero on my début,' he
admits, 'and to score the goals in a win for Wednesday. I

had stood on the Kop at Hillsborough in all weathers, dreaming of doing just that. Yet when I played my first League match against Preston in March 1950, I had a stinker! I had scored goals at all levels, whether it was the YMCA or the RAF, Wednesday reserves or Owler Lane school, but I did not get one in the League. We lost 0−1 [Tom Finney scored] and I knew I had blown it. What's more, I got barracked by the Kop.

'It was a good thing we did not have a fourth team at the time as I would have been in that. But it made me even more determined to get back and show 'em. It was eight months before they gave me another chance, at Charlton, and I blew that one, too. Sam Bartram's brilliant goal-keeping did not help, but I had failed again, and again I was dropped.'

It was the 'yo-yo' era in Sheffield with both Wednesday and United rarely able to remain in the same division from one season to the next. Wednesday ended the 1950−51 campaign being relegated from Division One by a fraction of a goal, in spite of desperate attempts to stay up. They had courted striker Jimmy Hagan but were repulsed by neighbours United and, in the end, broke the transfer record by paying Notts. County £35,000 for Jackie Sewell. Three months into the following season Wednesday were languishing in the lower half, having tried no less than four players in the No.9 shirt. None of them had made it their own and Dooley was recalled.

'I knew that this was my last chance as I ran on to the pitch,' he remembers. 'It was against Barnsley, and things did not look good at half-time. We were losing 0−1. But five minutes after the break I took a pass from Eddie Gannon and just hit it straight into the top corner. About 20 minutes later I hit another almost identical goal. We won 2−1 and on the way home I couldn't wait to buy the *Green 'Un*. The headline was, "He'll Dooley all right." '

It was now Dooley's turn to deliver and, helped by his goals, Wednesday began to climb the table. But the match that really made his name was the one at home to Notts. County. In goal for the visitors was Roy Smith, a former Owl. When asked by his team-mates about the still largely unknown Wednesday centre-forward, the 'keeper uttered the now famous reply: 'Oh, that big, useless bugger. Don't worry about him, he'll never score.'

He didn't, at least not until the second half. Up against Leon Leuty, a classy former England centre-half, and with Tommy Lawton also playing, Dooley hardly had a kick early on. 'But we played towards the Kop in the second half and I always fancied that,' he recalls. 'It was like a magnet to me. It was also an awful day and the heavy going suited me as I was a bit quick. Anyhow, with Albert Quixall and Sewell alongside, I managed to score five in 32 minutes! Three times I ran on to through-balls while one was a header and the other I chested in. I even got a sixth but that was disallowed for off-side!'

Dooley's goals came in the 50th, 62nd, 68th, 78th and 82nd minutes, and it was the first time anyone had scored five for Wednesday since Douglas Hunt in 1938. An adoring Kop duly saluted the birth of a legend, and Dooley kept his place. 'Yes, I was fairly confident after that,' he smiles. And Smith? 'I remember him coming up afterwards and putting his hand on my shoulder. It meant a lot, did that.'

After the match Dooley went home for his tea in the time-honoured manner, queuing in the rain for a No. 2 bus. 'Don't be late,' his mother had told him. 'There were no cars for footballers in those days,' he says, 'and I lined up like everybody else. Five goals in the second half and you got the bus home! I remember this old fellow, who was absolutely soaked to the skin, getting on and the conductor asking him: "How did you get like that?" The fellow said: "I was at the match and was just going to leave when this young Dooley scored. I thought I'd stop to see if he got another. When he did, I said, blow me, maybe he'll get three. And so it went on. I just stood there and got ruddy soaked." '

Leuty had a dousing of a different kind, and it would have been scant consolation to the cultured international to read the rave notices about his unstoppable young opponent. 'Speed . . . build . . . temperament . . . even the ability to tackle the centre-half' were among Dooley's suddenly discovered attributes. The strapping 14-stoner from Firth Park in Sheffield was, quite simply, a scoring sensation, a different kind of leader who did not rely on the wingers' crosses but would run through the middle, using his electrifying pace to skin lumbering defenders before finishing with a pulverising shot. He was undoubtedly raw, but few could fathom his awkward style or halt his direct runs. The fans loved him, and he was soon called 'The Hillsborough Juggernaut', or, if you preferred, 'Dreadnought Derek'.

One contemporary columnist wrote: 'He is as explosive as a pail of petrol pitched on a bonfire.' When Dooley scored twice against Swansea at the end of November, it was the fourth match in which he had found the net on two occasions. He had now scored 14 goals in eight games, and Wednesday rocketed up the table. Opponents began to dread meeting the Yorkshire side and tried various methods to combat this scoring phenomenon. Dooley's next match was at Upton Park against Malcolm Allison who had already established himself as the thinking man's centre-half and would later found the famous West Ham 'academy'. Surely Dooley would be tested here. Result: Hammers 0 Owls 6. Dooley scored three.

Sheffield became Dooley-daft, and the fans even altered the words of songs to suit their hero: even *Rudolf the Red-Nosed Reindeer* was not immune, developing 'a very awkward style', while *Truly, Truly Fair* became *Dooley, Dooley's There*. The local paper, whose emblem was the vulcan on the Town Hall, printed a picture of Dooley in its place. Just before Christmas, Dooley fired in four against Everton and, benefiting from the influence of manager Allan 'Brownie' Brown, he rattled up an unbelievable 47 goals in 31 matches to take Wednesday to the title.

'On the way home from [the deciding match at] Coventry, I sampled champagne for the first time in my life,' he says. He had much to celebrate: promotion in his first season, marriage in the summer and the prospect of First Division defences quaking in their boots the following season. 'They used to call me a tearaway,' he says, 'but I simply went one way: straight for goal. For me there was no greater thrill than when I belted that ball between those posts. That was my target. That was my life.'

Little did anyone know that less than a year later Dooley would be fighting for that life in a Preston hospital. Luckily he won, but not before the football world had been devastated by the news. 'It was an awful sensation lying there after the operation,' he says. 'I couldn't walk. I knew I would never play again. I'd been married only six months, and I had no trade. But I soon realised that it was no use worrying; that wouldn't bring the leg back.' So he fought back. In six months he had tossed away his crutches; in a year he had tossed away his stick. Derek Dooley lost a leg, but they could not take away his big heart.

Sheffield Wednesday: McIntosh, Bannister, Kenny, Gannon, Packard, Davies, Finney, Sewell, Dooley, Quixall, Rickett.

Scorers: Dooley 5, Quixall.

Notts. County: Smith, Southwell, Deane, Brunt, Leuty, Robinson, McPherson, Jackson, Lawton, Wyllie, Crookes.

Alex Ferguson

Aberdeen 2 Real Madrid 1 (aet)
European Cup-Winners' Cup final, Gothenburg, 11 May
1983

*Born 31 December 1941. Son of a Glasgow shipyard worker,
Ferguson represented Scotland at schoolboy, youth and
amateur levels. An aggressive centre-forward, he signed for
Queens Park in 1957, and then joined St Johnstone as a part-
timer in 1960. Four years later he went to Dunfermline as a full-
time professional before moving on to Rangers in 1967. After
two and a half years at Ibrox, he left for Falkirk where he
became player-coach. After spells at Ayr and East Stirling, he
took St Mirren to the First Division title in his first season in
1976–77 and became Aberdeen boss in 1978. In the most
glorious period in the club's history, Fergie led the Dons to three
Premier League titles, four Scottish Cups, the Scottish League
Cup and the European Cup-Winners' Cup. Was awarded the
OBE and joined the Pittodrie board. After Jock Stein's untimely
death during Scotland's qualifying campaign for the 1986
World Cup, Fergie took over and led the squad in Mexico.
Succeeded Ron Atkinson at Old Trafford in 1986 and in his first
full season United finished runners-up in Division One. Won the
FA Cup in 1990 and the European Cup-Winners' Cup in 1991.*

During his early days of management in the granite city,
Alex Ferguson would sometimes placate his players by
saying: 'Don't worry, you're not playing Real Madrid.'
After Aberdeen had knocked out Waterschei in the semi-
final of the European Cup-Winners' Cup, he had to change
the script. With the possible exception of North Sea oil,
Fergie's arrival had already proved the best thing to
happen to Aberdeen in living memory. His nous and

never-say-die spirit had provided the once unfashionable club on the east coast with the audacity to challenge the dominance of Rangers and Celtic. But Real Madrid?

'It was like a fairy tale,' he says. 'When we started the campaign, we were put into the qualifying round – that's how highly we were rated! But we beat Sion, a Swiss team, 11–1 on aggregate and I remember their manager telling me, "You can win this." I said, "Come off it, we're too young." Anyhow, we stumbled through 1–0 on aggregate against an Albanian side [Dinamo Tirana], then beat Lech Poznan and suddenly found ourselves in the quarter-final against Bayern. They had players like Rummenigge and Breitner and we thought, "Oh, Christ." We felt that we'd done well to get that far. But when we beat Bayern and came through the semi easily enough, we really fancied it. We had now got some momentum, and the great thing about winning is that it builds confidence. By that stage it really was a case of "Bring on Real Madrid". '

Perhaps the only thing the two clubs had in common was that they were both managed by former centre-forwards; Fergie had been a formidable leader of the Rangers line while the Spaniards were under the tutelage of the imcomparable Alfredo di Stefano. But even there the contrast in their respective styles reflected the gulf between the clubs. It was Real's eleventh European final and Aberdeen's first; the cantilevered splendour of Real's Stadium had a capacity of just 100,000 more than Pittodrie; Real's team had been expensively assembled from the four corners, Aberdeen's largely home-grown; the Madrid trophy room resembled Hatton Garden, Aberdeen had the northern lights . . .

But Ferguson is not a man to be overawed. 'I decided we needed a bit of presence in our party, someone whom the press would respect to counter all the attention di Stefano was bound to attract,' he explained. 'So I invited Jock Stein. It really was a Scottish clan thing. The whole country was behind us, and we believed that with our spirit nobody could beat us. We kept it low-key and light-hearted before the game, having a quiz the night before. I remember that was a great night with lots of laughs, so the boys went to bed in a good frame of mind. I felt they were mentally attuned for the match.'

Real probably were not. They had just beaten Gijon 6–0 in the Spanish Cup semi-final but had lost to Valencia the previous weekend and been pipped for the Spanish title by Atletico Bilbao. They had injury worries, too, and although Uli Stielike had been passed fit, the young forward Francisco Pineda was definitely out. Aberdeen were without Dougie Bell, which placed a heavier burden on midfielder Gordon Strachan, but striker Eric Black had recovered after being out for a month with an ankle injury. 'A tremendous bonus,' said Ferguson. He told his players: 'One goal is often enough to win a European final, and I'm sure we'll get one. We must be patient, though, and Real Madrid have just lost the League: they'll be looking for consolation.'

Gothenburg's Ullevi Stadium was awash with Aberdeen's red and white favours and torrential rain. The pitch had been protected but still looked like the North Sea when play began. Aberdeen took to it like trawlermen and almost scored before Real had left port. Black's fierce volley was tipped on to the bar by Augustin in the third minute. Three minutes later, Black, aged only 19, did even better, pouncing on a loose ball in the Real goal-mouth after Alex McLeish had got his head to a Strachan corner. One-nil, and Real not happy in conditions that were barely playable. But it was those conditions that brought them level in the 15th minute. A mortified Willie Miller watched in horror as his back-pass to Jim Leighton stuck in the Swedish mud. Santillana raced on to it and Leighton brought him down. Juanito struck his spot-kick firmly.

But the goal failed to lift Real above the oozing surface and Aberdeen, roared on by some 14,000 supporters, were playing out of their skins – although they were soaked to them. Strachan streaked across the water as if on water-skis, his red hair matted to his face and his eyes ablaze. With Peter Weir a wonderful accomplice on the left wing, he ran the waterlogged legs off the Spaniards. 'Gordon had a magnificent game,' says Ferguson. 'He never stopped.' The little red terrier deserved a goal and should have had one in the 55th minute after volleying against the 'keeper's legs. Driven on by the inspirational captaincy of Miller, the ceaseless running and probing of Strachan and Weir, and the invention of Black, Aberdeen were in total command. Real had Augustin to thank for keeping them interested as twice more he saved what looked like certain goals. In contrast, Jim Leighton had little to do.

The brave Black, having fully justified his selection, took a knock and was replaced by John Hewitt with three minutes of full-time remaining. The Scottish Under-21 international provided a lively presence and, with four goals already in the competition, eagerly sought a fifth. He got it in the 113th minute, a diving header at the far post which Real never looked likely to come back from. They didn't, and as the rain continued to fall on the almost entirely open stadium, no Scot in the ground noticed it. Aberdeen were the sixth British club to win the Cup-Winners' Cup and the first Scottish club to collect a European trophy since Rangers in 1972. Thankfully, the behaviour of their supporters was in marked contrast to the Rangers followers on that ill-fated occasion in Barcelona.

'It was a marvellous achievement for us to defeat Real Madrid to win our first European trophy and to do it in style,' said Fergie. 'Bobby Robson was telling me how important it is to win in Europe, and I agree whole-heartedly. We had now reached that same high platform as others who have tasted European glory, and no one can say we got through the back door.' Di Stefano, always the gentleman, said: 'Aberdeen deserved to win but they were fortunate in that the conditions suited them better. It really was only fit for swimming.'

Aberdeen, whose fighting qualities landed them three successive Scottish Cups from 1982 to 1984, turned their attention to the Scottish League Championship which they won in 1983–84 and 1984–85 to break the Old Firm stranglehold. After Gothenburg, Fergie could revert to his original script, albeit with a slight variation: 'Don't worry – it's only Real Madrid.'

Aberdeen: Leighton, Rougvie, Miller, McLeish, McMaster, Cooper, Strachan, Weir, McGhee, Black, Simpson.

Sub: Hewitt (Black)

Scorers: Black, Hewitt.

Real Madrid: Augustin, Metgod, Bonet, Camacho, Juan Jose, Angel, Gallego, Stielike, Juanito, Santillana, Isidro.

Subs: San Jose (Camacho), Salguero (Isidro).

Scorer: Juanito (pen).

Tom Finney

Italy 0 England 4
Turin, 16 May 1948

Born 5 April 1922. Made his League début in 1946 after his career was delayed by the war, and hit the target 187 times in 433 League appearances. Versatile winger who played in four forward positions in his 76 England matches. Never won a major honour but was the first man to become Footballer of the Year twice, in 1954 and 1957. Retired in 1959 at the age of 38, and earned this unique tribute from former team-mate Bill Shankly: 'If pressed, I would say Tommy was the best player ever born.' Now president of Preston North End.

Long before Michael Caine went near the place, the ultimate 'Italian job' was done by a Preston plumber. Italy were World Cup-winners in 1938 and, although it was ten years since they had lifted the trophy, they were still the undisputed masters of Europe. When England visited them in the cauldron of the Stadio Municipali in Turin, the Boys in Blue were expected to make something akin to bolognaise sauce out of the English defence. They nearly did, but Frank Swift's size 10 hands somehow kept them at bay, and with their own rearguard looking more like a colander than an impregnable *catenaccio*, it was the peerless Tom Finney who delivered the final counter-punches. In pin-drop silence, England won 4–0.

'After playing us off the park for most of the first half,' Finney recalls, 'yet finding themselves 0–2 down, they started arguing with each other. Morty [Stan Mortenson] gave me a nod and a wink and said: "We can beat these." And we did.' Nods ... winks ... goals against the run of play . . . It was the sort of victory of which Caine himself would have approved. Yet a character further removed from that chirpy, celluloid Cockney would be harder to imagine than Finney, a tradesman who was to turn down a prince's ransom for 'a proper job' in Italy: £30,000 from the Prince di Trabia to play for Palermo. But it was Finney whose two goals in the second half twisted the knife as far as the home fans were concerned.

The match had all the trappings of a major continental football occasion. A searing sun, a packed partisan crowd, a perfect pitch and, from England's point of view, their skipper Frank Swift's farewell appearance. They also had quite a side arrayed against them. 'Very skilful,' says Finney. 'We hardly had a kick.' In his self-deprecatory Lancashire manner, Finney would have us believe that Walter Winterbottom had sent the boy scouts over on a recce – until you ask him the composition of England's forward line. 'Oh, well, er . . . Stan [Matthews] were on right, Wilf Mannion, Tommy Lawton, Morty and me.' Load of rubbish, really.

The defence wasn't bad, either. The giant 'keeper, Frank Swift, massive of presence and paw, demanded a quick goal 'to shut this lot up', as he motioned toward the din filtering into the tunnel before the teams took the field. Billy Wright and Neil Franklin were at the heart of that defence, but still it was all but overrun in the first half. England had, however, granted Swift his wish by taking a four-minute lead through the mighty Mortenson. 'Atomic' was how the *Daily Mail*'s Roy Peskett described him, but even atoms needed luck, thinks Finney.

'Morty made this tremendous run down the right early on and shaped as if he were going to cross. The goalie came out and the ball sailed into the top corner. Morty will never admit it, but I think it were a fluke.' England were 1–0 up, and the game had hardly begun. Roared on by 85,000 fans and their coach 'Dictator' Pozzo on the bench, the Italians then produced some bewildering stuff. Carapellese, Gabetto and Parola, a centre-half who 'locked up' Tommy Lawton and still had time to launch attacks, were outstanding. Finney hardly got a look in as wave after azure wave lashed upon the England barricades but, with Swift inspired and Franklin and Wright rock-like, the visitors' defences were not to be breached.

Then in the 24th minute Mortenson cut another characteristic dash and, after a mazy and electrifying dribble over half the length of the field, he crossed for Lawton to ram home. The crowd had long since recovered from the first goal, but this was a body-blow and, with the courageous Spanish referee Escartin disallowing two offside goals, the Italians began to show the first signs of panic. 'We sensed at half-time that they were becoming agitated with one another,' Finney recalls. 'Walter [Winterbottom] did not have any geeing up to do as we felt at that point we could win it, but we knew they'd come at us early in the second half.' They were right.

England got the anticipated roasting, from a boiling Italian sun and some pretty hot footballers. 'They fought like tigers,' Finney recalls, 'and the crowd created a right old racket.' But England had the slice of luck they needed when a back-header by Gabetto hit the bar and bounced on to the line. While the Italians were screaming for a goal, Swift plucked it off the line and tossed it into the crowd. No goal, said the ref. Still 2–0 and only half an hour to go.

By now the crowd had become incensed, the Italian players were fraying at the edges and England knew that they had only to keep their heads and their stamina in the intense heat. 'Morty looked at me and we both knew that it was on,' says Finney. 'But we still needed another goal as, even with only 20 minutes to go, anything could have happened.'

Finney, with a wonderful sense of timing, provided not just one goal to soothe England's nerves but a second to turn the remainder of the match into a kick-around. 'Wilf Mannion laid one inside the full-back and I ran on to it, rounded the 'keeper and drove it in,' he says. A minute later, the irrepressible Mortenson supplied the pass, the peerless Finney the finish to a silence, he recalls, 'so eerie you could hear a pin drop. After that we just knocked it around to one another, but the crowd did give us a good reception at the end and the whole match was pretty sporting. There was a bit of shirt-tugging but nothing really dirty, and it was a pleasure to be a part of one of England's greatest victories.'

Italy: Bacigalupo, Ballarin, Eliani, Anrovazzi, Parola, Grezar, Menti, Loik, Gabetto, Mazzola, Carapellese.

England: Swift, Scott, Howe, Wright, Franklin, Cockburn, Matthews, Mortenson, Lawton, Mannion, Finney.

Scorers: Mortenson 2, Finney 2.

Tommy Gemmell

Celtic 3 Benfica 0
European Cup second round, first leg, Celtic Park, 12
November 1969

Born 16 October 1943. Signed for Celtic in 1961 after learning his trade at Meadow Thistle (Wishaw) and Coltness United. Was a member of the great Celtic side of the late 1960s and scored in the European Cup final triumph in 1967 and the defeat in 1970. Won six Scottish League champions' medals, three Scottish Cup-winners' medals and four in the League Cup with Celtic. Earned 18 caps for Scotland as a powerful, overlapping full-back who could play on either right or left. Joined Nottingham Forest in 1971 but returned to Scotland to win another League Cup with Dundee, whom he later managed, in 1974.

Discovering a Celtic fan who is prepared to admit that he was not present in Lisbon on the night the Lions destroyed Inter Milan in the 1967 European Cup final is probably the most hopeless quest in Scottish football's endearing sociology. As it happened, only some 7,000 actually attended the famous match but two seasons later all those tens of thousands who swear that they, too, witnessed the great victory were provided with some substance for their arguments. Tommy Gemmell fired another artillery shell into a Portuguese net that was so similar in velocity and range to his celebrated equaliser against Inter Milan in the Stadio Nacional that even sober Celtic fans can be forgiven for getting the two confused – with the inevitable consequences.

The second explosion occurred at Celtic Park, Glasgow, and the opposition was Benfica. But toss in a wee dram or two down the years, and most of the 75,000 fans assembled that night can convince themselves that they had also been there when the European Cup was lifted, and so they too are somehow tinged with immortality. For Gemmell the goal was especially sweet, for it came after he had been left out of the side by Jock Stein following a previous dismissal. And it came very quickly: just 75 seconds into the first leg. 'You could say that I had a point to prove,' smiles Gemmell.

'It was one of those great European nights in Glasgow,' he adds. 'Full house, terrific atmosphere, glamorous opposition, Eusebio, you name it . . . but it was the night Celtic also proved that we were still a great team.' One or two names had changed from 1967, but most of the major players were still there. Jock Stein was still at the helm, the crowd had lost none of its passion and Gemmell none of his power. Indeed, it was vintage Celtic. The consensus was that they would have routed anybody in Europe on that form. It was the Celtic that had eventually prevailed over Inter Milan, the Celtic that had won six successive Scottish League titles, an irresistible force carried by a tide of emotion; one of the great club sides of all time.

'I'll never forget that night,' says Gemmell, 'as the atmosphere was special even by Celtic standards.' Perhaps it was the Portuguese 'connection'; perhaps it was the presence of the Black Panther, Eusebio; perhaps it was the magnificent start Gemmell had given them. Whatever it was, it was a night that went into Celtic folklore. 'I don't know if it was because I remember it so well from a personal point of view,' offers Gemmell, 'but the fans seemed to roar as they never had before.' But then, he did give them the perfect excuse.

Celtic won a free-kick on the edge of the penalty area when Bobby Murdoch was impeded. Benfica duly assembled their wall, and they of all people must have been aware of the artillery Celtic possessed. But the Portuguese might have been confused by the reputation that Bobby Murdoch had built with his own blockbusters.

Judging by their obvious apprehension, they appeared to
be expecting a blast but looked unsure as to where it might
come from. They fidgeted nervously.

Gemmell had loaded his shells, his eagerness
heightened by the 'just about perfect' range. When Bertie
Auld laid the ball back to him, he had already released the
safety catch. The Portuguese spotted the danger too late. A
sudden awareness crept over the wall. Gemmell fired, and
'keeper Henriques seemed alert to the danger. But beyond
flapping a helpless arm in the general direction of the
missile, he was powerless to prevent it giving Celtic a 1–0
lead. 'It was a very special moment,' says Gemmell. Some
observers felt it was a better goal than the one against Inter
Milan. 'Different class,' wrote one Scottish scribe, who
definitely was at both matches. 'A real thunderer,' wrote
another. 'No goalie alive would have got near it,' added
another.

The impact on the game was enormous, for while
Benfica wondered what had hit them, Celtic sprayed the
ball around like men possessed. With Auld a magnificent
general and Jimmy Johnstone in jaunty mood, it took
Benfica all their time to absorb Celtic's attacks without
even conceiving any of their own. Eusebio? There were
times when Celts were entitled to ask whether he was
actually playing. He was, and had a good chance before
slicing uncharacteristically wide from fifteen yards. Celtic
were rightly wary of the great man, for he punctuated
periods of apparent indifference with a lightning strike
and all but struck with a darting header late in the first
half. John Fallon, in the Celts goal, dived to thwart him
with a reflex save.

In between the green and white waves which crashed
upon the Portuguese defensive shore, Benfica were able to
demonstrate their pedigree with some classy moves but
they never looked as threatening as Celtic. Just before the
break, the home side got a deserved second when Willie
Wallace drove home from an acute angle. 'It was just the

lift we wanted,' remembers Gemmell, 'as we had given 'em a pounding and were worried we might not have much to show for it. We knew we still had to go to Lisbon.'

Gemmell was right to be wary of the second leg, but Celtic gained a psychological boost when neither Eusebio nor Simoes came out for the second half. When Harry Hood, who had earlier set up Hughes only to see the winger miss a gilt-edged chance, powered a great header beyond the redoubtable Henriques in the 69th minute, the tie looked over. 'We certainly thought we'd won it,' recalls Gemmell. 'Not just because we had a 3–0 lead, although that was a great cushion, but through having outplayed them. We just felt that we had nothing to fear. We were not complacent, though; Jock wouldn't allow that.'

Permissible or not, Celtic were to surrender their lead in Lisbon, if not like lambs, then in a manner of which Stein did not approve. After Eusebio had headed Benfica back into the tie in the 36th minute of the second leg, Graca drove home from long range two minutes later. Celtic, helped by Eusebio's now customary second-half absence, held on until the last minute but, with the referee looking at his watch, substitute Diamantino equalised. Celtic finally made it to the last eight all right, but on the toss of a coin. Few of their fans claimed to have witnessed the final scene, however; not even those who were there.

Celtic: Fallon, Craig, Gemmell, Murdoch, McNeill, Clark, Johnstone, Hood, Wallace, Auld, Hughes.

Scorers: Gemmell, Wallace, Hood.

Benfica: Henriques, Malta, Humberto, Zeca, Fernandez, Graca, Coluna, Simoes, Torres, Eusebio, Diamantino.

Subs: Jorges (Eusebio), Augusto (Simoes).

Bobby Gould

Wimbledon 1 Liverpool 0
FA Cup final, Wembley, 14 May 1988

Born 12 June 1946. A fiercely competitive, old-fashioned inside forward, Gould never gave less than 100 per cent in over 600 games for his many clubs. As a youngster, he made a sufficiently big impact with his first club Coventry City to persuade Arsenal to pay £90,000 for his services. Major honours eluded him, however, most notably in the League Cup final in 1970 when Swindon Town staged their remarkable triumph. Returned to the West Midlands and had spells with Wolves and West Brom before joining Bristol City, West Ham, Wolves again and Hereford. Became manager of Bristol Rovers, then Wimbledon, where he won the FA Cup; joined QPR as coach and returned to the Hawthorns as boss in March 1991.

When Wimbledon took the field against Liverpool at Anfield in a previous season, their players displayed an inglorious disdain for both the place and Liverpool's reputation. As they ran down the steps under the famous 'This is Anfield' sign, they spat on it. It is perhaps not something the perpetrators will look back on with pride but, besides epitomising the contempt in which these common-man footballers from this unfashionable club held the aristocrats of the game, it showed they were quite capable of making intimidatory statements of their own. Wimbledon's subsequent 2–2 draw earned them a respect which was to become greater, albeit more grudging, the longer they remained in the top flight. The way they muscled in on Wembley confirmed that they were capable of anything. Well, almost anything.

The 1987–88 season had been a vintage one for

Liverpool. With John Barnes and Peter Beardsley bringing extra attacking flair to the time-honoured efficiency, Liverpool had never been so appealing. Their 5–0 demolition of Nottingham Forest in the League earned rapturous reviews, not least from Tom Finney who called it: 'The finest display I have ever seen from a British club side.' It was a month before Wimbledon were wheeled on to face them at Wembley. As far as the bookmakers were concerned, the trophy could be handed to Liverpool there and then. Most football purists agreed. Such was Wimbledon's reputation for ruggedness and lack of etiquette that their presence at Wembley's show-piece final was prompting the sort of reaction a country squire might reserve for the local tramp who gatecrashes his favourite daughter's wedding.

'Liverpool have a duty to stop them,' screamed one headline; 'For football's sake,' pleaded another, while a third screeched: 'Wimbledon must be halted.' The South Londoners had collected as many bookings as the Wembley box office, and neither their football nor their antics enhanced the reputation of the beautiful game. But the big plus in their favour was that Liverpool did not like playing against them. Bobby Gould was well aware of this and he did not have to remind the squad, which he had inherited from Dave Bassett, of its tremendous psychological advantages. What is more, the Dons loved to play against Liverpool. Gould has since said: 'There was never a moment when I thought we wouldn't win.'

It was a confidence that only a dream decade can inspire. Eleven years earlier Wimbledon were in the Southern League, and both the dog track and speedway team were better-known local sporting institutions than Plough Lane. The All England Club? A different world. But now Wimbledon were in a different galaxy and they arrived at the twin towers feeling that overturning Liverpool was well within their orbit. The gist of Gould's pre-match pep talk was: 'Nobody thinks we can win it.'

But they still went up Wembley Way as the most denigrated team since the 1966 Argentinians. Five sendings-off and fifty-one cautions was a clear sign that, in the retaliation stakes, Wimbledon were never likely to be second.

As is often the way of Wembley finals, the underdogs were not in the least overwhelmed by the occasion and gave as good as they got in a tense opening which contained more football than anyone had dared hope. To the amazement of many, the dreaded Dons behaved impeccably – apart from one tackle by Vinny Jones on Steve McMahon in the ninth minute. It was a steamy, claustrophobic afternoon, and Liverpool's normally rampant attack had been well and truly stifled. Playing as if anti-personnel mines, trip-wires and barbed wire had been strewn about the hallowed turf, the champions had clearly lost the propaganda war. But they still looked capable of winning the match.

In the 26th minute Beardsley and Ray Houghton produced a rare moment of fluency to leave leading scorer John Aldridge unmarked in front of Dave Beasant in the Wimbledon goal. The 'keeper went the wrong way but stuck out a leg to block the shot and then, in a marvellous double save that evoked comparison with Jimmy Montomery's for Sunderland in 1973, scooped the ball to safety. Eight minutes later it did not appear that Beasant's acrobatics would hold the same significance, for Beardsley netted after being fouled by Andy Thorn – only to discover that referee Brian Hill had blown for the infringement. The disadvantage law? An irate Liverpool wasted the free-kick, but worse was to come for the champions. Much worse.

Lawrie Sanchez was to add his unlikely name to a long list of unsung Wembley heroes when he headed home Dennis Wise's superbly floated free-kick a minute later. As surprising as that lead, however, was Wimbledon's refusal to indulge in the rough-house tactics which had besmirched their season. They could scarcely be faulted in the first 45 minutes but, surely, there was still time enough for Liverpool to put the upstarts in their places. Kenny Dalglish had much to say at half-time. Gould, with masterly understatement, merely told his team: 'It's very hot; make sure you drink plenty of water.'

If Gould's way of preparing his men for the Liverpool onslaught was refreshingly simple, tactics had not been neglected. The master-stroke of coach Don Howe, who had detailed Dennis Wise to cut off Barnes's supply line, continued to thwart the increasingly frantic Merseysiders. But the decisive moment of the match occurred in the 61st minute when, after an extremely harsh penalty award against Clive Goodyear, Beasant dived to save Aldridge's kick. It was the first penalty to be missed in a Cup final at Wembley.

There were inevitably more Liverpool assaults, more heroics from Beasant and more palpitations for Gould, but his Dons held on for one of the greatest upsets in Cup history. 'Don Howe just hugged me when we had won it,' remembers Gould, who was tearfully to dedicate the success to his family. He deserved his magical moment. Arguably, his greatest achievement had been in not just beating Liverpool, but doing so in a manner the Marquess of Queensberry would have admired. The critics had to hand it to him: there was nothing untoward about the Dons' behaviour on the day, and some of their football bore a quality that belied its pre-match reputation.

'I'm working hard to get the club accepted,' said Gould. 'Nothing has been easy in my life, and I've had to fight for everything I've ever had. As a player I gave 100 per cent, I didn't mind getting hurt and I'd like to think I was appreciated by my clubs. But I was never sent off in over 600 games. Hard, fair, and with a smile. That's how I saw myself. That's how I want to see Wimbledon.' That's how Wimbledon had played it. His players had done as they were told and had drunk enough water. Never has it tasted as sweet.

Wimbledon: Beasant, Goodyear, Young, Thorn, Phelan, Wise, Jones, Sanchez, Cork, Fashanu, Gibson.

Subs: Cunningham (Cork), Scales (Gibson).

Scorer: Sanchez.

Liverpool: Grobbelaar, Nicol, Gillespie, Hansen, Ablett, Houghton, Spackman, McMahon, Barnes, Aldridge, Beardsley.

Subs: Molby (Spackman), Johnston (Aldridge).

Andy Gray

Everton 3 Rapid Vienna 1
European Cup-Winners' Cup final, Rotterdam, 15 May 1985

Born 30 November 1955. From the Gorbals, Glasgow, Gray joined Dundee United as a schoolboy and scored 36 goals for them before moving to Aston Villa for £110,000 in 1973. Four years later Wolves paid a record £1,460,000 for him, and he notched the winner in a League Cup final triumph over Nottingham Forest in 1980. A courageous, rampaging centre-forward and an ebullient character, Gray played 20 times for Scotland but made his greatest impact at Everton who captured the FA Cup, the League and the European Cup-Winners' Cup during his brief twenty-month stay. Returned to Villa to make way for Gary Lineker, but Everton fans never really understood why one of their favourite sons had to go.

Andy Gray won a few medals in his time, those in the FA Cup, European Cup-Winners' Cup, League and League Cup being the most celebrated quartet. But he should have been able to fill his house, let alone his mantelpiece, with awards for his bravery. Like the great centre-forwards of the past, Gray was never afraid to venture into that part of the opposition's penalty area which Hugh McIlvanney calls 'the bad place' – where boots fly, bones crunch and nets sometimes burst. But what distinguished the Everton folk hero from even his courageous predecessors was that he was prepared to do so head first.

'Rotavating the ground with his nose,' was how Howard Kendall described his classic horizontal header against Notts. County at a rainswept Meadow Lane in the FA Cup in 1984. At 1–1 and County with their tails up,

Everton could easily have lost. Thanks to Gray, they survived to win the Cup and now found themselves in a major European final. Thanks to Gray, they never thought they could lose that, either. 'It never crossed my mind that we could get beat,' he says. 'We had an air of self-belief about us after the semi-final that nothing was going to break.' It had been Gray, with perhaps his finest performance for the club, who had led the glorious fight-back against Bayern Munich to book the passage to Rotterdam's Feyenoord Stadium.

'Just as we had been so confident of beating Watford in the Cup final the previous year, we know we would beat Rapid. We also knew that the eleven that started that match would go down in history as the side who won Everton's first European trophy. The Bayern match was more exciting as a contest, but this was the one which would be remembered,' he adds. Indeed, it was the match when Everton finally emerged from Liverpool's shadow. 'We had already won the League,' he reminds us, 'but until Rotterdam, Liverpool could always say they'd done it in Europe whereas we hadn't.'

Everton were strong favourites to beat a side who had won few friends by the manner of their dismissal of Celtic in the second round. After Celtic had apparently clinched the tie with a 3−0 win at Parkhead, Rapid came up with evidence to suggest that one of their players had been injured by a missile in Glasgow. UEFA ordered the match to be replayed at neutral Old Trafford, and the Austrians won 1−0.

Rapid subsequently proved a resilient outfit by removing Dynamos Dresden and Moscow respectively in the quarter-final and semi-final, and in Hans Krankl they possessed a striker of the highest class. 'Nae bother,' insisted Gray and, in an Everton side which had already captured the League title in style, there were no dissenting voices. 'Another reason for our confidence,' Gray explains, 'was the fact that 25,000 Evertonians had travelled to Rotterdam, and they outnumbered the Rapid fans about ten to one. It sounded more like fifty to one. Although it's a big, open stadium that doesn't keep the sound in, the noise was tremendous and was definitely a factor in our favour.'

With twenty-seven Austrian League titles to their credit and over 100 games in Europe, Rapid were well-versed in the art of containment. That was how they thought they could win this tie, relying on Krankl to provide occasional counter-attacks from a deep position. Such tactics were never likely to unhinge Everton, however. As if the Merseysiders did not have enough to motivate them in bidding for a unique treble – they were to play Manchester United in the FA Cup final three days later – the prospect of out-Liverpooling Liverpool in such conquests was guaranteed to ensure a gung-ho performance.

'We attacked right from the start,' remembers Gray, 'whereas all they could was defend. We respected them, but they were obviously more afraid of us than we were of them. Krankl hardly had a kick, but we needed a goal. I had one disallowed for off-side in the first half but I've seen it dozens of times on video since and I swear there was nothing wrong with it. At half-time, we had played quite well but just needed that goal to settle us and make them come out.'

With Peter Reid masterminding the relentless Everton attacks and Trevor Steven an able lieutenant, Gray and Graeme Sharp both went close. But Rapid somehow survived, and those Evertonians of a nervous disposition took little comfort in the Austrians' ability to come back from the dead. Besides the technical knock-out inflicted by Celtic, Rapid had recovered from a three-goal deficit to defeat Dresden and had contrived to miss a penalty but still come from behind to beat Moscow. As soon as the second half started, they suggested that their name just might have been engraved on the trophy. Further Everton attacks were repulsed while they began to mount a few of their own. They even hit the bar via Pat van den Hauwe and forced a corner.

But Rapid found Neville Southall in stubborn mood and in the 57th minute knew that they would have to come from behind once more when Gray was on hand to slam home the crucial opening goal. Sharp seized upon a terrible back-pass, rounded the 'keeper and squared to his fellow-striker in front of an open goal. Joyously, triumphantly, Gray whacked it home. 'It was a formality after that,' insists Gray. 'We were able to relax and really start knocking it around. We played some super stuff, and the fans made an incredible din. When Trevor [Steven] made it 2–0, it was like a celebration. They'd taken two defenders off and brought on two attackers, but we were never going to lose a two-goal lead.'

As the Evertonians roared the Rotterdam night away, one could almost feel the yoke of Liverpool domination being lifted. 'The fans really came out of the cupboard and walked around with their heads held high,' said Gray. 'For fifteen years they had suffered a lot of ribbing from Liverpool supporters but now they could get their own back.' Finally, Everton had a team that had won a European trophy, and they had done it in style. Or had they?

Krankl, who had been effectively handcuffed by Kevin Ratcliffe, managed to pull a goal back. But before coronary failure on a massive scale could sweep Merseyside, let alone Rotterdam, Kevin Sheedy clouted a stunning third within a minute. 'The overwhelming reaction from the crowd was relief rather than jubilation; that came later,' remembers Gray. 'But not much later.'

It was Everton's sixty-second match of an epic season. But that was two out of an incredible potential treble in the bag, and Gray was fulfilling his promise to the reporters who had witnessed his signature less than two years earlier. 'When I was introduced to the local press,' he remembers, 'I was asked by one, "What is going to change?" When I told him that I had joined Everton to win things, someone said, "We've heard all that before." Only when I added, "You haven't heard it from me," did they take me seriously.'

1. Ivor Allchurch (left), seen here in action for Swansea against Hull City, played 68 times for Wales and was a key figure in the last Welsh side to have reached the final stages of the World Cup, in 1958.

2 & 3. (left) Ossie Ardiles went straight from a successful World Cup final in 1978 to White Hart Lane, where he was in the Spurs side which won the FA Cup three years later. (right) Jimmy Armfield, the best full-back in the world in 1962, now a broadcaster and reporter for the BBC.

4. The greatest save of all time. Gordon Banks claws away a goal-bound Pele header during the England-Brazil game in the World Cup finals in 1970.

5 & 6. (left) 'Slim Jim' Baxter, the millionaire midfielder for Rangers and Scotland who tormented the 'auld enemy' England at Wembley in 1967. (right) Manchester City's Colin Bell battles to recover from the horrific knee injury that nearly finished his career in 1975.

7. George Best, 'a living James Dean', is thwarted by Chelsea's Peter Bonetti during a League match in November 1966. Eddie McCreadie (centre) and David Sadler look on.

8 & 9. (left) Luton's Billy Bingham is chaired from the field by supporters celebrating their side's 2–1 win in the 1959 FA Cup semi-final replay. (right) Tony Book was taken away from the building site by Malcolm Allison in 1964 and went on to win the League with Manchester City in 1968.

10. Stan Cullis (right) completed a successful transition from centre-half to manager with Wolves, and steered them to victory in a series of unforgettable friendlies against foreign opposition under floodlights in the mid-1950s.

11. Derek Dooley's professional career lasted only fifteen months before a broken leg tragically led to amputation. In that short time, however, he scored 63 goals in 59 games for Sheffield Wednesday.

12 & 13. (left) Raich Carter, whose 24 goals before Christmas in 1935 propelled his Sunderland team towards the League title. (right) Alex Ferguson, who piloted both Aberdeen and Manchester United to European Cup-Winners' Cup triumphs, in 1983 and 1991 respectively.

14 & 15. (left) Tom Finney, described by Bill Shankly as 'the best player ever born', and still a legend in his native Preston. (right) Tommy Gemmell, the Celtic full-back with the cannonball shot, whose goals illuminated his side's European successes in the late 1960s.

16. Wimbledon's Dave Beasant pulls off an extraordinary double save to deny Liverpool and John Barnes during the 1988 FA Cup final. Wimbledon crowned their phenomenal rise from obscurity to the top flight with a 1–0 win under Bobby Gould's management.

17. Peter Reid (left), Trevor Steven and goal-scorer Andy Gray celebrate the opening score in Everton's classic 3–1 victory over Rapid Vienna in the 1985 European Cup-Winners' Cup final in Rotterdam.

18 & 19. (left) Rangers captain John Greig, without his famous beard, who led the Light Blues to a European Cup-Winners' Cup triumph in 1972. (right) Fulham's Johnny Haynes, the pass-master whose understanding with Jimmy Greaves destroyed Scotland 9–3 in 1961.

20. Glenn Hoddle, 'the white Pele', in League action against 1981 Cup final opponents Manchester City. The replayed match, won 3–2 by Spurs, saw one of the great Wembley goals from Argentinian midfielder Ricky Villa.

21. Pat Jennings played over 1,000 first-class matches in his career, but had to wait until he was 37 to appear in the World Cup finals, when he was the rearguard in Northern Ireland's memorable campaign in Spain in 1982.

22 & 23. (left) Derek Johnstone, at 16 the youngest goal-scorer in a national Cup final, gave Rangers a 1–0 victory over Celtic in 1970. (right) Howard Kendall, at 17 the youngest player to appear in an FA Cup final, could not save Preston from a 2–3 defeat in 1964.

Gray carried an enormous burden donning the Everton No. 9 shirt, but had been bought as much for his inspirational qualities as his goals. 'Maybe it was the ghosts of the Deans, the Lawtons, the Royles and the Latchfords, but I felt enormous pressure,' he says. 'The fee had only been £250,000, whereas when I went to Wolves it was a British record of almost £1.5 million. Yet I had never felt any pressure there.'

Capturing the European Cup-Winners' Cup was certainly an excellent way to answer the sceptics, and a wonderful night was had in Holland. 'The only disappointing thing was not being able to do our proper lap of honour,' he remembers. 'There were just too many photographers in the way, and it took a little of the shine off it.' Little did he know that Norman Whiteside and Manchester United would take away even more lustre with an extra-time Cup final win. But it had still been Everton's finest hour for years. Gray had kept his promise.

Everton: Southall, Stevens, van den Hauwe, Ratcliffe, Mountfield, Reid, Steven, Sharp, Gray, Bracewell, Sheedy.

Scorers: Gray, Steven, Sheedy.

Rapid Vienna: Konsel, Kienast, Garger, Weber, Lainer, Hristic, Kranjcar, Weinhofer, Brauneder, Pacult, Krankl.

Subs: Panenka (Weinhofer), Gross (Pacult).

Scorer: Krankl.

Alan Green

Barcelona 2 Manchester United 3
European Cup-Winners' Cup quarter-final, 7 & 21 March
1984

For Sir Matt Busby, this was the tie when 'the memories came flooding back'; for Graeme Hogg, the youngster who put through his own goal, it was a quiet sob behind the team bus; and for Alan Green, the BBC radio commentator, it was the match of his broadcasting life. 'But I would have to choose the whole tie as both games were so memorable,' he insists. Over to you, Alan.

'I remember going with Jimmy Armfield to the Nou Camp Stadium the day before the match,' says Green, 'just to get the feel of the place. We had a look around the dressing-rooms and then went up the steps on to the touchline and looked up at this great bowl. It nearly took my breath away. Quite phenomenal. It rises up above you and is both mightily impressive and intimidating. There was a tingle about the place, and that was when it was empty. But it also had the worst commentary position in the world. It was about seventy yards to the right of the right corner flag so, as we looked at the pitch, the goal on our left was about 200 yards away. What made it worse was the fact that United wore an unfamiliar all-white strip. Now seeing a familiar side in a strange outfit is one thing; to see them in it at such a distance is quite another, but what really made it a challenge was finding that by kick-off the players were shrouded in mist!'

Manchester United, who had qualified for the European Cup-Winners' Cup by beating Brighton after an FA Cup final replay, had been plagued by injuries since comfortably negotiating the second-round hurdle presented by

Varna of Bulgaria. There had been a long gap between November and March, and in it a lot had happened to Ron Atkinson's team. Among the youngsters thrown in was a certain Mark Hughes, who had scored on his first-team début in the Milk Cup but had yet to start a League game. It was to be the start of his eventful association with the aristocrats of Catalonia. 'I'll never forget that night,' he said. 'It was a bit frightening, but I was all right once I had started.' Green wishes he could have said something similar.

'I was doing the commentary on my own,' he recalls, 'and spent a lot of time before the kick-off trying to find out whether Maradona was going to play or not as he had been injured. But I just could not get confirmation. So the time came to be shown up to the commentary box and I still didn't know. But when I arrived there, Maradona was the least of my problems. It was so high, I felt dizzy. It was like commentating on a Subbuteo match from 100 yards. I did recognise Maradona but, of the United players, Ray Wilkins was the only one I could tell, because of his bald patch. I was going what we call a "lift and lay commentary", which you do as if you're on the air but which is edited later to include just the most significant moments. After 35 minutes we had one: a United own goal.

'Carrasco sent in a high cross which was lashed into the United net by one of their defenders. I thought it was Hogg, who was 19 and making his European début, but the moment I had said it was him, I had my doubts. In fact, I was sure I was wrong. I looked at Jimmy Armfield. "Oh, Kevin Moran," he said. "Definitely." I needed a third opinion. In the next box was Gordon McQueen who was doing commentary for Piccadilly Radio. I thought that, as a former United player, he would be sure. "Arnold Muhren," he said confidently. Meanwhile, the scoreboard was flashing up "Moran". There was no way of checking, so I did the classic get-out: "United have gone 0–1 down to an own goal. We're not certain who put it in, but does it really matter? The important thing is . . ." '

United played well, producing a thoroughly disciplined 'European' performance which reduced the fanatical 90,000 crowd to silent frustration. At 0–1, the tie was very much in United's hands. If it finished like that, one goal would not be too much to overcome before a full house at Old Trafford in a fortnight's time. But it did not stay like that; Rojo added a stunning second from twenty-five yards in the dying seconds. Skipper Bryan Robson, who had missed a couple of chances he would normally have buried, said: 'We can't believe it. It just wasn't our night.' Manager Ron Atkinson agreed: 'It's an incredible situation when you look at the way we played.' That was not the only thing on which captain and manager saw eye-to-eye: 'We'll still get through,' they insisted.

It was not until some 45 minutes after the final whistle when he walked past the United team coach that Green was sure of the identity of the player who had scored that own goal. 'At that point,' he says, 'I spotted Graeme Hogg crying his eyes out. Then I knew I had been right all the time.'

Later, much later, Robson, bitterly disappointed by his wayward finishing, vowed: 'The only way I can repay my team-mates is to get two goals in the return.' It did not take him long. Before a packed 58,457 crowd at Old Trafford, United tore at the Spanish defence and, after 21 electrifying minutes that evoked memories of the late 1960s, the Red Devils had scored the goal they craved. 'Back in a more familiar commentary position,' says Green, 'with United in their normal strip and the late Peter Jones, the doyen of radio commentators, at my side, I started off and the first goal fell in my slot. United had a corner which Wilkins took to the near post. Norman Whiteside flicked it on and, right in the middle of a crowded penalty area, Robson got down to head it home. Old Trafford erupted.

'With Maradona playing but hardly leaving the centre circle, Barcelona were forced back as Muhren, Wilkins, Robson and Remi Moses ran the show. Barcelona had a great side in those days, but this was a pretty good United team and, with the crowd creating a fabulous atmosphere, it was rapidly becoming one of those nights. One of those nights to savour.' Barcelona held United to one goal at half-time, but it was only five minutes into the second half when Robson grabbed his second, courageously forcing a loose ball past Urruti. At 2–2, the Reds were not to be denied, and Frank Stapleton grabbed the winner in the 52nd minute when he joyously smashed home after Whiteside had pushed back a cross from Arthur Albiston. With its epicentre at the Stretford End, Manchester shuddered at the sound, on a par with the great days of twenty years earlier. Old-timers admitted that the performance was not far off, either.

'I was fortunate enough to describe all three goals,' recalls Green. 'The noise and the emotion that night were something very special. Robson was carried shoulder-high off the pitch. He had carried the United team in stark contrast, it must be said, to Maradona. Barcelona were simply overwhelmed.' That Saturday afternoon against Brighton ten months earlier when every commentator at Wembley said, 'And Smith must score . . .' seemed a millenium away. Indeed, on a night like this few spared a thought for the luckless Brighton forward who missed that last-minute open goal. But Graeme Hogg might have done.

In Barcelona, 7 March:

Barcelona: Urruti, Gerardo, Moratalla, Julio Alberto, Victor, Alexanco, Carrasco, Schuster, Rojo, Maradona, Marcos.

Scorers: Hogg (og), Rojo.

Manchester United: Bailey, Duxbury, Albiston, Wilkins, Moran, Hogg, Robson, Muhren, Stapleton, Hughes, Moses.

Sub: Graham (Hughes).

At Old Trafford, 21 March:

Manchester United: Bailey, Duxbury, Albiston, Wilkins, Moran, Hogg, Robson, Muhren, Stapleton, Whiteside, Moses.

Sub: Hughes (Whiteside).

Scorers: Robson 2, Stapleton.

Barcelona: Urruti, Gerardo, Moratalla, Alexanco, Julio Alberto, Victor, Alonzo, Schuster, Maradona, Rojo, Marcos.

John Greig

Rangers 3 Dynamo Moscow 2
European Cup-Winners' Cup final, Barcelona, 24 May
1972

Born 11 September 1942. A Heart of Midlothian fan and an apprentice plating engineer, Greig was playing for Edina Hearts in Edinburgh before he joined Rangers. Originally an inside forward, he made his name on a tour of the Soviet Union in 1962 before dropping back to wing-half. Versatile, brave and an inspirational leader, Greig was to play a staggering 857 times for Rangers and was captain of the team that won the European Cup-Winners' Cup in 1972. Earned five League champions' medals and five Scottish Cup-winners' medals plus 44 caps for Scotland. A magnificent servant of the game, he was twice Scottish Footballer of the Year, in 1966 and 1976, and was awarded the MBE in the Jubilee Honours List.

The closest Rangers fans have ever been to going green was in the late 1960s, and it was because of envy, not the environment. Celtic's success in Europe was hard for the average Light Blues fan to take, let alone the religious zealots; but then it was equally so for 'Catholic' Hibernian, superstitious Leeds United and atheist Eastern Europe. Who wouldn't be a wee touch jealous of a club that had proved itself at the highest level? By reaching the European Cup final in 1970, three years after winning it, Celtic confirmed that they were anything but one-season wonders on the continent. Rangers had only themselves, Franz Beckenbauer and Gerd Muller to blame for blowing their chance to emulate Celtic's great win in 1967 by losing the Cup-Winners' Cup final to Bayern Munich a week after their arch-rivals had disposed of Inter Milan.

The extra tingle generated by the Old Firm divide was a further, poignant factor, and John Greig was well aware of how religious bigotry could manifest itself. Once, in a works canteen after signing for Rangers, he found his haddock and chips dramatically substituted by steak pie. When he looked up, he was told firmly: 'Rangers players don't eat fish on Fridays: it's a Catholic habit!'

'The Dynamo game was absolutely vital for the club,' admits Greig, 'as we had not just been beaten by Bayern in the 1967 final but also by Fiorentina in 1961. I was not in that team, having only just signed as a boy, so this was the club's third Cup-Winners' Cup final and my second, and we did not want to fail again. We had matched Celtic round for round in 1972 – them in the Champions' Cup and us in the Cup-Winners' – just as we had in 1967, which is not bad for a small country like Scotland. But they had gone out in the semi-finals while we had got our own back on Bayern. Our biggest worry was that many of our fans thought that we'd won it with that result. But I did not have any problem about complacency; I was struggling to get fit.

'I was injured in the Scottish Cup semi-final, and it was a race against time. I'd played in the first leg of the semi-final, but not the second as I had broken a bone in my foot. If it had been any other game but the Cup-Winners' Cup final I would definitely not have played. But we were already without two central defenders in Colin Jackson and Ronnie McKinnon, so we were a wee bit short at the back.'

Earlier in the campaign, Greig had sustained another injury which, although it never threatened to keep him out, illustrated what European glory meant to him. 'It happened in the kick-about before the first-leg match against Sporting Lisbon at Ibrox,' he says. 'I had a gash on the chin and it needed nine stitches. It meant that I couldn't shave for a while, and I vowed not to shave again while we were in the competition. That was way back in the autumn, and by the time the final came round I had quite a growth. As it was unusual for a Rangers player to have even a moustache, there were cries of "Get that beard off". But as we progressed, there was no way I would take it off. In fact, as it proved to be a lucky omen, it's a wonder we didn't take the field with a team of Rasputins the following season.

'As it was, we were not having a great time domestically but had the sort of team that could rise to the occasion and was capable of adapting to continental opposition. We knew that Russian sides were always well-prepared but could be a bit of an unknown quantity. Whatever the supporters felt, we were on our mettle and felt the weight of history on our shoulders.'

Judging by the size of the light blue hordes who had found their way to Catalonia, Rangers fans, too, appeared to appreciate the game's significance. Having passed himself fit on the eve of the match, Greig recalls the coach journey from the hotel to the ground. 'It was only two or three miles, but there were thousands and thousands of our supporters lining the route. We hardly needed reminding of what the match meant to the club but we were so moved by the cheering and well-wishing that we all had lumps in our throats; it was unbelievable. We said to ourselves, "we cannae let these people down".'

Even before the kick-off there was an invasion of the pitch, and the start had to be delayed while thousands of over-exuberant fans were persuaded to return to the terraces by manager Willie Waddell, who had already spotted that the Spanish police were looking longingly at their truncheons. Up to 20,000 Rangers supporters were in the Nou Camp compared to a token 400 from Moscow. The Scots soon had cause to think their journey had been worthwhile.

'We made a great start,' says Greig, 'and were 2−0 up in no time from goals by Colin Stein and Willie Johnston. Both players were superb for these European occasions,

Stein running all over the park and pinching vital goals, while Johnston's speed was enough to worry anybody.' It had the makings of a great night for Rangers but for those fans, who greeted each goal with a pitch invasion. Sensing the threat and realising that the Guardia Civil possessed neither the patience nor the humour of their Glasgow counterparts, the Rangers players helped to persuade their admirers to leave on each occasion, but not without difficulty. When the brilliant Johnston appeared to have clinched the Cup with a thrilling third goal after latching on to a long punt from Peter McCloy five minutes into the second half, the celebrations reached a climax. The Soviets, however, had other ideas.

'We became a bit careless,' admits Greig, 'and they upped their game. We lost one unnecessary goal on the hour, and it became harder to bear after that. For us and our supporters.' When the Russians pulled another back with three minutes to go, it was heart-failure time for the travelling hordes. Shrieking, whistling and drunkenly imploring the referee to end their agony, they exploded at the first free-kick that was given, thinking it was the final whistle. With the Spanish police powerless, on they came in scenes that evoked comparison with the Moorish invasion – a final act which effectively spoiled the party. There was still a minute to go.

With Greig's captaincy holding the line, Rangers hung on when play resumed, but the bedlam going on around meant that what should have been the finest moment in this magnificent player's career ended in a shambles. During the final pitch invasion, one over-zealous fan actually trod on the skipper's foot – his other one – and ensured that Greig had a matching pair by breaking it. But what hurt him much more was being prevented from receiving in the grand manner the major European trophy he and his club had craved. Greig had dreamed of parading it around the ground before the fans and all of watching Europe. Instead, as the Spanish police and

Rangers hooligans were embroiled in what was now something much more serious than chucking-out time in Sauchiehall Street, Greig was handed the trophy in a dingy little room behind the stand.

'It was about 8 foot by 6 foot and very much a case of "here it is and get out as quick as you can",' he remembers. 'I was in tears. It was the biggest anti-climax of my career, and all so unnecessary. What made it worse was being banned for the next two years. Even though we got a year knocked off the sentence when we appealed, it still meant we couldn't defend the trophy. Although some of the behaviour was inexcusable, I felt that the police brought a lot of it on themselves. It was a sad way to end.'

Rangers: McCloy, Jardine, Mathieson, Greig, Johnstone, Smith, McLean, Conn, Stein, MacDonald, Johnston.

Scorers: Johnston 2, Stein.

Dynamo Moscow: Pilgui, Basalev, Dolmatov, Zykov, Dobbonosov, Zhukov, Baidatchni, Jakubik, Sabo, Mahovikov, Evryuzhikin.

Subs: Gerschkovitch, Eshtrekov.

Scorers: Eshtrekov, Mahovikov.

Johnny Haynes

England 9 Scotland 3
Wembley, 15 April 1961

Born 17 October 1934. Haynes was the pass-master for England in 56 internationals, 22 as captain. A one-club man, his loyalty to Fulham led to his being made the first £100-a-week footballer in 1961. Became player-manager at Craven Cottage but relinquished the post after just seventeen days to concentrate again on playing. Finished his career with Durban City in South Africa after a broken ankle in a car crash prematurely ended his England days.

The laser was unknown in the late 1950s, but something similar must have been attached to the boots of Johnny Haynes. From thirty, fifty, even seventy yards, the Fulham maestro could pierce a defence with passes that were not merely perfectly weighted and custom-made for the recipient, they might have contained a greeting card.

Haynes was an artist whose sweeping brush-strokes illuminated the broad canvas of English football for eighteen years. Strikers such as Jimmy Greaves accepted so many gift-wrapped chances that they thought playing alongside the pass-master was akin to accompanying Santa on Christmas Day. Haynes, of course, required finishing to match and in Greaves found the ideal accomplice. Building on the sound foundations that manager Walter Winterbottom had laid for the England team of 1960–61, the pair colluded in many of the 40 goals scored in a scintillating six-game unbeaten run.

Winterbottom had settled on his side and vowed not to disrupt it unless forced to do so by injuries. Ron Springett was a reliable 'keeper, Jimmy Armfield and Mick McNeil were a classy pair of full-backs while Peter Swan and Ron Flowers effectively bottled things up in the middle. In the engine room of midfield, Bobby Robson was an able ally for Haynes, Bryan Douglas dazzled on the right wing, Bobby Charlton was just bursting on to the scene down the left, while the rapier thrusts of Greaves were the perfect complement to the bludgeoning Bobby Smith at centre-forward. Wales, Luxemburg, Spain and Northern Ireland had all been hammered. Still, the Scots were not impressed.

Under the tutelage of Ian McColl, still a Rangers player at 33, the Dark Blues possessed the rich skills of Denis Law and Davie Wilson, the dynamism of Dave Mackay and the towering strength of Billy McNeill. And while England had Greavsie, Scotland had the Saint. England at Wembley? It was, as ever, 'Nae bother'.

The tartan army was right. It was nae bother at all, but for England. Once Robson opened the scoring with a low drive from the edge of the box after a neat tap-back by Greaves, the home side always looked likely to get a goal. Haynes began to split the Scottish defence at will and, sure enough, two more were added before half-time. Inevitably, Greaves notched both.

'They had come with a very attack-minded side,' recalls Haynes, 'and there were a lot of gaps to exploit. I suppose you could say we exploited them pretty well.' Indeed, it was as if, one contemporary report suggested, the England mastermind was 'equipped with some private computer', so precise and calculating was his distribution. Roaming Wembley's vast acreage virtually unchecked, Haynes's uncanny knack of unlocking the Scottish defence from long range was such that the unfortunate 'keeper Frank Haffey felt he was under constant siege, even when the ball was in England's half.

As Law later admitted: 'Haynes and Greaves could not believe their luck: we gave them the freedom of

Wembley.' And how they took it. Haynes's ability to deliver not just an inch-perfect pass but one that would behave itself made one think that, had he lofted one toward the royal box, he would have made it bow before entering.

'But don't get the idea it was all one way,' Haynes warns. 'Far from it. For almost an hour it was anybody's match, and they caught us on the hop once or twice.' Just after half-time Mackay's ferocious free-kick was deflected off the wall past Springett, and then Wilson capitalised on English uncertainty to peg the score back to 2–3 with half an hour still to play. But Greaves, determined to put one over 'the Jocks', caught the visitors on the hop by sending a swiftly-taken free-kick to Douglas who gently dispatched it beyond Haffey to restore daylight between the teams. Haynes, spraying the ball about with the relish of a graffiti artist and the aim of a sniper, restored England's command of midfield, and five goals in 11 minutes was the result.

'I had a very good understanding with Jimmy and sometimes did not even have to look up when I hit a long pass,' Haynes explains. 'I just knew he would be on the end of it.' With Greaves causing havoc, Smith grabbed the fifth and then the skipper, as if to prove that his accuracy was not confined to passing, drove two long-range shots powerfully past the hapless Haffey. 'I lost count near the end,' insists Haynes, denying that they tried for double figures. 'It's not the sort of thing you think about on the field.' But it looked as if it had crossed the minds of Greaves and Smith who added the eighth and ninth to complete the biggest Scottish massacre since Culloden.

'As a ritual,' wrote one eminent Scottish commentator, 'devotion to the Scottish cause sometimes offered all the joys of self-flagellation.' But this was surely one of the Dark Blues' darkest hours. The Scottish coach was much abused by the tartan army's angry remnants when it made its escape down Wembley Way, the players keeping their heads down below window level. In stark contrast, Haynes had been hoisted on to the shoulders of his team and carried as a hero around Wembley and before Her Majesty the Queen. Generously, he gave his team-mates the credit. 'There have been few better England sides than that one,' he insists. 'It was a privilege to lead them, and I think we would have beaten anybody that day.'

Not surprisingly, the Scots made Haffey the scapegoat, and it was his performance that probably launched the jokes about Scottish goal-keepers, with Greaves leading the jesters. Haffey never played for his country again, doing well to survive the wrath of his team-mates, the tartan army and that scathing band of supporters with irate type-writers, the Scottish press. Haynes, however, has a word of sympathy. 'It's so easy to blame the 'keeper. He might have been to blame for one or two, but I'm sure we would have run away with it whoever was in goal.'

England: Springett, Armfield, McNeil, Robson, Swan, Flowers, Douglas, Greaves, Smith, Haynes, Charlton.

Scorers: Greaves 3, Haynes 2, Smith 2, Douglas, Robson.

Scotland: Haffey, Shearer, Caldow, Mackay, McNeill, McCann, McLeod, Law, St John, Quinn, Wilson.

Scorers: Mackay, Wilson, Quinn.

Glenn Hoddle

Tottenham Hotspur 3 Manchester City 2
FA Cup final replay, Wembley, 14 May 1981

Born 27 October 1957. The only Spurs player to win England honours at four levels: youth, Under-21, 'B' and full, where he played 53 times. One of the most talented players of the modern era, Hoddle was never given the opportunities his natural genius deserved. Scored a memorable goal on his England début against Bulgaria and was dropped for the next match. Such treatment set the tone of an unfulfilled international career, and it took him another five years to come close to establishing himself in the England side. Played out his twilight years with Monaco where his sublime gifts were more appreciated and where he won a French champions' medal. Took over from his former Spurs midfield partner Ossie Ardiles as manager of Swindon Town.

They called him 'the white Pele' and 'a South American-style player', but Glenn Hoddle was as Home Counties as they come. The kid from Harlow could caress a ball like they do on the Copacabana and could bend free-kicks like ripe bananas but paid a heavy price for doing the equivalent of the samba in a working men's club. A delicious irony, then, that he should choose a match in which a South American player stole the show.

'The 1981 Cup final replay has to be the outstanding team memory,' he says. 'I had better games as an individual – Spurs v Feyenoord, for example, when I laid on four goals in the first half after Johan Cruyff had said he would mark me out of the match – but winning the Cup beats that. Having been a Spurs fan since I was a kid, it really was a dream. Although I went back and won it again, nothing will top that first time.'

The tie had begun in anti-climax, a dull 1–1 draw necessitating a return on the following Thursday, only the second Wembley FA Cup final to require a replay. On the Saturday, two hours of mediocrity were relieved only by the quirk of Tommy Hutchinson scoring both goals – at either end. Hoddle at least had a hand in one, his free-kick being deflected by Hutchinson into his own net for an equaliser with half an hour of normal time remaining. But Hoddle had an undistinguished match and was looking forward to restoring his reputation. So, too, was Ricky Villa.

The big, bearded Argentine had been pulled off by Spurs boss Keith Burkinshaw just before the fateful equaliser and had suggested that he was not best pleased by producing the sulk of the century. Although his piratical appearance may have exacerbated his tantrum, Villa's chances of making the replay did not look bright. However, Burkinshaw, who had brought Villa and Ossie Ardiles to Britain in the first place, stood by his man.

Immediately, the replay was unrecognisable from its disjointed precursor. 'Saturday had been a bit of a let-down,' acknowledged Hoddle who soon established his presence in the return. Curling long through-balls, collecting and cradling the loose stuff, he was in his element, as were Ardiles and Villa. It did not take the reprieved Argentinian long to show his gratitude. In the seventh minute, after Ardiles and Archibald had been thwarted, Villa stabbed the ball home from close range. But the goal – and his subsequent celebration – were merely a taste of things to come.

'We lost it a bit after that,' recalls Hoddle, 'and then Steve MacKenzie scored a great goal to level it.' A right-footed volley from outside the penalty area, it was one of Wembley's finest. 'It was a real shock to the system as we had started so well and felt really comfortable,' says Hoddle. 'I thought we played some super stuff but faltered a little after that goal.' Worse was to come, as City's Dave Bennett was brought down and Kevin Reeves, another of Malcolm Allison's expensive buys, slotted the spot-kick home. Incredibly, Spurs were behind. 'I remember thinking we had never lost a Cup final at Wembley and just at a vital time in the game we had gone behind after having the upper hand. It seemed that we had to do something or we'd lose it.'

Hoddle's riposte was, as ever, a cultured one. The midfield maestro, whom skipper Steve Perryman memorably accused of 'having feet like golf clubs – a different iron for every pass', chipped what he called 'a nice little ball' into the City defence. Steve Archibald failed to fasten on to it, but Garth Crooks did. Twenty minutes to go, 2–2, and tension at fever pitch. Spurs really did possess the firepower to clinch it in the dynamic duo of Archibald and Crooks and, with Hoddle now giving a command performance and the Argentinians finding the freedom of the wide open spaces, the Cup looked more likely to go to White Hart Lane than Maine Road. But City, with big Joe Corrigan between the posts, were in no mood to surrender.

Villa, pleased just to have survived for 76 minutes, then took a pass from Tony Galvin and began to run at the packed City defence. Switching direction and riding tackles like a drunken gaucho, Villa jinked his way into the penalty area, inside one hapless City defender, outside another, then another. Wembley held its breath in wonder as he finished in the grand manner, ramming the ball past Corrigan for one of the Cup final's greatest individual goals. Villa celebrated in a style more befitting Buenos Aires than Brent, and Spurs' record was preserved. 'The greatest goal of my life,' was how he rated it. 'On Saturday I was so unhappy. Tonight I am the happiest footballer in the world. But I must thank the manager. . . at last I have luck in England.' Burkinshaw said: 'I think I have found the way to get the best out of him.'

So Hoddle, who had supported the club since he was 11,

finally had a Cup-winners' medal, something he would treasure more than any subsequent triumph. 'There's nothing like the Cup and nothing like winning it for the first time,' he says. 'It was a great team performance, but there will never be another goal like Ricky Villa's.'

Tottenham Hotspur: Aleksic, Hughton, Miller, Roberts, Perryman, Villa, Ardiles, Archibald, Galvin, Hoddle, Crooks.

Scorers: Villa 2, Crooks.

Manchester City: Corrigan, Ranson, McDonald, Caton, Reid, Gow, Power, MacKenzie, Reeves, Bennett, Hutchinson.

Sub: Tueart (McDonald).

Scorers: MacKenzie, Reeves (pen).

Emlyn Hughes

Liverpool 3 St Etienne 1
European Cup quarter-final, second leg, Anfield, 16 March
1977

Born 28 August 1947. Joined Blackpool as a junior before becoming one of Bill Shankly's more inspired bargains, being introduced at Anfield as 'a future captain of England'. The Scot was right: the versatile Hughes played 62 times for his country and over 650 for Liverpool. Nicknamed 'Crazy Horse' by the Kop for his upfield gallops, he was a player of unbridled enthusiasm and captained Liverpool to their first European Cup triumph. After collecting every domestic and European honour in the game, he added another – the League Cup – during his twilight years with Wolves.

When Emlyn Hughes was snapped up by Bill Shankly and taken to Anfield, there was a slight hint of regret in his wide eyes. 'I had been there as a kid a couple of times and seen the great European nights of the 1960s with Ian St John, Ron Yeats and all those stars. I just felt that as a player I might have missed out on all that,' he explained. 'One of the matches I had seen was against Ajax after they had murdered Liverpool 5–1 in Holland,' he says. 'I was a junior with Blackpool and I'll always remember reading that Bill Shankly felt Liverpool could hammer four past the Dutch and still win it. As it turned out, the return was a 2–2 draw, and I never forgot how difficult it can be to recover from a deficit in Europe.'

The 0–1 first-leg deficit to St Etienne in the 1976–77 European Cup quarter-final was not regarded as insurmountable, but the French champions had earned the Liverpool players' respect in Paris. 'They had kept a clean sheet and were reckoned to be one of the best sides in the competition,' says Hughes. 'Borussia and us were the others and, really, it was between us three.'

The Kop agreed that the return was far from a walkover, the anticipation of a hard struggle providing the sort of electric atmosphere which Hughes had only previously experienced as a youthful spectator. 'We knew we had to win by two clear goals and did not have the comfort of an away goal,' he recalls. 'But we got off to a cracking start, scoring after just two minutes. We had a short corner and Kev [Keegan] hit one of his specials which surprised the 'keeper from about twenty-five yards. It was the perfect start, and we were on our way. We were storming away with the League and had a good side, but what the Kop wanted above all else was the European Cup. We sensed, there and then, that if we could beat these we were halfway there.'

Liverpool, urged on by the customary packed house, poured forward in waves, playing some scintillating football, and it seemed only a matter of time before a second goal came. It was a perfectly balanced Reds side, with powerhouses Jimmy Case and Tommy Smith a fearsome hub, skipper Hughes a driving force alongside, Keegan's buzzing augmented by the strong running of Ray Kennedy, Steve Heighway and Terry McDermott, and old head Ian Callaghan there to calm it all down. But these were the days before the cutting edge was provided by Ian Rush and Kenny Dalglish, and the second goal continued to elude them. St Etienne, it must be said, showed organisational qualities of which Liverpool themselves would have been proud. 'But still, nobody was pressing the panic button,' says Hughes. 'Yet.'

Five minutes into second half the French, who had shown glimpses of being able to counter-attack with some conviction, suddenly broke out of defence, and Bathenay ran from the half-way line before unleashing a twenty-five-yarder that soared over Ray Clemence and dipped under the bar. 'It was a killer blow,' says Hughes, 'as it meant we had to score two more.' For all their mastery, Liverpool had not really looked like scoring since the second minute but continued to take the game to the Frenchmen. With the Kop now baying for a goal, the patient build-up from the back gave way to cavalry charges, and caution was thrown into the Anfield night as the elusive European Cup threatened to escape Liverpool once more.

As the minutes ticked away Liverpool became frantic, but the French lines held. Then John Toshack flicked on a Callaghan centre for Kennedy to rifle home. One more goal would surely be enough, but still the French resisted. 'We knew we only wanted one at that point,' says Hughes, 'but we wondered where it was going to come from.' Liverpool, however, did have one ace still up their sleeve in David Fairclough, a tall, rangy red-head whose unpredictability kept him out of the starting side but whose lethal speed and rescuing of lost causes meant that he was permanently wearing the substitute's jersey – hence the nickname 'Super Sub'. If ever he were needed, this was the moment, and Bob Paisley sent him on with 15 minutes to go.

'The mere sight of him gave us a lift,' says Hughes, 'as we knew they would not know what to expect. We didn't either. He was impossible to play with at times – most of the time – and we couldn't compensate for what he did. That's why he was seldom in the side from the off. He never made a regular player.' But with the unthinkable of another failed European Cup campaign staring Anfield in the face, Paisley's irregular seized his chance.

'I remember it well,' says Hughes. 'We were well inside our own half and he got the ball. I was alongside him and screaming, "Pass it, pass it", but either he couldn't hear in the din or didn't want to. He carried on into their half, and I screamed even louder. There were only about five minutes to go, and we couldn't afford to waste another chance like this. But he kept going. He had about six defenders between him and the goal and couldn't get anywhere. But he was a hopeless case. They kept coming at him and he just kept beating 'em. He finally got inside the box and slotted the ball home. I've never seen anything like it. He'd saved us, the Kop went wild, we went wild, we were through. The European Cup was there for the taking, thanks to Super Sub ignoring me and everybody else.'

So Hughes had his night of Anfield nights, one which compared with anything he had seen from the terraces in the 1960s. Indeed, 'the semi-final was an anti-climax after that; we battered FC Zurich and went on to beat Borussia in the final. But we owed it to Dave Fairclough. Of all the other Liverpool matches and England appearances, that is the night I remember most.'

Liverpool: Clemence, Neal, Jones, Smith, Kennedy, Hughes, Keegan, Case, Heighway, Toshack, Callaghan.

Sub: Fairclough (Toshack).

Scorers: Keegan, Kennedy, Fairclough.

Saint-Etienne: Curkovic, Janvion, Farison, Merchadier, Lopez, Bathenay, Rocheteau, Larque, P. Revelli, Synaeghel, Santini.

Sub: H. Revelli (Merchadier).

Scorer: Bathenay.

Geoff Hurst

England 4 West Germany 2 (aet)
World Cup final, Wembley, 30 July 1966

Born 8 December 1941. A converted wing-half, Hurst played 49 times for England, scoring 24 goals. He is still the only man to have scored a hat-trick in a World Cup final, yet he had been only a squad member until an injury to Jimmy Greaves gave him his chance. Notched 180 League goals for West Ham before adding 22 with Stoke City. Played first-class cricket but failed to trouble the scorers in his only game, making 0 and 0 not out for Essex against Lancashire.

'All I wanted to do,' insists Geoff Hurst, 'was hit it as hard as I could. Over the bar and into the crowd at the back end of Wembley would have done nicely. That would have kept it out of German hands for a few precious seconds. On that I am very clear.' The only man to score a hat-trick in a World Cup final admits to being 'blank' about many other aspects of that memorable day, but that was how he felt moments before unleashing the shot that made him immortal and guaranteed English football's finest hour.

Hurst had latched on to a pass from Bobby Moore, who had eschewed similar thoughts about booting the ball into the stands. The striker, two goals already in the bag and the Germans now spent, found himself virtually unchallenged on the edge of their penalty area. 'I knew there were only a few seconds left, but we'd been through that before,' he remembers. 'My instinct was just to settle for 3–2 and waste as much time as I could.'

It was at this point that TV commentator Kenneth Wolstenholme observed: 'There are people on the pitch

. . .' Hurst strode on. A lone defender gave up a hopeless chase. The goal-keeper Tilkowski stood rooted in his six-yard box. The referee had the whistle between his lips. 'They think it's all over,' crackled Wolstenholme. Hurst, the ball bouncing kindly for him, let fly. Tilkowski stretched, but the net billowed. Above Wembley's roar, Wolstenholme informed the nation: 'It is now.'

Martin Peters was the first to congratulate Hurst. Then came Alan Ball. Then the rest of the team forgot their cramps and other pains, their fatigue and their sheer desperation, to swarm around the hero. Hugging, back-slapping, sobbing. Jack Charlton sank to the turf. Bobby wept. Nobby Stiles danced a jig. Others tried to believe it, but the enormity of what they had achieved would need time to sink in. Elsewhere it was different, and impromptu celebrations began around the living rooms of the land. They went on into the night on a scale that surpassed VE Day. Hurst's life would never be the same again. What did he make of it?

'As any sportsman will tell you,' he says, 'the immediate reaction to a triumph is one of relief, even more than a sense of achievement. That's how it was for me: it was a job done. Admittedly, it was a very big job and done very well, but that's how I felt when it was all over. Relief, sheer relief.' You almost feel that he is reliving the agony twenty-five years later, for this was no ordinary victory: it was the most tumultuous ever seen on a football field and had been earned at great cost. It had been earned twice.

With the last kick of normal time West Germany had scrambled an equaliser that was almost too cruel to bear for England and their fans. The Germans scarcely deserved it; outplayed in the second half, they were fortunate to be awarded a free-kick and then, in the ensuing fracas, a German hand made contact with the ball. The referee did not see it, and Weber somehow forced the ball beyond Banks. Even the twin towers seemed to shed a tear.

Surveying his distraught troops after the final whistle, Alf Ramsey, inwardly raging but still employing those quiet, clipped tones of his, delivered the now-famous address: 'Look, you have won it once. Now go and win it again.' Ramsey, like the great general he was, knew his men. He knew that they would not let either him or the nation down. Summoning strength perhaps from what he had called their 'moral superiority' or simply from the sight of the Germans with their socks at their ankles, England, driven on by the 20-year-old legs of Alan Ball, socks at his ankles but a heart of oak in his chest, tore at the old enemy yet again.

Just before the break in extra-time, Ball slipped a short, square pass inside to Hurst who crashed it first time against the crossbar. The ball bounced down, and the crowd roared in salute of what they thought was the winner. Hurst wheeled away thinking it was, too; so did Roger Hunt, the closest to the goal. But the Germans thought otherwise. Angrily, desperately, they appealed that it had not crossed the line. Ball dragged the Swiss referee over to the Russian linesman who pointed to the centre-spot, and Wembley erupted again. 'I have seen it dozens of times, from all angles and in slow motion,' says Hurst, 'and nothing proves it conclusively either way. All I have gone by is Roger Hunt's instinctive reaction that it was a goal.' But Hunt has since said he was not sure, either.

Neither side had the energy to mount penetrating assaults after that, and most of Wembley was simply waiting, hardly daring to look, torn between the tortuous action and the agonisingly slow tick of the clock. England appeared to be holding firm, but no one could be too confident. There was one more despairing German raid, but Bobby Moore won the ball. There was no better man to have it. Surely, now, Moore would not let the Germans in from here. Anywhere would have done. But not for Moore, ever the perfectionist: he had spotted Hurst in space, and the final act in the drama at least ensured that two magnificent teams were separated by more than one highly controversial goal.

During the momentous two hours of the match and the ensuing bedlam, Hurst cut a dignified figure. Older, much older, professionals were engulfed by tension and then tears, but the converted wing-half from the West Ham 'academy' was conscious of 'a funny, peaceful calm inside. What definitely helped was not expecting to be in the side. It took all the pressure off me.' In another of those excusable 'blanks', he does not recall the moment he learned of his selection although, by all accounts, it was the night before the match on the way to the obligatory cowboy film. Ramsey told the players one by one, as he had told those who did not make the final twenty-two after a training camp at Lilleshall.

'I remember that,' says Hurst, recalling the stroll past the landscaped shrubbery and stately flower beds of the national training centre. 'It was the longest walk of my life.' Hurst had not made his England début until February – against West Germany of all people – and remained a fringe player until he was drafted in for the quarter-final against Argentina. Then a glancing header of which Tommy Lawton would have been proud – 'the most satisfying of all,' he says – from a Peters cross and much subsequent unselfish running and ideal dovetailing as a target man aroused a national debate as to whether he or the fit-again Jimmy Greaves should play in the final. 'It still haunts me a bit,' admits Hurst on what happened to Greaves. But, as Moore acknowledges, 'Alf had no alternative. Geoff scored against Argentina, had a hand in the second goal against Portugal and, with him, we'd played our best football so far.'

'I certainly didn't feel any pressure at all,' says Hurst. 'I was just glad to be out there playing. It was a bonus to be in the squad and a bigger one to be in the team. I went into the final satisfied, like a win at the races; you're now betting with the bookies' money. It would have made the Greaves thing more horrible if I had had a total shocker. You have to remember that not many agreed with Alf on the morning of the match, and I had to astonish half of Britain just to stop them wanting to string Alf up for leaving out Jimmy.'

Any such thoughts subsided just before half-time when Hurst headed his first and England's equaliser. Moore took a free-kick with laser accuracy and Hurst, catching the Germans before they had regrouped, nodded home. 'We did it at West Ham all the time,' says Hurst; nothing to it, really. It had looked fairly straightforward when Peters prodded home a second in the 78th minute. England were in command, and 2–1 would have done for most of the 93,000 present. It would have done for Hurst, too, but the gods decreed otherwise.

England: Banks, Cohen, Wilson, Stiles, J. Charlton, Moore, Ball, Hunt, R. Charlton, Hurst, Peters.

Scorers: Hurst 3, Peters.

West Germany: Tilkowski, Hottges, Schulz, Weber, Schnellinger, Haller, Beckenbauer, Overath, Seeler, Held, Emmerich.

Scorers: Haller, Weber.

Pat Jennings

Northern Ireland 1 Spain 0
World Cup finals, Group 5 match, Valencia, 25 June 1982

Born 12 June 1945. Brought up on Gaelic Football in Newry, Jennings soon switched to soccer as a goal-keeper and was snapped up by Watford for just £6,500. In 1964 he was bought by Bill Nicholson and enjoyed the best years of his career at White Hart Lane, playing 472 of his 757 League games for Spurs. Was transferred to Arsenal in 1977 and played in three successive FA Cup finals. Won the FA Cup with Spurs in 1967 and with Arsenal in 1979, the League Cup twice and the UEFA Cup (all with Spurs). Played more than 1,000 first-class matches which included 119 for his country. Capped his career with an international finale against Brazil on his 41st birthday.

Wielding those massive, magnetic shovels that are his hands, Pat Jennings had clasped everything football could throw at him: high, swirling crosses, blockbuster free-kicks and 'hospital' back-passes. With Watford, Spurs and Arsenal, he had also clawed every trophy in the domestic game. But for much of his career it looked as if the greatest honour of all would slip through even his reassuring grasp.

'Appearing in the World Cup finals has to be the pinnacle of any player's career,' he says, 'and when you look at the size of our country, you realise how difficult it is for us to get there. Even George Best didn't manage it, and long before 1982 I thought it had passed me by, too.' Being a goal-keeper, the frustration was probably even greater for Jennings. Unable to do much about it at the other end, he could only watch, quietly curse and silently fume. He had done plenty of that as three generations of journeymen in front of him had failed to capitalise on his genius between the posts.

It had looked that way again when Northern Ireland had lost 0–1 in Sweden in the qualifiers for the 1982 World Cup. 'I thought that was us,' said Jennings, but the latest team that Billy Bingham had assembled was of sterner stuff. Jennings thought it was 'us' again after a 0–0 draw with Scotland in Belfast had seen Jock Stein's men celebrating, leaving Jennings & Co. to contemplate a missed opportunity and to drown their sorrows in an adjoining dressing-room – until they heard that Sweden had won in Portugal to leave the door of their group still ajar. A 1–0 win over Israel was then enough to secure a place in the finals for the first time since Danny Blanch-flower led his 1958 side to Sweden.

Jennings had been in most of the teams who had failed to make it since. 'I had been trying for twenty years to get there; that's why it was so special to me,' he says. 'At 36, the best of my career was over, and I was pretty well resigned to not making it. That's why it surpasses anything I ever did for Spurs or Arsenal.' The big man from Newry had performed a hero's role in getting the tiny nation (population 2.3 million) through, playing in six of the eight qualifying ties and conceding a niggardly two goals. But even after Israel, the agony was not over for Jennings.

'I aggravated an old groin injury in January,' he says, wincing at the memory even now. 'I only played two or three games between January and May. I remember having half a game against Wales, and Billy Bingham saying: "You've still got a few weeks." I was determined to get there as I sensed it was my best ever chance. Being drawn in the same group as the hosts added some spice, as everybody was interested in them and thought they would qualify automatically. Spain and Yugoslavia were the favourites, while Honduras and ourselves were supposed to be soft touches. But Honduras gave us a tough game. There were no mugs in our group.'

Northern Ireland drew with both Honduras and Yugo-slavia to throw Group 5 wide open. With Spain having beaten the Yugoslavs, Northern Ireland needed to beat the hosts to top the group and go through to the next round. 'Spain could afford to lose but only by one goal,' recalls Jennings. 'But there was no way they were going to take it easy in front of that crowd in Valencia. And we certainly weren't. I'll never forget that day, even out of the 1,000-odd matches I've played. The atmosphere was electric, the stadium packed with people hanging from everywhere, and we knew exactly what we had to do. The pressure was all on Spain and we were determined to increase it.

'It was a very physical game but we were not going to be intimidated, either by the team or the fans. Spain came at us early on, but our defence was up to it.' So, too, was the 'keeper, although he is too modest to admit it. As the game wore on, the Spaniards – and their fans – became frustrated with their forwards' failure to break through this unfancied opposition with their ageing goal-keeper, and at half-time it was Billy Bingham's boys who enjoyed their cuppa more.

Just a minute into the second half the Irishmen hit the Spaniards with a sucker-punch. Spain's own celebrated 'keeper, Arconada, was caught in two minds by a cross from Billy Hamilton, only pushing it weakly into the path of Gerry Armstrong. The striker, already a hero for his goal against Honduras, hammered it home from near the penalty spot and entered Ulster folklore. The Ulstermen still had much to do, however, as Spain, badly stunned and realising that another goal could put them out and Yugoslavia through, stormed towards Jennings's goal like the Moors of old. In the Luis Casanova Stadium in Valencia no love is normally lost for the visitors, but with the home side fighting for their World Cup lives, it called for something a bit special from the men in green. His name was Pat Jennings.

'Somewhere in there,' wrote Eamonn Dunphy of the

great man, 'the grace of a ballet dancer joins with the strength of a SAS squaddie, the dignity of an ancient king, and the nerve of a bomb disposal officer.' Jennings needed all those qualities that night in Valencia. It was bad enough having to withstand the rampant red and blue assaults with a full complement of players, but after an hour Mal Donaghy was sent off for his part in a mêlée with full-back Camacho, who had brought him down. But this dismissal only stiffened Irish resolve and, with Jennings forgetting he could not do the splits and grabbing everything, they held out.

'It would have been one of the longest half-hours of my life had I not been so busy,' he laughs. 'I hardly had a chance to think of what we were on the verge of achieving or anything like that. It was just a case of hanging on and hanging on. In a rare moment, I might have asked myself, "Can we do it?" ' Thanks to a magnificent rearguard and Jennings's own virtuosity and improvisation, they did. There was one memorable moment when Jennings, eschewing the punch or the catch, just pushed the ball gently in the air and manoeuvred around a Spanish forward to snatch it, thus avoiding a collision.

'I got some stick for that afterwards,' he recalls, 'as people said it was too risky. But I knew exactly what I was doing. If I'd caught it, I could easily have been bowled over by this bloke who was rushing in at me, and in those situations you can't depend on the referee to give you anything. The ball could have been knocked from me and gone anywhere, so I decided to knock it round him, avoid a collision and go and pick it up. Fortunately, it worked.' But that was one of countless acts of agility and quick thinking that Jennings performed on the night and through which Northern Ireland achieved their finest victory. It eclipsed even the feat of Blanchflower's team, of which Bingham had been a sprightly member twenty-four years earlier, and, in doing so, it shook the whole competition and brought a few fleeting hours of joy to the troubled province.

Northern Ireland: Jennings, J. Nicholl, C. Nicholl, McCreery, Donaghy, M. O'Neill, McIlroy, McClelland, Hamilton, Armstrong, Whiteside.

Subs: Cassidy (McIlroy), Nelson (Whiteside).

Scorer: Armstrong.

Spain: Arconada, Camacho, Tendillo, Alexanco, Gordillo, Sanchez, Alonso, Saura, Juanito, Satrustegui, Lopez-Ufarte.

Subs: Quini (Satrustegui), Gallego (Lopez-Ufarte).

Derek Johnstone

Rangers 1 Celtic 0
Scottish League Cup final, Hampden Park, 24 October
1970

---

*Born 4 November 1953. A schoolboy prodigy from Dundee, 'DJ'
won Scottish honours at all levels after starting his career with
St Francis Boys and St Columba's FC. Signed schoolboy forms
for Rangers at 15, turning professional two years later. Made a
sensational start by scoring the winner in the League Cup final
against Celtic in only his second game, and before his 17th
birthday. Powerful, confident and superb in the air, Johnstone
was just as at home at centre-half as centre-forward. Earned
only 14 Scottish caps, a poor reward when set against three
Scottish League Championship medals, five Cup-winners'
medals and four successes in the Scottish League Cup. Was
Player of the Year in 1978.*

It was something that Messrs Grimm and Hans Christian
Anderson would have hesitated to script, while Roy of the
Rovers would surely have waited another couple of
seasons. But Derek Johnstone's leap into Old Firm folklore
at the tender age of 16 years and 355 days was real enough
to rewrite the record books. 'I became a legend BEFORE
my own lifetime,' he laughs of his 40th minute header that
decided not only a Scottish League Cup final, but made the
strapping Dundonian the youngest player ever to score a
winning goal in a national final. It was Rangers' first
trophy for four years. A disbelieving 106,263 people,
including his mum and dad, were there to see it. Yet six
months earlier, Johnstone had been poring over his 'O'
levels.

'I only found out that I would be in the team on the

Friday,' he recalls. 'I was reading the paper in the boot room when Willie Waddell and Jock Wallace came in. I was still living in Dundee at the time and used to spend my lunch hours at Ibrox before getting the train home late in the afternoon. I was thinking about leaving when the gaffer stuck four complimentary tickets in my top pocket and told me to bring my mother and father to the final. I was playing in it.' Was it such a sensational gamble? Johnstone had made his début a month earlier in a 5–0 win over Cowdenbeath, and had scored two goals. Tossed in to replace the injured Colin Stein, the youngster remarked: 'I just kept looking around the field, staring at the men I was playing with and finding it hard to believe I was out there.'

Cowdenbeath at Ibrox was one thing; the Celtic of Jock Stein at Hampden quite another. Says Celts striker Harry Hood: 'It did our morale no harm to hear that Rangers had thrown in a teenager. They were already without John Greig and had now put a kid in to face Billy McNeill. But it was not true that we took the game lightly. You never take an Old Firm game lightly.' Under Stein, that would have been impossible, but it is worth reflecting on Celtic's omnipotence. Rangers had not won a trophy since 1965 while Celts were bidding for their sixth League Cup in succession. Besides that, the League Championship was also in seemingly permanent residence at Parkhead. Celtic's hold on the Cup, however, was altogether more tenuous; they had won it only three times in the last five years.

Such a period of dominance by one half of the Old Firm is unprecedented in modern times. After all, as Archie McPherson writes in his introduction to *The Great Derbies – Blue and Green*, this contest 'has uplifted the depressed, depressed the uplifted, mortified bookies, influenced the Scottish divorce rate, survived riots, created legends, spawned a million jokes and bored hardly anybody.' As far as Rangers fans were concerned, second-best WAS boring and they could not stand it any longer. But in Waddell and his assistant Jock Wallace, Rangers had a fresh management team. The dynamic duo had promised a new dawn and had gone some way toward halting Rangers' decline. But after a nearly a year in office, they had won nothing; a week before the League Cup final, Rangers had been humiliated at Ibrox by Aberdeen.

The portents were not good for the clash with Celtic on 24 October; in fact, they were awful. But Johnstone was undaunted. 'I actually slept well the night before and dreamed of scoring the winner. I just hadn't had enough time to take in what was happening to me; I was too young,' he says.

It was raining as Johnstone's mum, dad and a busload of relatives, who had made the journey from Dundee, settled into their seats. Rangers, fired up by the two Ws and disregarding the form book, set about Celtic from the kick-off. With wingers Willie Johnston and Willie Henderson in full cry, Johnstone was getting his head to a few crosses and actually beating the mighty McNeill in the air. 'It just seemed like any other game of football,' he says. Five minutes before half-time he knew that it wasn't.

'Alec MacDonald started the move by sending Willie Johnston away down the right wing,' is how he remembers the build-up. 'Just before he crossed, I tried to get a little bit away from their defenders. When it came over, it was between Billy McNeill and Jim Craig. I jumped. They hesitated just long enough for me to get my head to it as I turned towards the goal. It was a bit of a blur, and the next thing I knew the ball was in the net. The rest of the game just passed me by.' Although some pundits claimed it was a fluke, most praised Johnstone for a fine goal and Rangers, gamely overcoming the absence of Greig, dominated the match. Celtic, responding belatedly to the Stein half-time sermon, came back into it later on and had chances, Wallace hoofing the best over the bar from six yards, but it was not their day. It very definitely was Derek Johnstone's, though.

'It was a beautifully taken goal,' says MacDonald. 'I still call it the "good morning" header for the simple way he just nodded his head and glided the ball in. I still tell players about it today.' Hood agrees that it was a fine piece of opportunism: 'You can say he wasn't covered properly but at the end of the day it was a great leap and a superbly directed header.'

So the Light Blues had finally won something, and the first crack in the Celtic supremacy had been made. Mafeking had nothing on the relief Rangers fans felt. As for Johnstone, he insisted: 'I honestly didn't feel nervous. In fact, I felt nothing.' But that was not the reason he did not give a press conference afterwards. Anxious to keep their teenaged match-winner's feet on the ground, Rangers refused to let him speak to the eager scribes. 'I was just hustled out of the door by Jock Wallace who answered the questions for me,' he recalls. When asked about the goal, Wallace rasped: 'What about the ones he missed?' Clearly, Rangers valued their new starlet very highly.

Johnstone felt the same way about his medal. When spirited away for a youth match in Iceland a few days later, he took it with him. 'I didn't want to have it stolen so I hid it in a drawer in the hotel room. Then I forgot it. We came back, and I was almost in tears when I told Willie Waddell. He just said, "Leave it to me." I got it back in three days.' Later Johnstone was to collect enough silverware to open a small jewellers and was in the side that won Rangers' first European trophy. 'Beating Moscow Dynamo was the most significant win of my career,' he says, 'but the League Cup final was the game that endeared me to the supporters.' He was just old enough to be allowed up to stay up to watch the highlights on TV.

Rangers: McCloy, Jardine, Miller, Conn, McKinnon, Jackson, Henderson, MacDonald, D. Johnstone, Stein, Johnston.

Scorer: D. Johnstone.

Celtic: Williams, Craig, Quinn, Murdoch, McNeill, Hay, J. Johnstone, Connelly, Wallace, Hood, Macari.

Sub: Lennox (Hood).

Joe Jordan

Scotland 2 Czechoslovakia 1
World Cup qualifying match, Hampden Park, 26
September 1973

Born 15 December 1951. A bustling target man whose aggressive mobility, unselfishness and courage more than compensated for a modest scoring rate. Started his career with Blantyre Victoria and joined Morton in 1968. Snapped up by Leeds United for £15,000 two years later and spent his best years at Elland Road. Forced his way into the Scotland side before he had established himself at Leeds and scored some crucial goals for his country. Was the only Scottish player to score in three World Cup finals (1974, 1978 and 1982) and notched seven World Cup goals in all. Began to travel when he moved to Manchester United for £350,000 in 1978, being lured by the lire of AC Milan in 1981 and then by Verona. Returned to Britain with Southampton in 1984 before finishing his playing days at Bristol City, where he became manager. Appointed boss at Hearts in 1990.

If a week is a long time in politics, sixteen years is an eternity to a Scottish football fan. For that is how long Scotland were out in the World Cup wilderness, that wasteland of non-qualification that is populated by no-hopers and non-entities. As one notable observer of Scottish life commented: 'Football is the arena where Scots and Scotland assert themselves and play a role in international affairs.' It is perhaps a reflection of how hard they had been trying to return to that role that the man who finally achieved it was a young bull of a centre-forward with three front teeth missing.

Inevitably, Joe Jordan was nicknamed 'Jaws'. There was an aggression and stature about him that his 5ft 11in and relative lack of goals only hinted at. At full cry, he could be a terrifying sight for opposing defenders and, if he did not snaffle that many goals himself, he would put himself about sufficiently to ensure that someone else did. 'A great man to have on your side,' was how colleagues, whether it was at Blantyre Victoria or Bristol City, Scotland or AC Milan, appreciated his rampaging presence. For there was more to Big Joe than merely flying elbows, a hungry look and an open mouth. He was an extremely unselfish player and a fearless one, the kind of guy to ruffle the most rugged centre-back and give even a nerveless goal-keeper a sleepless night.

Jordan was also an excellent man to have on your bench for the numerous occasions when softer options had failed and his harder attributes were needed to save the day. But with 26 minutes remaining against Czechoslovakia in the autumn of 1973, nothing was needed as badly as a goal. When manager Willie Ormond replaced Kenny Dalglish with Jordan, he thought the kid could exploit an obvious Czech weakness in the air. The occasion was a World Cup qualifier and, in spite of a rare pummelling, the Czechs were on level terms and looking forward to the return in Bratislava. It was only a three-nation group, and Scotland had already dealt convincingly with the Danes, beating them twice. As Denmark had drawn with the Czechs, a win at Hampden would secure a place in the World Cup finals in West Germany in 1974 and a return from that wilderness. There was a lot on young Joe's shoulders when he raced from the bench to join the fray.

'I realised the significance all right,' he recalls, 'but, if I'm honest, it probably didn't mean quite as much to me as it did to some of the more experienced players like Denis Law and Billy Bremner. They were coming to the end of their careers, whereas I was only just beginning mine. I certainly hoped to be appearing in the World Cup finals at some stage.' Some stage was not enough for the crowd which had been kept to 100,000 on the advice of the police.

Well down on Hampden's record attendances, it would more than compensate in decibels. Sixteen years was the time span on everybody's mind and marked a new sophistication among Scottish football fans in the 1970s. Perhaps a walloping of the English was no longer sufficient compensation for missing out on the big one.

Since Sweden in 1958, the life of a Scottish football supporter had been a traumatic one, with supreme humiliation dovetailing with unconfined joy, and 1961 and 1967 at Wembley being the prime examples of each. But not even those who regarded the beating of England's World Cup-winning side as *nirvana* could maintain that such wins were adequate compensation for not seeing the sublime talents of Jim Baxter, Jimmy Johnstone, Willie Henderson and Denis Law shine on the world stage. For Scotland never seemed to get as fired up for matches with foreign opposition as they did for those with the 'auld enemy'. This night, however, it seemed that they had.

Urged forward by that firebrand of a skipper, Billy Bremner, Scotland tore at the redoubtable Czech rearguard in which Victor was soon to display why he was rated a world-class 'keeper. The visitors were penned in their own half; indeed, they seldom escaped from their own penalty area for much of the first half as Scotland swept forward in dark blue waves. Roared on by the massed banks of Hampden, attack after attack cascaded on the Czech defence. But the line held.

Then came the kind of nightmare scenario against which Scottish football fans have long steeled themselves: a breakaway and a speculative shot catching the 'keeper unawares. After 34 minutes the speedy Nehoda produced precisely that nightmare double, letting fly from wide on the right, yet finding the net through Alistair Hunter's groping gloves.

There have been times when such a happening was regarded as fatal and, while never causing a lessening of resolve, might have been too much of a hurdle to overcome. But not tonight. With the Hampden hordes finding new voice and Bremner fresh fire in his belly, Scotland were level seven minutes later as Big Jim Holton rose to head home a Tommy Hutchinson corner. The explosion of sound might have interested Mr Richter. The Scots attacked with even more fervour now but, with Colin Stein and Derek Johnstone missing, they found penetration difficult against stout opponents. The ominous thought that 'if they can defend like this here, they're going to be tough to beat over there', was beginning to enter Scottish consciousness. Another goal was needed.

After another 15 minutes of unrelenting assault on the Czech goal, Ormond decided to gamble on the raw, unbridled aggression of Jordan. 'I had already been blooded,' he remembers, 'but it was still quite something to run on the field as a youngster in that atmosphere, in those circumstances.' Earning his living in Leeds reserves, it should have been a major culture shock for Jordan but it did not seem to bother him. He began to win balls in the air, and already Scotland were looking more dangerous. But still the goal would not come.

Only 15 minutes remained when Bremner, still battling, still sniping, hammered a shot against the Czech post. 'The ball rolled out,' remembers Jordan, 'and was cleared to the edge of the box. Willie Morgan latched on to it and crossed from about eight yards. I rose and headed it in. We were through!'

The goal was acclaimed in the most tumultuous fashion. So loud was the crescendo of sound that one wondered if the decaying old mausoleum could cope with it. The Czechs, who had done well, could not maintain their threat any longer, and Scotland held on to clinch one of their most famous and long-awaited victories. 'It was my first goal for Scotland and good to break my duck in that way,' reflects the scorer. 'Nearly twenty years later, the cheers are still ringing in my ears.'

Scotland: Hunter, Jardine, McGrain, Bremner, Holton, Connelly, Hay, Law, Morgan, Dalglish, Hutchinson.

Sub: Jordan (Dalglish).

Scorers: Holton, Jordan.

Czechoslovakia: Victor, Zlecha, Samek, Pivarnak, Beldl, Adamec, Kuna, Bicovsky, Nehoda, Stratil, Penenka.

Subs: Capkovic (Beldl), Dobias (Kuna).

Scorer: Nehoda.

Howard Kendall

West Ham 3 Preston North End 2
FA Cup final, Wembley, 2 May 1964

Born 22 May 1946. An outstanding youngster, Kendall earned England honours at schoolboy, youth and Under-23 levels but never won a full cap. At 17 years and 345 days, he became the youngest player to appear in a FA Cup final when Preston lost to West Ham in 1964. Joined Everton for £80,000 in 1967 and, with Colin Harvey and Alan Ball, forged a famous midfield trio which became known as 'Los Tres Magnificos'. Returned to Wembley in 1967 but was again on the losing side in a Cup final. Was more successful as Everton manager, winning the FA Cup, the League Championship (twice) and the European Cup-Winners' Cup before taking charge of Atletico Bilbao. Returned to the reins at Goodison via Maine Road, where he enjoyed a brief spell as boss of Manchester City.

It was Benjamin Disraeli who declared, 'Youth is a blunder.' But it might well have been a football manager, such is the reluctance to toss youngsters in at the deep end. Fortunately for Howard Kendall, Jimmy Milne had no such compunction, and the Preston boss threw the kid on to the hallowed turf when others felt he was barely out of his play-pen. Blunder? Preston lost, but no blame could be attached to Kendall; the match was the making of him.

However, Kendall maintains: 'I should never have been given the opportunity to play in a Cup final at that age. It was a complete shock to get selected but, even with starting so young, I never won a Cup-winners' medal as a player. I got in because of a disciplinary measure against Ian Davidson, who was a regular at the time. I think it was very harsh to leave him out, and the decision was so sudden that I didn't have the chance to get that nervous. Nor did I manage [to get] tickets for all my relatives. There were big fall-outs at the time, and I think there are some members of the family who are still not speaking . . .'

Born in Crawcrook in the North East, Kendall's initial allegiance was to Sunderland but he switched to Newcastle once his cousin Harry Taylor had joined them. The Magpies belatedly tried to persuade young Kendall to sign for them, but Preston had already made an approach. It was the Lancashire club, he says, 'which made the best impression on my mum and dad, and I became an apprentice for them at 15.' Less than three years later the family were squabbling over who would go to Wembley.

Kendall, being carefully nurtured in the reserves, was thinking he might wangle a ticket for himself when the call came. 'Davidson,' claimed chairman Allan Harrison, 'was chosen to play in the home game against Northampton, but was given leave of absence by the manager on the Friday after asking to be allowed to attend a funeral in Edinburgh the following day. However, when the manager reported the facts to the board, there was no option but to suspend the player.'

'I had played in a few League games and one or two Cup matches,' recalls Kendall, 'and I was on stand-by for players who were injured or whatever.' But he had never anticipated that 'whatever' would include Davidson's subsequent admission, when pressed, of going to Edinburgh to help a relative who was in debt. 'Even so,' says Kendall, 'it seems very harsh. I was elated for myself but gutted for Ian.

'Instead of it being me who felt nervous,' he remembers, 'I remember my team-mates feeling concerned for me. Apparently, they were worried that I might freeze on the day and had come up with this plan to make sure I didn't. It involved giving me an early touch straight from the kick-off and, sure enough, the ball came back in my direction. The only trouble was,' he chuckles, 'it went whizzing straight past me. So it was Plan X after that.'

Plan X, however, was soon working splendidly. Holden put Preston ahead after just ten minutes when Jim Standen, the Worcestershire wicket-keeper, fumbled an Alex Dawson shot as if it had risen off a green top at New Road instead of the greensward of Wembley. 'I didn't know where I was in the first half,' admitted the 'keeper. 'Everything seemed so unreal.' 'For me,' recalls Kendall, 'the most important thing was not to make a costly mistake. I don't think I did.' Even when that gnarled veteran of 18, John Sissons, levelled for West Ham, Kendall looked cooler than the scorer. 'I was in a daze,' admitted Sissons. 'Even scoring didn't help.'

'It hadn't sunk in that I was playing,' says Kendall. 'But I think the whole business helped the rest of the team as it stopped them worrying about their own individual performances. We were playing quite well and yet, when I think back, people had been chasing me for all kinds of things before the kick-off. Photographers wanted to take pictures of me in bed on the morning of the match and having my breakfast. Strangely, I didn't feel the pressure: I was too young.'

As the match wore on, Preston effectively smothered West Ham's smoother First Division touches and had the audacity to go in front again through Dawson, the 'Black Prince', just before the break. The former Manchester United striker headed home following a corner to leave the Londoners with a lot to do – and an interesting team talk. Manager Ron Greenwood ensured that his hand would be writ large on Wembley's history by his half-time reshuffle. 'We were giving them too much space,' he said. 'In the second half we played 4–2–4, and things worked a little better for us.'

It was typical of this most urbane of managers to refer to Preston's ultimate weakening in such terms. After seven minutes of the second half, Geoff Hurst headed the second equaliser and, with the Second Division side wilting visibly, it was Hurst again who bore through to set up the opening for Ronnie Boyce to head the winner. Throughout all this second-half turmoil, it was Kendall as much as anyone who maintained the pride in Preston, tackling, passing, chasing and harrying like the classic wing-half he was to become. It was Kendall, too, who made it into the headlines – not easy when you've lost. 'Preston lose the Cup but discover a star', was the way many northern editions looked at a memorable match.

But poor Preston had been pipped for promotion, too, and it was sad to see them trail despondently away from Wembley with, as they say at Deepdale, 'nowt'. 'We were all very down in the dressing-room,' Kendall recalls, 'and then our skipper Nobby Lawton turned and said: "Eh, we should be proud of ourselves; we've shown people we can play." And that lifted us. On the way home, as we approached Preston, I remember all these people lining the route. At first I didn't think it was anything to do with us as we had lost, and someone shouted out, "Do they know the result?" It was absolutely unbelievable. I just never expected a reception like that, and then there was an official do. The people were just tremendous, and I don't think it could have been much better if we'd won. Even Tom Finney said, "Well done", but, of course, I was just in awe of him at the time.'

Kendall, a realist even then, did not attempt to console himself with the thought that time was very much on his side when it came to capturing a Cup-winners' medal. 'Oh, no,' he remembers, 'I just thought of Stanley Matthews and how long it had taken him. And then of all the top internationals who never won one. I thought I might end up the same.' For a 17-year-old wing-half, his remarkable perception was not confined to the field.

West Ham: Standen, Bond, Burkett, Bovington, Brown, Moore, Brabrook, Boyce, Byrne, Hurst, Sissons.

Scorers: Sissons, Hurst, Boyce.

Preston North End: Kelly, Ross, Smith, Lawton, Singleton, Kendall, Wilson, Ashworth, Dawson, Spavin, Holden.

Scorers: Holden, Dawson.

Denis Law

Manchester United 3 Leicester City 1
FA Cup final, Wembley, 27 May 1963

*Born 24 February 1940. Joined Huddersfield as a schoolboy and
made his League début on Christmas Eve 1956, aged 16 years and
10 months. Fetched a British transfer record of £55,000 when he
moved to Maine Road in 1960. Won his first Scottish cap at 18 – the
youngest post-war débutant – and was sold to Torino for £100,000
after 21 League goals in 44 games for City. After a miserable
twelve months in Italy, Law found his spiritual as well as
footballing home at Old Trafford, being signed by Matt Busby for
£115,000. Won his only FA Cup-winners' medal in 1963 and twice
won the League Championship but cruelly missed the European
Cup triumph of 1968, which he watched from a hospital bed as he
recovered from a knee injury. Scored 30 goals in his 55 internationals, a record he shares with Kenny Dalglish. For United Law
scored 171 goals in 305 League games but was even more lethal in
Cup competitions, notching 28 in 33 matches in Europe and 34 in
44 in the FA Cup. Ended his career back with Manchester City and
with the famous back-heeled goal that put his beloved United into
the Second Division.*

Whether he was exercising a scissors-kick or a suicidal,
head-down dash into an undergrowth of defending studs,
Denis Law was not a man to have in your six-yard box.
Lethal of foot, lightning of reflex, he did not merely score,
he carried out a commando raid. Not even the cast-iron
defences of the Italian League were immune, which was
one reason why Manchester United paid a ransom
£115,000 for him in 1962. Law did not take long to show his
gratitude. Linking up with David Herd, recently acquired
from Arsenal, the Aberdonian notched 23 goals in 38

League appearances that year in a struggling side. 'We only just avoided relegation,' he chuckles. 'But that is easily forgotten when you win the Cup.

'Even though it was early in my career, I go for the 1963 Cup final win over Leicester as my most memorable match. We had not played well in the League yet had a spirit in the side that carried us through in the Cup. For me, it was nice to crown my first season back from Italy with a medal – my only winners' medal – but, more importantly, it was the first thing the club had won since Munich. It was a sign that Manchester United were being rebuilt, and so it was great for Sir Matt. It was one of the greatest games I ever played for United.'

It had been Busby who awarded Law his first Scottish cap as an 18-year-old, but it had been another managerial great from the Scottish coalfield who had first recognised his potential. Legend has it that, when Law went to Huddersfield for a trial as a 15-year-old, the Yorkshire club sent an official to the station to meet him. After carefully perusing all the disembarking passengers, the gentleman finally returned to the ground empty-handed, swearing that no one who looked remotely like a footballer had stepped off the train. Fortunately, a pale, cock-eyed kid in thick glasses had since presented himself and, as he scarcely resembled a healthy human being, let alone one of the greatest forwards of all time, the official was forgiven. One wonders whether Bill Shankly, shortly to take over at Huddersfield, would have been as kind.

'He was a skinny little whippet,' said Shankly later. 'I thought: "How can he play?" ' The vision of the red or dark blue shirt worn loosely outside his shorts, the sleeves pulled down and the cuffs curled into his fist, arm raised in triumph, must have seemed a fantasy then. 'But after you'd seen him with a ball,' said Shanks, 'you realised that he was something unusual. It is debatable if anyone was better than him. He could dance on egg-shells.'

In knock-out competitions there was no one better. The

sudden-death drama of the Cup brought the best out of
Law's predatory instincts. Lurking in the dark recesses of
the penalty area like a viper in the bracken, he would
suddenly leap, dart or dive into devastating action, a
blond blur that defences would have found difficult to
stop even if he had been in slow motion.

Leicester were renowned for the composure and
organisation of their defence, which was marshalled by
the rugged Frank McLintock and had Gordon Banks in
goal. But they did not know what had hit them on Cup
final day. 'I can see Paddy Crerand finding me with a
perfect ball from the left wing now,' Law says. 'I turned
quickly and shot past Banksy's right hand. It was the first
goal, and one I had always dreamed of scoring at
Wembley.' Condemned as 'spiritless, unenterprising and
content to live on the reputation of their predecessors' by
Donald Saunders in the *Daily Telegraph*, United were
underdogs on the day. Ninety minutes later, the same
judge wrote: 'The football they played suffered little in
comparison with the artistry of Milan and Benfica . . .
Even Eusebio and Rivera, the bright young stars of
European soccer, did nothing on Wednesday [in the
European Cup final] that Law did not do on Saturday.'

Leicester, who were content to remain in their defensive
fortress for most of the game, were made to pay for
spurning several early chances when United went in front
in the 29th minute. Crerand seized the ball in front of
Gibson after Banks had blocked a Bobby Charlton drive.
The cross was controlled by Law on his left foot and then,
with that marvellous pivot, he swung round to hammer it
home with his right. United were in control, and Saunders
commented: 'I have never seen Law play better. Auda-
cious, slippery as an eel, driven to greater and greater
effort by a very Scottish determination to succeed, this
volatile young man unravelled Leicester's defensive web
and cast it contemptuously to the winds.'

After United had added a second through Herd, who

knocked the ball over the line after Banks had failed to hold a Charlton 'special', Leicester kept their hopes alive when Keyworth scored with a diving header. But Banks, having a rare nightmare, then dropped a Johnny Giles centre and a grateful Herd gobbled his second. However, the match was not lost by Leicester's lapses; it was bravely and gloriously won by United's adventure. This rebuilt side displayed sufficient zest and guile to suggest that Manchester United could be a force in Europe again, rewarding Busby with a vintage display, with his bolder and bigger purchases finally coming good.

Besides Law's virtuoso performance, Herd, Quixall and Crerand displayed the class of thoroughbreds to bring the great manager his first trophy since the air disaster of 1958 had destroyed the 'Busby Babes'. 'This was why it was so special,' says Law. 'I had joined during this rebuilding phase, and it was immediately obvious to me just how everybody at the club craved success.' Lying in the Rechts der Isar Hospital in Munich after the crash, Busby had been convinced by his wife Jean that the players who had died would have wanted him to go on. 'It was hard,' he said, 'but I did.' Now thanks to the quality and commitment of new boys like Law, the recovery of old ones like Charlton, and finally the emergence of Best, the elusive European Cup would eventually be lifted.

Beating Leicester was an important step on that road, but the direction had been pointed by a fellow who once wore thick, round National Health specs and had an hereditary squint. As a boy, Law had gone through matches with one eye closed, but the complaint was happily corrected by an operation at 15. The youngest of seven children, Law's first boots were bought on credit by his hard-up mum, and it was in adversity that he developed his fighting instinct. After Munich, United needed all of that.

Manchester United: Gaskell, Dunne, Cantwell, Crerand, Foulkes, Setters, Giles, Quixall, Herd, Law, Charlton.

Scorers: Law, Herd 2.

Leicester City: Banks, Sjoberg, Norman, McLintock, King, Appleton, Riley, Cross, Keyworth, Gibson, Stringfellow.

Scorer: Keyworth.

Tommy Lawton

Scotland 1 England 2
Hampden Park, 15 April 1939

Born 6 October 1919. Played for Burnley as an amateur at 16 and notched a hat-trick on his professional début at 17. Further goals persuaded Everton, who saw him as the long-term successor to his idol, Dixie Dean, to pay £6,500 for him – a lot for anyone in those days, let alone a teenager. Scored four in his first representative game, an 8–2 win over the Irish League, when he was only 18, and in 1939, after replacing Dean, hit 34 goals in 38 games to help Everton to the League Championship. After the war Lawton played for Chelsea, Notts. County, Brentford and Arsenal. Scored 231 League goals in 390 games, 22 in 23 for England plus 24 in 25 wartime and Victory internationals.

Wingers, not to mention opposing defenders, should have known just by looking at Tommy Lawton: anyone with such an immaculate parting was bound to be particular about his headers. Lawton, of the sleek, raven thatch and neck muscles of a Salamanca bull, used to like the lace facing away from his forehead on impact. At least that is what he told Stanley Matthews after that prince of wingers had sent in a pearl of a cross for Lawton to head a famous winner at Hampden in 1939. The maestro was taken aback as the young leader appeared to admonish him in the moment of victory. 'Tha did it all wrong, Stan,' he insisted in his best Lancashire brogue. 'Tha put it over with the lace facing my forehead.' Then he grinned and joined the celebrations.

Lawton's goal gave England their first win at Hampden for twelve years and was a typically heroic effort from the

Everton centre-forward who had used his 'stepladder' to soar above the Scottish defence before unleashing a header that left the 'keeper helpless. 'I think that match gave me more satisfaction than any other,' he says 'as it had been a long time since we'd won there, you know.' Lawton was 19.

Although the goal was greeted with silence by all but a handful of the 134,000 fans, Lawton was not the only one to appreciate its significance. An unusually animated England team knew what it meant to them, not least Matthews and Eddie Hapgood, the celebrated Arsenal full-back. After doing a passable impression of a Highland fling on the pitch after the match, Hapgood threw his boots around the dressing-room. 'I've played all these years and this is the win I've longed for,' he said. With a possibly epoch-making quote, he added: 'I could have jumped over the moon.' It may have been original in 1939 . . .

As for Matthews, who had fashioned the winning goal, it was one of the most memorable moments, too. A draw was written all over the match when he latched on to a pass from inside-left Len Goulden with a minute to go, and waltzed past McNab and Cummings on his way to the Scottish line. 'I was actually going for the corner flag,' recalls Matthews, 'and I could see Tommy racing parallel with me down the middle. But then the ball stuck in the Hampden mud and I remember thinking, "I must get this off the ground and try to drop it on Tommy's head." I looked toward Tommy once more, but the Scottish defenders were now closing in on me. I just hit it to where I thought he'd want it, and he rose to knock it in the net. It was not the hardest header he scored, but it was perfectly placed, and typical of the best centre-forward I ever played with.'

'I was very happy that night,' says Lawton, 'as I thought I'd played pretty well – I must have done because I got picked for the continental tour afterwards. Yes, it was a big day for a 19-year-old, and I had a head to match – it wouldn't go through the goal-posts. I was a bit cocky in those days.' Lawton had even been 'cocky' enough to tell Dixie Dean that he would not get his No. 9 shirt back at Everton once he had replaced him. But he denies that he was disrespectful to the great man: 'No, I was just young and confident and, anyway, I used to watch Dixie play whenever I could. He's still No. 1 in my book.'

For all his bounce, Lawton was a good learner and, before studying 'Dixie's every move, every mannerism', he acquired his legendary heading ability in a most painstaking and painful manner. 'We used to hang a ball from the rafters under the stand at Burnley and the coach, Ray Bennion, would stand behind me with a cane. If I didn't jump high enough he would hit me on the backside. That's where I developed the ability to "float".' But that was not all that Lawton, who was renowned more for his heading than his shooting skills, learned. 'I could put topspin and back-spin on the ball, too, you know, but that took hours and hours, and many was the night when I went home with the skin bleeding on both sides of my head.'

Lawton claims he was pretty good with his feet, too, but it was his ability in the air that became the stuff of legends. 'I scored more with my boots,' he still insists; but people were used to long-range shots, and it was the headers that set them talking, headers from outside the penalty area. Soaring and then hanging in the air, Lawton could somehow find the power to beat 'keepers from a distance with his head. Even the most feared centre-halves and agile goal-keepers would be wary of Lawton's 'step-ladder'; for that is what he seemed to use when he rose to meet those high centres he loved so much, regardless of where the lace was.

Although not yet 20, Lawton was beginning to make a name in the England side and was relishing the prospect of taking on the Scots at Hampden before the massed ranks of the 'auld enemy' and that famous swirling wind which always seemed to be accompanied, he said, 'by a blood-curdling roar'. It was not a place for the faint-hearted and, with a capacity crowd undeterred by a downpour before and during the match, Lawton needed all his confidence, especially when the Scots went ahead midway through the first half. With the pitch resembling a Hebridean peat bog, the ball stuck obligingly in the mud in the English penalty area for Dougall to send a simple shot past Woodley. The conditions deteriorated as the swirl became a gale, but the teams contrived to produce a feast of good football, and the excitement reached fever pitch when Huddersfield's Pat Beasley rifled past the redoubtable Jerry Dawson with 20 minutes remaining.

Urged on by their fanatical followers, the Scots tore at England but found the Sassenachs in resolute mood. A classic match was thus ended by a classic goal, and the reputation of Dixie Dean's successor was firmly established. 'Bill Shankly was playing,' says Lawton, 'and he just couldn't believe it. I always remember his reaction: I think he nearly fainted from the shock. We were all good mates afterwards, though, and we had a do in Glasgow that night. But then it was back to reality with the midnight train south. It was so packed that we could not get a seat until Preston. It was a different world then. We were national heroes having just beaten Scotland at Hampden, and yet we had to stand in the corridors for half the journey home.'

Scotland: Dawson, Carabine, Cummings, Shankly, Baxter, McNab, McSpadyen, T. Walker, Dougall, Venters, Milne.

Scorer: Dougall.

England: Woodley, Morris, Hapgood, Willingham, Cullis, Mercer, Matthews, Hall, Lawton, Goulden, Beasley.

Scorers: Beasley, Lawton.

Franny Lee

Born 29 April 1944. A Lancashire lad from Westhoughton, Lee joined Bolton Wanderers straight from school and made his début at 16. Scored 92 goals in 189 appearances, but won 'only a couple of clocks' in his seven years at Burnden Park. Threatened to quit football and concentrate on his burgeoning business interests after a dispute with Bolton but signed for City in 1967 for £60,000. As a central striker, he was dynamite in the penalty area, making up for a comparative lack of height and modest heading ability with tremendous acceleration, an intimidating presence and a fierce competitive spirit. Helped City to their great triumphs under Joe Mercer and Malcolm Allison, when the League, FA Cup, League Cup and European Cup-Winners' Cup were captured in three years. In 1971-72 he converted 13 penalties, a record at the time. Scored 112 goals in 249 League matches for City and 10 in his 27 appearances for England. Was sold to Derby County in 1974 and played an enormous part in taking them to the title in 1975. Scored 25 goals in 62 games for the Rams before retiring at 32 to run his successful paper business and train horses.

A barrel chest is no encumbrance when inside it beats the heart of a lion. Franny Lee, of the slightly portly appearance, occasionally puffing cheeks and chunky thighs, was VC material. No matter what the situation, the goals deficit, the state of the pitch, the state of the opposition or his colleagues, he would never surrender. Lee went in where it hurt and invariably came out with the ball before blasting or bundling it past a bemused 'keeper and a bruised defence. He did not merely shoot, he fired

mortar shells. Just as his effervescence was much appreciated by his team-mates and loved by the fans, it could nark
the opposition into momentary neglect of the spirit of the
game. So much so that Lee was nicknamed 'the Chinaman' because of the number of scorelines that read 'Lee
One Pen'.

For City, up against West Brom in the League Cup final
in 1970, the portents were not good, but his colleagues still
felt that Lee was at his formidable best. City had already
collected the League, the FA Cup and the Charity Shield,
and were well on the way to adding the European Cup-
Winners' Cup when they found the hallowed Wembley
turf looking more like a waterlogged Wincanton. The
Horse of the Year Show had only just hoofed off in
midweek, and the groundsman confessed that the pitch
was in the worst state he had known before a big match.
On top of that, City were late back from a European
adventure. Albion started favourites.

'The weather was so bad when we returned,' says Lee,
'we had to land in Birmingham in the early hours of
Friday. It was not ideal preparation for a final.' It showed
when City went behind after just five minutes, when Jeff
Astle headed a goal gifted by Joe Corrigan. The 'keeper
failed to collect a long centre from Wilson, and the big
striker nodded home. There was a suspicion of pushing,
but a lenient referee would have none of it.

City were muted for 20 minutes and West Brom, who
had made their name as cavaliers of attack, were uncom-
promising defenders in difficult conditions. 'The game
must have come very close to being called off,' says Lee.
But, with the recalled George Heslop now effectively
shackling Astle, City finally cracked the whip, and it was
Albion who suddenly found the going heavy. Never one to
hang around snooker halls or golf courses in his youth,
Lee did not hang around on the field either, least of all when
his team were behind in a Cup final. He was irrepressible:
coming back to help out in midfield, tearing down both

flanks, boring through the middle, he positively buzzed and lifted downcast City heads.

It was riveting stuff and, with Colin Bell also covering every glutinous sod, City assumed command. But it took the Blues over an hour to find the net. The fans were beginning to fret when Glynn Pardoe's corner was hooked in by Summerbee, nodded down by Bell and driven home by a delirious Mike Doyle. Suddenly, there was a feeling that City could finish it without having to resort to the extra-time which might favour the fresher Albion team. Lee and Bell strove mightily but neither side could break the deadlock. So it went to a final half-hour on what was now a quagmire more suited to the sliding tackle than the slide-rule pass.

In the 102nd minute it was Lee who laid on a short cross for Bell to head down and Pardoe finished the job. The massed City hordes were besides themselves and, even though there was the inevitable nail-chomping near the end, City had the strength of sinew and character to hold on. Lee was indefatigable.

A year earlier he had told commentator Kenneth Wolstenholme: 'I used to say that I would pay a year's wages to play in the Cup final: that's how much it means to me.' He had also said: 'To play for England at Wembley is the experience of a lifetime.' He had done all that and more, but his appetite was far from sated. He had now won a few 'clocks' but did not intend to let time stand still. City were pursuing another 'clock' in Europe, and Lee saw that they got that, too.

Back at Wembley for the second consecutive year, Tony Book ascended the thirty-nine steps to receive the League Cup, and the City bandwagon rolled on. It had got a little bogged down in the mud, but Lee had lifted them over it. 'He never played a better game for us,' said Bell, 'and that's saying something.' 'The Chinaman' was still at it, but this time the headlines read 'Lee Won Cup'.

Manchester City: Corrigan, Book, Mann, Doyle, Booth, Oakes, Heslop, Bell, Summerbee, Lee, Pardoe.

Sub: Bowyer (Summerbee).

Scorers: Doyle, Pardoe.

West Bromwich Albion: Osborne, Fraser, Wilson, Brown, Talbot, Kaye, Cantello, Suggett, Astle, Hartford, Hope.

Sub: Krzywicki (Hartford).

Scorer: Astle.

Larry Lloyd

Nottingham Forest 1 Malmo 0
European Cup final, Munich, 30 May 1979

Born 6 October 1948. Joined Bristol Rovers as a junior and made just 43 first-team appearances as pivot before being spotted by Bill Shankly. At 6ft 2in and almost 13 stones, he was seen as a successor to the great Ron Yeats and went to Anfield for £60,000 in 1969. He was ever-present in the 1972–73 Championship-winning side, won three England caps and scored in the first leg of the 1973 UEFA Cup final against Borussia Münchengladbach which Liverpool won 3–0 on aggregate. After being unloaded to Coventry in 1974, a subsequent £60,000 switch to Nottingham Forest heralded an incredible spell in which Lloyd collected medals in the League, two League Cups, two European Cups and a fourth England cap. Managed Wigan and Notts. County before becoming a licensee in Nottingham.

The place: a *bierkeller* in Munich, a sophisticated city with a world-wide reputation for fine lager. The date: the afternoon of the twenty-fourth European Cup final. A Forest supporter, one of some 20,000 who had found their way to the Bavarian capital, leans on the bar. In a broad Nottingham accent, he asks: 'Two pints o' Shippos, please.' Such naivety is perhaps excusable among fans for whom a mid-table spot in Division One was once cause to sup several pints of the local Shipstone's ale, and who regarded the FA Cup win of 1959 as a once-in-a-lifetime occurrence. But such days were over. What John Robertson called 'a team of rag-tags' were about to become masters of a continent.

For Larry Lloyd, it was perhaps even harder to believe. 'I had been to a European final with Liverpool,' he says, 'and, when they sold me, I obviously wasn't expected to go to another.' But Lloyd had been joined at the City Ground by another considerable cast-off, Kenny Burns, and the two were to form one of the most feared 'they-shall-not-pass' central defensive pairings of the modern era. 'If I wanted someone to go through a brick wall for me,' said Forest's co-manager, Peter Taylor, 'I would ask Kenny Burns.' As for Lloyd, he WAS a brick wall.

With Peter Shilton behind them and the likes of Viv Anderson and Archie Gemmill also at their peak, Forest were a formidable unit. Robertson was a revelation on the left wing and, with Peter Withe and Tony Woodcock a potent strike force, they had amazed everyone and won the League Championship in their first season back in the top flight in 1977–78. 'But we didn't get the credit we deserved,' says Lloyd, 'and when the draw was made for the first round of the European Cup, the knockers all said we'd get put in our place. We drew Liverpool. People obviously looked to me for a bit of guidance, but it was the gaffer who did it. Brian Clough just refused to accept that we could be beaten. He said, "If we have to meet them sometime – as we probably will – it may as well be now as later." Even when we beat them 2–0 in the home leg, most people still thought Liverpool would do us. Liverpool certainly did.'

Ray Clemence, the Liverpool 'keeper, remembers: 'Our dressing-room was a different place compared with what it was like a fortnight earlier. And Anfield was buzzing as only Anfield can. There was a sense of optimism, a feeling of total concentration and determination. We were pre-pared to sweat blood that night.' They did, but Forest, inspired by the magnificent Lloyd and Burns, were a cut above. Lloyd, delighted to be back where he had experienced so many European nights with the Kop on his side, had to face its full blast, while on the field he had the small matter of Kenny Dalglish to take care of. But, on the receiving end of an almost constant barrage, Forest's colossus was up to it. 'Liverpool's physical commitment was frightening,' said Clough. 'But we did not waver.'

'That altered a few opinions,' says Lloyd, 'and we started to get more respect, but there were still those who felt that England's best chance of lifting the European Cup had gone with Liverpool going out. But by the time we got to the final we were favourites, and the gaffer was warning us about complacency. That's why the whole campaign is so memorable for me, rather than just one match.' Lloyd's own part in it almost ended in the next round over the celebrated 'blazer incident' after Forest had beaten AEK in Athens. Fined £200 by Clough for not wearing the club blazer, Lloyd, ever his own man, put in a transfer request. Sanity somehow prevailed, and Forest's European express was kept on the rails. But it was a close thing.

AEK and Grasshoppers of Zurich were duly dispatched, but then Cologne gave Forest a shock by grabbing a two-goal lead in the opening minutes in Nottingham. Courageously, the Reds fought back to go 3–2 up, but then appeared to blow it completely by conceding a third late in what Lloyd calls 'an unforgettable game'.

'Nobody gave us a chance over there,' says Lloyd, 'except ourselves. We had tremendous belief in those days with all the trophies we were winning, and then there was the 42-game unbeaten run in the First Division. So when Ian Bowyer headed us into the final, it really was a great moment. According to almost everybody, we were out, and then suddenly we were in the European Cup final. That away leg was probably our best ever performance.'

Forest's build-up to the final was vintage Clough: low-key and quirky. The manager decided to go to Crete on holiday – booked, apparently, a long time ago, so how was that for confidence? – and left the running of the club to Taylor. 'I'm the shop window, he's the goods in the back,' Clough was fond of saying. It seemed a strange carry-on before the biggest date in the club's history, but Lloyd, smartly clad in the club blazer, revealed: 'I would take a diving header through a plate-glass window for our gaffer. I have more respect for him than any man I know.'

After playing Mansfield in their final warm-up game to win the Nottinghamshire County Cup final, Forest flew to Munich to be joined by their manager and, it seemed, by about one in every ten citizens of Nottingham. 'They outnumbered Malmo fans about three to one,' says Lloyd, 'and it was tremendous to see so many of our own fans there for the biggest match of our lives.' But as the fans made their way to the daunting Olympic Stadium, whose spider's-web roof and steepling masts make it look like a fleet of trawlers caught in a storm, there was unease about the team. Neither of the midfield anchors, Gemmill and Martin O'Neill, had been able to shrug off injuries, and both were on the bench. But one man who was on the park was Trevor Francis, now eligible after the transfer that made him Britain's first £1 million footballer.

'Being favourites put extra pressure on us,' says Lloyd, 'and the opening was very dull. We were being patient, and they were being negative. It did not make for a very good match.' Indeed, it was the poorest of the twenty-four finals to date, with Malmo's off-side tactics taking much of the blame. Forest, however, were not to be denied, and just before the interval Bowyer found Robertson wide on the left. 'Robbo' jinked past two defenders in his inimitable way and then curled over a superb cross to the far post. Francis, revealing that wonderful acceleration of his, darted into the six-yard box to meet it and repaid a hefty slice of his fee by heading joyously into the roof of the net.

After that Malmo revealed their paucity of attacking ideas, and Forest could and should have had more goals. Garry Birtles put a volley well over, and Robertson hit a post with the 'keeper Jan Moller beaten. But Malmo seldom threatened, and Forest coasted to their magnificent milestone. 'It was one of the easiest games we ever had at the back,' says Lloyd. 'But we didn't mind one bit.'

'To say the final was disappointing is an understatement,' says Robertson, 'but we felt the campaign was great.' Lloyd agrees: 'We had to beat two of the toughest teams in Europe to get there and one of them, Cologne, we beat on their own ground. So nobody can argue we didn't deserve it.' Lloyd, the lanky lynch-pin of Forest's impenetrable rearguard, had played his part in a fairy-story outcome. Modest Forest, the European champions. It did not quite ring true to certain establishment types. So, with typical Clough cussedness, Forest went out and retained it.

'The Hamburg game [the following year] was probably better,' acknowledges Lloyd, 'but there is nothing like the first time. For a club like this, it was a fantastic achievement. Fantastic. The fans must have thought anything was possible, and it was for a couple of years.' Everything, that is, except Shippos in Munich.

Nottingham Forest: Shilton, Anderson, Clark, McGovern, Lloyd, Burns, Francis, Bowyer, Birtles, Woodcock, Robertson.

Scorer: Francis.

Malmo: Moller, R. Andersson, Jonsson, M. Andersson, Erlandsson, Tapper, Ljungberg, Prytz, Kinnvall, Hansson, Cervin.

Subs: Malmberg (Tapper), T. Andersson (Hansson).

Nat Lofthouse

Austria 2 England 3
Vienna, 25 May 1952

Born 27 August 1925. The youngest of four sons of a coalbagger, he scored a club record 256 goals in 452 League matches for Bolton Wanderers. Won 33 England caps and scored 30 goals as an 'old-fashioned' centre-forward. Footballer of the Year in 1953 when on the wrong end of the 'Matthews final', but captained Bolton to an FA Cup win over Manchester United in 1958, scoring twice. Devoted his life to Bolton where he has been coach, scout, manager and 'kicked upstairs', but will always be a legend.

When music lovers think of Vienna, they can almost hear the masterpieces of Mozart, Strauss and Beethoven; when English football fans think of it, they see only the rampaging figure of Nat Lofthouse. On an unforgettable afternoon in the Austrian capital in May 1952, and before a division or two of khaki-clad British soldiers who had swelled the disbelieving home ranks, the rawboned Bolton Wanderers and England centre-forward rifled his and the city's name into football folklore. 'Lion of Vienna' does not have so much a ring as a roar, and was perhaps the most enduring line ever written by Desmond Hackett, the illustrious football correspondent of the *Daily Express*, who concocted it after England's memorable 3–2 victory. Thereafter, opposing centre-halves trod more warily when facing 'Lofty', while goal-keepers everywhere knew that they were fair game.

Better known for its waltzes than its wildlife, this lovely cultural mecca thus became inextricably linked with the coalbagger's son from the back-streets of Bolton. Even now pride of place on the Lofthouse mantelpiece goes to a trophy in the shape of a lion, presented years later by a local football association. 'It is like the lion from the old five pound notes,' he says, 'and even has an outstretched paw over the ball. It is one of my most prized possessions. This lion business all started in Florence after the previous game on our summer tour. We had drawn 1–1 with Italy – not a bad performance on a hot day against one of the best teams in Europe – but I did not have a very good game. Afterwards, I learned that Fiorentina were interested in me so I couldn't have been that bad, but I did not impress everybody.'

Lofthouse, whose shoulders were broad enough to send a shiver down the sturdiest 'keeper's spine, suddenly found that he had an unexpected burden to carry on this World Cup warm-up tour: a bad press, with Hackett among his critics. 'I always used to ring my wife in the evenings when we were abroad and was staggered to hear her say the papers were calling for Jackie Milburn to be sent over "on a Comet". This made me more determined than ever, and I have to admire our manager Walter Winterbottom for sticking by me. I did not intend to let him down.

'Austria had knocked in an amazing number [57] of goals in their last few [sixteen] matches and fancied themselves a bit, you know. In fact, they reckoned they were the kings of Europe, while we were always the team the continentals most wanted to beat. But what made the atmosphere for me was having over 10,000 British soldiers in the crowd. They roared their heads off.' Vienna was still an occupied city after the war, and adding to the cosmopolitan flavour were many Russian troops. The vast majority of the 65,000 crowd were Austrians, however, and they had come along to witness the unofficial championship of Europe.

The build-up to the game was extraordinary, and the tension was all the more marked by the presence of the sizeable and vociferous contingent of away supporters – a

rare occurrence for a continental fixture in those days. It
was just the lift Lofthouse needed with his place allegedly
at stake. The Lancashire lad had a habit of sizing up the
opposition during the national anthems and, as the Vienna
Boys Choir did their stuff, the England No. 9 knew he was
up against 'a big 'un', as he put it. As he soon discovered,
Ernst 'Clockwork' Ocwirk was a good 'un, too.

In unfamiliar red shirts, England were on the receiving
end for much of the first half and, against the uncomp-
romising Ocwirk, one of the game's great 'attacking'
defenders, Lofthouse was making little headway. But
before the cry for 'Wor Jackie' could be raised by the
British press, the Bolton star scored with England's first
shot of the match after 26 minutes. 'I finally gave our boys
something to cheer when I got a pass from Jackie Sewell
and just shoved it in,' he explains in that modest way of
his. When pressed about the 'shove', he admits he hit it
'pretty hard', with his left foot, 'which was normally just
for standing on.' He was on the edge of the penalty area at
the time: the Lion had begun to growl.

But the Austrians, with Ocwirk doubling as a marauding midfielder, levelled within a minute through a
dubious penalty. Huber scored from the spot after Dienst
had tumbled when tackled by Portsmouth's Jack Froggatt.
But in the end-to-end football that was typical of the day,
the pendulum swung England's way. Sewell dummied
two defenders before scoring a spectacular second after a
pass from Froggatt, and England were back in front. Three
goals in two minutes kept the troops entertained but, just
when England had assumed control, Dienst equalised on
the stroke of half-time.

The second half was not quite as frenetic and, after a
relatively quiet opening when England seemed the more
authoritative side, the magificent Ocwirk rallied his men
to throw everything at Gil Merrick and his defenders. But,
with Austria committed, the classy Birmingham 'keeper
caught yet another corner, spotted Tom Finney and

Lofthouse lurking in their own half with nary a defender in sight and threw an immaculate pass to the Preston winger.

'Tom was about half-way inside our half, drew their lone defender and plonked a long ball through for me to run on to,' Lofthouse recalls. 'He always knew exactly how I wanted 'em and I latched on to it with nobody but the 'keeper to beat.' The Austrians tried desperately to get back, but it was a hopeless chase as Lofthouse, the roars of famous regiments ringing in his ears, bore down on the home 'keeper. The troops in the crowd stood transfixed as the centre-forward pinned his ears back and raced onward, always in control of the ball. Without a moat around the penalty area and a raised drawbridge in front of goal, Austria had little hope of avoiding their fate, and even that was lost when their 'keeper hesitated.

'I remember him [Musil] stopping and then finally coming for me, and we both ended up in a heap. But not before I'd hit it past him from thirty yards. I was down and out for a few minutes and never saw where it went. I heard second-hand from our trainer Jimmy Trotter that I'd scored the greatest goal of my career.'

England clung on for a famous victory; the press scribbled their eulogies, appropriately laden with humble pie; and the soldiers carried their heroes shoulder-high from the field. Blue-coated Austrian police and stone-faced Russian soldiers looked on in awed silence. So began what Lofthouse later acknowledged was, 'the greatest night of my life.' If it had been the Vienna Boys Choir that had launched his finest hour, it was the British army who were now in full cry. The lion had roared all right.

Austria: Musil, Roeckl, Happel, Scleger, Ocwirk, Brink, Melchior, Hanappi, Dienst, Huber, Haummer.

Scorers: Huber, Dienst.

England: Merrick, Ramsey, Eckersley, Wright, Froggatt, Dickinson, Finney, Sewell, Lofthouse, Baily, Elliott.

Scorers: Lofthouse 2, Sewell.

Billy McNeill

Celtic 2 Inter Milan 1
European Cup final, Lisbon, 25 May 1967

Born 2 March 1940. Joined Celtic from Blantyre Victoria in 1957 for £250, and went on to play 831 times for the club. Earned every honour in the game, including a European Cup triumph, nine successive Scottish League Championship medals, seven Scottish Cup-winners' medals and six League Cups. Earned 29 full caps as a rock-like central pivot and was a dangerous addition to the forward firepower at set-pieces, scoring some vital goals. Has enjoyed a successful managerial career at Aberdeen, Celtic (twice), Manchester City and Aston Villa.

With their numbers on their shorts and their hearts on their sleeves, Celtic were an unlikely bunch of path-finders. But for their glorious impression of eleven rampant lions on a balmy night in Lisbon in 1967, the game of football will be eternally grateful. Until then, the European Cup had been the exclusive preserve of Latin clubs. Only the incomparable Real Madrid of Puskas, Gento and di Stefano, the Benfica of Eusebio and, more cynically, the two Milanese teams had captured the continent's most coveted prize in its twelve-year history. Even though England's 'wingless wonders' had won the World Cup in 1966, there was a perceived naivety about British club football in Europe that was not supposed to trouble the maestros from the Med. Not even Celtic's magnificent monopoly of Scottish titles altered the near-unanimous verdict that their attacking style would be custom-made for those Italian aristocrats, Inter Milan, the defending champions.

'Everybody but ourselves made us total underdogs,'

remembers McNeill. 'They were kings of Europe, but it meant that we had nothing to lose and, from the moment we had a cavalcade send-off in Glasgow, we were very relaxed about the whole thing. When we arrived in Lisbon, we found that the Portuguese had adopted the Celtic fans. It was a great boost to have the locals on our side. Besides ensuring the support of Britain's oldest ally and swelling the crowd in the sun-lit Stadium of Light, the Celtic faithful had boosted the 'gates' in local churches as intervention from the highest authority was sought. But they need not have worried: when it came to football, authorities didn't come any higher than Jock Stein.

'Win or lose, we want to make the game worth remembering,' the late and great man said. 'We don't just want to win, we want to win playing good football, to make the neutrals glad we've done it, glad to remember how we did it.' Nothing could have been in greater contrast than the approach of his overpaid and overrated opposite number. Like an even more celebrated bricklayer from down the road in Ancient Rome, Helenio Herrera was into walls: defensive walls. Like Hadrian, the Inter Milan coach was concerned with keeping out marauding Scots. 'But,' says McNeill, skipper and one half of a central defensive bulwark with John Clark, 'he had reckoned without our spirit and our skill. We sang Celtic songs in the tunnel on the way to the pitch, and that really shocked them. I know it's a daft thing to say, but they looked sombre and were more nervous than we were.'

But the masters of *catenaccio* soon settled. After just seven minutes Mazzola converted a penalty awarded when Jimmy Craig tackled Cappellini from behind. 'We thought it was harsh and so did the crowd,' says McNeill, 'but when I saw it on TV, I had to agree that the referee was right. At half-time, though, we were more aggrieved by that than by having twice hit the woodwork. Although it gave them the lead they wanted, the incident probably did us more good as we just declared there and then: "We're not going to let this outfit get away with it." It was constant traffic towards their goal afterwards. We were going forward so much, I had one of the easiest games I had in the whole competition – and I was marking Mazzola, the Italian star!

'We had thought Sarti, their 'keeper, might be a weak link, but he had a magnificent game and, although they were past masters at soaking up pressure and we left it a bit late, I can honestly say that we never once felt that we were going out.' Eventually, not even the agility of Sarti could resist the irresistible. Based – in spite of his modest recollection – on the rock-like solidity of McNeill and Clark at the back, the ceaseless promptings of Bertie Auld in midfield, the magic of Jimmy Johnstone on the wing, the selfless running of Steve Chalmers and Bobby Lennox augmented by the formidable overlaps of Craig and Tommy Gemmell, Celtic were not to be denied.

When Gemmell, glimpsing a chink of light in the black and crimson barrier, rifled home from twenty-five yards in the 63rd minute, Herrera's edifice was profoundly shaken. But with seven men hardy veterans of three European Cup finals, they were not about to crumble just yet. However, the goal was the signal for Celtic to up their already ferocious tempo and for McNeill to add his considerable aerial power at the set-pieces. 'We were going for broke,' he says. With half of Europe watching entranced on TV, the classic contest came to an inevitable conclusion.

Following yet another Celtic surge, Chalmers triumphantly turned in Murdoch's diagonal shot five minutes from time to trigger scenes of delirium that have probably never been surpassed on a foreign field. 'You know,' says McNeill, 'I don't think anyone was in command of himself to remember what Jock said to us as we came off. The dressing-room was bedlam and the feeling was . . . ecstasy.' But that was nothing to what was happening on the terraces.

A party that had begun when the advanced guard of the Celtic hordes had arrived on the Monday and had become a trifle subdued between the Mazzola and Gemmell goals, only to erupt when Chalmers scored, was now in full and unstoppable flow. What was left of the whisky was washed down with *vinho verde*, and only when the taverns were drunk dry did a bleary-eyed, bedraggled queue begin to form at the British Embassy, not one but two dawns later. As the red-faced, rumpled remnants of the tartan army attempted to return home – many had lost their passports as well as their money and marbles in a joyous spree – Hugh McIlvanney described the evacuation as 'a Dunkirk with happiness'.

The Italians could scarcely believe the pummelling they had taken, while the hosts were overwhelmed by the flair of the Scots: 'The real meaning of the game,' commented one observer on Celtic's attacking style. 'Sooner or later,' wrote Lisbon's *Mundo Desportivo*, 'the Inter of Herrera, of negative football, and of marginal victories, had to pay for their refusal to play entertaining football.' Even a former Rangers manager, Willie Waddell, generously wrote: 'This was the greatest day in our history.' It was for Scottish football, and it was one of the best for Britain, too. It was to be English clubs who would capitalise on the breach of Latin domination more than most, and in the eighteen years after Celtic's triumph the European Cup left northern Europe only once.

It was also a triumph for passion over paranoia, for flair over fear, and if the sheer ebullience of the football has not been matched since it at least brought a temporary respite from the cynicism. 'It was the ultimate,' enthused McNeill. The magnitude of the deed was probably best summed up by Bill Shankly, who told Stein: 'You're immortal now.'

Celtic: Simpson, Craig, Gemmell, Murdoch, McNeill, Clark, Johnstone, Wallace, Chalmers, Auld, Lennox.
Scorers: Gemmell, Chalmers.

Inter Milan: Sarti, Burgnich, Facchetti, Bedin, Guarneri, Picchi, Domenghini, Bicicli, Mazzola, Cappellini, Corso.

Scorer: Mazzola (pen).

Peter McParland

Aston Villa 2 Manchester United 1
FA Cup final, Wembley, 4 May 1957

Born 25 April 1934. Graduated from Gaelic football to Shamrock Boys via a summer soccer league. Played for Dundalk before joining Aston Villa in 1952. Known as 'Mac the Knife', McParland was a fast, direct left-winger with a lethal shot. Notched 123 League goals and ten for Northern Ireland after finding the net with his first international kick against Wales in 1954. Scored five in the 1958 World Cup where he was one of the tournament's outstanding players. Hero/villain of the 1957 FA Cup final with two goals in Villa's 2–1 win over the 'Busby Babes' and scored the winner for Villa in the 1960 League Cup final. Spent his twilight years with Wolves, Plymouth and then Atlanta in the United States before managing Glentoran in the 1970 European Cup.

Taking on the 'Busby Babes' at Wembley was the sort of challenge Peter McParland relished. 'We didn't mind being the underdogs,' he recalls. 'In fact, we quite liked it: most teams do. We fancied ourselves all through the competition. You know how you get a bit of a feeling . . .'

Neither the bookmakers nor the public shared the Irishman's sentiments. Manchester United were overwhelming favourites, having won the League by a massive 11 points and boasting the legendary 'Babes' whom Matt Busby had already nurtured into a marvellous side. People only had to mention the names: Roger Byrne, Duncan Edwards, Tommy Taylor, Bill Foulkes, 'Billy' Whelan, David Pegg, and it looked as if the first League and Cup double of the century would be theirs. 'Send the trophy to Manchester now,' was the general verdict, 'and give the kids their place in history.' But that gave the Midlanders an extra incentive: the last club to win both competitions was Aston Villa. 'So we had a bit of club history to protect as well as playing for our pride,' quips McParland. But in the Irishman's case, pride would have been more than enough.

In spite of McParland's 'feeling', Villa had hovered near the exit sign throughout the campaign. Three times they survived after replays and, on each occasion, it had been their dashing left-winger who had saved them. 'Yes, we had a little bit of luck,' he acknowledges. They also had his indomitable spirit and his dynamic left foot. 'The worst moment was at Luton in the third round,' he remembers. 'We were 0–1 down and it was injury-time. The ref was about to blow, and I just got my foot to one in the six-yard box. I'll never forget it as it was so muddy and the ball almost stuck in the mud. But somehow I managed to force it over the line. It was the last kick of the match.

'After that we gained a lot of confidence from beating a good Middlesbrough side at Ayresome Park but then got the sixth-round draw we didn't want: Burnley away. They were our bogey side, and I remember watching it live on the television news as I had my tea. I nearly swallowed my sausage when our name came out of the bag last and we had to go there. But, backs to the wall, we held 'em, won 2–0 at Villa Park and then scraped through against West Brom after a semi-final replay. So we had a few flutters, but then that's the Cup, isn't it? After all that, we were not worried about United. We had drawn with them at Old Trafford in the League, which did us a lot of good, and we were confident we could hold our own.'

The game got off to a dramatic start with the hallowed turf taking heavy toll and the stretcher bearers working an arduous shift. Ray Wood, the Manchester United 'keeper, and McParland collided with Wood coming off worse. In fact, Wood came off the field and, in many people's eyes, the incident turned the tie. McParland was blamed in some quarters for a reckless challenge, but it must be remembered that shoulder-charging of the 'keeper was more acceptable then. Substitutes, however, were not.

'It came about after Les Smith, our winger, had made a run down the right. He had put in many throughout the season and would usually follow with an excellent cross. I would come in from the other wing to capitalise and I was doing that and just picking my spot for this one. Over it came and I wanted to hit inside the far post from outside the six-yard box. Unfortunately, I didn't hit it quite right and sent it straight at Wood. He caught it. But he was moving forward as he did so and I followed up in case he dropped it. I was sideways on to him and was preparing to charge. Now he was a 'keeper who was not afraid of being hit and in we went.

'The trouble was that on impact our heads clashed, the side of my head with his cheek-bone. I was hurt, too, and lay there on the ground with the stadium spinning around me. Luckily, I recovered, but Ray had to go off. He came back and gave us a bit of trouble on the wing before going back in goal. But, of course, I had scored a couple of goals by then.' McParland vehemently denies that his charge was unfair, just as he maintains that a fit Wood would not have got near either of his goals. 'The first came from a lovely cross by Johnny Dixon. I sneaked in front of Duncan Edwards to get in a header. I thought it was a helluva goal,' he says. Certainly, the gallant Jackie Blanch-flower, who had donned the green jersey, had no chance. Nor did he with the second, five minutes later.

Again it was Dixon, playing a real captain's role, who had a hand in it after McParland, lurking on the far post, had headed a cross from the right-back across the face of the goal. Dixon drove it against the bar with Blanchflower beaten, and the ever-alert McParland nipped in to volley home the rebound. 'That was a great feeling,' declares the Irishman, who had had to put up with the inevitable boos of frustrated United fans. 'But it was not over by a long way. They were still battling, and Tommy Taylor headed a goal with seven minutes left. I wouldn't say there was panic in the Villa side, but there was definitely fear.'

With Wood – 'he could play a bit outfield, too,' says McParland – having returned between the posts, United threw everything at Villa's defence in those final minutes. But the Midlanders' line held and so did their proud record of being the last team to complete the League and Cup double. For McParland, the celebrations were hardly muted, even though the triumph was tinged with sadness, not to mention controversy. 'I felt very sorry that a fellow player had been injured in the Cup final,' he says, 'and should have to miss part of what was the supreme occasion of your career. The United fans gave me some stick, but our trainer Bill Muir had told me: "There's only one way to shut them up." He did not have to tell me what it was.

'The press were a little bit critical, but not too much because most of them had predicted that I was the main danger to United. So they had to stick by that, didn't they? As for the goals themselves, if Gordon Banks, Pat Jennings and Peter Shilton had all been standing on the line, they still would have gone in.'

But the controversy raged. Wood's injury, a fractured cheek-bone, had been the latest example of the Cup final jinx. In 1952 Wally Barnes had limped off with a wrenched knee; in 1953 Bolton's Eric Bell had been but a passenger; Manchester City had Jimmy Meadows injured in 1954; and Bert Trautmann broke his neck in 1956. The day before the 1957 Cup final, the FA had once again rejected the idea of substitutes. Leading scribe Peter Wilson screamed his reaction in the *Daily Mirror*: 'Obstinacy. Sheer damn pig-headed obstinacy. That's what's wrong with British sport.' He ended in a massive swipe at the FA by asking: 'Why should the winners' victory be tarnished for all time?' A player of McParland's class deserved a better fate.

Aston Villa: Sims, Lynn, Aldis, Crowther, Dugdale, Saward, Smith, Sewell, Myerscough, Dixon, McParland.

Scorer: McParland 2.

Manchester United: Wood, Foulkes, Byrne, Colman, Blanchflower, Edwards, Berry, Whelan, Taylor, Charlton, Pegg.

Scorer: Taylor.

24. Joe 'Jaws' Jordan, the scourge of goal-keepers, snatched the goal that put Scotland through to the final stages of the 1974 World Cup with a 2–1 victory over Czechoslovakia. Here he terrorises the Norwich defence in the colours of Leeds United in 1976.

25. Manchester United's Denis Law tries to take the ball round Leicester's Gordon Banks during the 1963 FA Cup final. Law scored the opening goal and David Herd struck twice to give United a 3–1 win.

26. Tommy Lawton uses his famous 'stepladder' to climb above Leeds's McCabe in a third-round FA Cup tie at Brentford in 1953. The immaculate Lawton had no doubt ensured that the lace in the ball was facing away from his forehead.

27. Franny Lee, in where it hurts in the penalty area. Lee helped Manchester City to the League, FA Cup, League Cup and European Cup-Winners' Cup, scoring 112 goals in 249 League matches, before winning the League with Derby County in 1975.

28. Nat Lofthouse, the 'Lion of Vienna', turns away after scoring the first goal in Bolton's 1958 FA Cup final win over Manchester United. Lofthouse's soubriquet was earned on a memorable afternoon in Austria, when England beat their hosts 3–2 and the centre-forward scored twice.

29 & 30. The European Cup in British hands. Larry Lloyd (left) in jubilant mood after Nottingham Forest's 1–0 win over Malmo in Munich in 1979; and Billy McNeill (right) raises the trophy after Celtic had beaten Inter Milan 2–1 in Lisbon in 1967.

31. The moment in the 1957 FA Cup final when Aston Villa's Peter McParland collided with Manchester United's Ray Wood, leaving the 'keeper with a fractured cheek-bone. Wood was stretchered off, but McParland got up to score twice to give Villa a 2–1 victory.

32. At the age of 38, Stanley Matthews at last received an FA Cup-winners' medal in 1953, when Blackpool recovered gallantly from a 1–3 deficit to beat Bolton 4–3, Stan Mortenson scoring a hat-trick and Matthews making two of the goals.

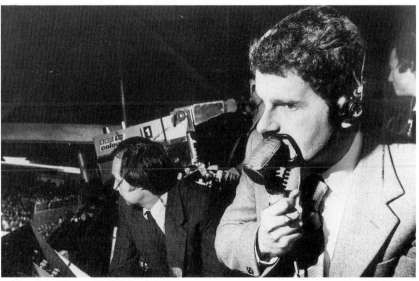

33. John Motson's first major commentary assignment was at humble Edgar Street in 1972, when non-League Hereford took on mighty Newcastle in the third round of the FA Cup. Thanks to a screamer from Ron Radford and an extra-time goal from substitute Ricky George, the minnows won 2–1.

34 & 35. (left) Bobby Moore lifts the European Cup-Winners' Cup after West Ham's stylish 2–0 win over Munich 1860 at Wembley in 1965. (right) England manager Bobby Robson, with his namesake Bryan, finally silenced his critics with World Cup glory in 1990.

36. Swindon Town players parade the League Cup in 1969 after they became the second Third Division club to win the trophy by beating Arsenal of the First Division by 3–1. Don Rogers (fourth from right) scored twice in extra-time to give his team victory.

37 & 38. (left) Len Shackleton scored six times on his début for Newcastle in a 13–0 win over Newport, but lasted only eighteen months at St James's Park. (right) Bob Stokoe and Sunderland captain Bobby Kerr celebrate their team's shock 1–0 win over Leeds in the 1973 FA Cup final.

39. Gordon Strachan, unloaded by Manchester United to Second Division Leeds, scores the goal that gave the Elland Road club a 2–1 victory over Leicester City in their drive for promotion in 1990.

40. The Wallaces, Danny, Ray and Rod, the first brothers to become £1 million players. Danny went from Southampton to Manchester United in 1989, and Ray and Rod joined Leeds in May 1991.

41 & 42. (left) Billy Wright, who played 105 times for England, captained his country in their revolutionary 3–6 defeat by Hungary at Wembley in 1953. (right) Terry Yorath, the Wales manager, who steered his country to an unforgettable 1–0 win over world champions Germany in June 1991.

Archie McPherson

Scotland 3 Holland 2
World Cup finals, Group 4 match, Mendoza, 11 June 1978.

When Bill Shankly said, 'My ideal Scottish team would have only three Scots in it,' there were some clansmen who thought that the Liverpool sage had lost touch with his marbles, let alone his heritage. Blasphemy, sacrilege and treachery were among the milder responses he triggered, but the great man had intended it as much a back-handed compliment as a criticism. 'Three's enough,' you could almost hear him rasp, 'tae beat most countries.'

Iran and Peru would certainly have been on Shanks's list of no-hopers, yet it was Scotland's failure to beat either country in the catastrophic campaign in Argentina in 1978 that led to the epic clash with Holland. It was at this match that the distinguished commentator, Archie McPherson, said: 'We experienced all the emotions . . . in the commentary box.' It had long been recognised that Scottish football writers were 'supporters with type-writers', but McPherson's inherent fairness and unbiased broadcasts of his country's fluctuating fortunes over three decades had established him as much more than a mere 'fan with a microphone'.

To begin to appreciate just how McPherson & Co., not to mention the Scottish nation, felt during that amazing match, one had to go back well beyond Glasgow and the false hopes of an open-topped bus send-off to South America. One probably has also to bring in Bannockburn and the Jacobites, for the Scotland team's behaviour has frequently mirrored the national characteristics, especially when it came to riding gloriously roughshod through cannon fire only to stumble over their own bayonets.

Being the only country from the United Kingdom to

qualify for Argentina inevitably meant that Scotland were going to be subjected to the closest scrutiny all over the UK, while in Scotland McPherson sensed, 'more than ever before that my every word was being listened to by people on the edge of armchairs.' But the wild, ill-considered claims of that charismatic but ultimately calamitous manager, Ally McLeod, were definitely shades of Bonnie Prince Charlie. After an encouraging, but not wholly convincing, run-up to the finals, McLeod was insisting: 'We'll win it.' His boasts later contained riders such as, 'Well, if we don't, we'll come back with a medal.' But when asked what he would do after the World Cup, he replied: 'Retain it.' The citizens of Glasgow cheered as if they had, but you could almost see McPherson cringe.

With such as Archie Gemmill, Kenny Dalglish, Joe Jordan and Graeme Souness in the team, a degree of optimism was justified, but not only did McLeod appear oblivious to such outstanding opponents as Holland, Argentina and Brazil, he had also ignored the Scottish tendency to slip up against also-rans; which brings us back to Shankly. For all the tartan wizardry he admired in his compatriots, the Anfield folk hero had lived south of the border long enough to appreciate the steadying influence that a leavening of foreigners, even Sassenachs, could have on Scottish footballers. Failures such as Scotland's against Peru and Iran in the group matches would not have been allowed to happen to any of his Liverpool sides. Shanks could see the shambles coming.

'We had a terrible time,' recalls McPherson. 'Losing to Peru was bad enough, but scraping a draw with Iran thanks to an own goal was worse – to think an own goal saved us against Iran! Then, of course, there was the Willie Johnston drugs business . . . It was awful, yet we knew that we could still qualify for the next phase – if we beat Holland. Suffice to say, there was not a lot of confidence.'

Indeed, one wag inquired: 'Where are we gonnae find three Dutchmen to score three own goals?' Ron Greenwood, who told the press matter-of-factly that, 'All Scotland have to do is to beat Holland by three clear goals,' was given short shrift. 'Hell, man,' retorted a Scottish scribe who recalled England's 1–0 win at Hampden before the team left Britain, 'What do you mean, beat Holland . . . we cannae even beat you.'

McPherson could detect the sorrow in the Highlands even from Argentina. 'I remember the magnificent stadium in Mendoza, a concrete bowl in the shadow of the Andes, and we were perched very high up. The pitch was actually below ground level and, looking down, I wondered just what I would be telling the viewers back home. There had been some pretty rotten things written by the South American press, some of which had filtered through to the British papers, so we badly needed to salvage pride against Holland. But no one seriously felt we could do any more than that.'

However, with the belated inclusion of Souness, who struck up an immediate understanding with Gemmill, there was a new spirit about the Dark Blues, and new hope in McPherson's voice. But when Rensenbrink slammed home an early penalty for the 1,000th goal in World Cup finals, Scotland needed a miracle. The poignancy of such a landmark goal being a penalty against Scotland was not lost in the press box, but just as more tearstained copy was about to be filed, Scotland scored. Kenny Dalglish slotted home from a Joe Jordan knock-down, and the improvement was no longer imagined. Soon after half-time Gemmill converted a spot-kick after Souness had been tripped, and Scotland had a chance.

'It was difficult to convey the mood,' says McPherson, 'after all we had been through, and we still needed something a bit special. But it was clear that suddenly there was hope, whereas before there had been only abject misery and pessimism.' Hope there was, for Gemmill was suddenly a man inspired. Seizing upon a loose ball on the right, the dynamic little midfielder launched himself upon a run. McPherson takes up the story: 'Turning inside and out, and then inside again, Gemmill beat three men and bore down on goal. The Dutch defence was in disarray. Then, with a searing shot every bit as good as the dribble, he scored one of the great goals of the tournament, one of the great goals . . .'

McPherson did not see a nation's collective leap off its armchair nor the raising of a million roofs, but he does vividly recall the reaction in Mendoza. 'I shall never forget the whole line of commentators leaping to their feet when the ball went into the back of the net, and you must remember that sitting next to me were David Coleman and Huw Johns, an Englishman and a Welshman.' For a few minutes the miracle looked on. One more goal would have done it, and McLeod, who had been a sorry shadow of the man on the Glasgow omnibus, had come back to life on the bench. But as the lion rampant went for the kill, it was unprepared for a swift Dutch counter. Johnny Rep latched on to a poor clearance and, with Alan Rough unawares, he sent it soaring over the hapless Scottish 'keeper. Abject misery and despair all over again.

'It was extraordinary,' says McPherson. 'We went from very, very low to top C and then, wallop, we came crashing down again – all in one game. Apart from all that, it was a great football match with a stunning goal.' But pride had been salvaged. The recriminations and resignation of McLeod did not take long, but all Scots felt a little better that night – once they had sorted out their emotions.

Scotland: Rough, Kennedy, Buchan, Donachie, Forsyth, Rioch, Gemmill, Hartford, Souness, Dalglish, Jordan.

Scorers: Dalglish, Gemmill 2 (1 pen).

Holland: Jongbloed, Suurbier, Krol, Rijsbergen, Poortvliet, Neeskens, W. van der Kerkhof, Jansen, Rep, R. van der Kerkhof, Rensenbrink.

Subs: Wildschut (Rijsbergen), Boskamp (Neeskens).

Scorers: Rensenbrink (pen), Rep.

Sir Stanley Matthews

Blackpool 4 Bolton Wanderers 3
FA Cup final, Wembley, 2 May 1953

Born 1 February 1915. Son of a featherweight boxer, Matthews signed as a professional footballer for Stoke City, his local club, at 17. An outside-right, he won a Second Division medal at 22 and another at 48, playing his last game for them at 50. In the intervening years, every left-back in football had nightmares about facing his bewitching skills. 'Playing Stanley Matthews is like playing a ghost,' said Johnny Carey, the Manchester United defender. Stoke sold him to Blackpool for £11,500 in 1947, and it was in the tangerine jersey that he enjoyed his greatest triumphs, although he had to wait until he was 38 before a coveted FA Cup-winners' medal was his. He had already secured ambassadorial status abroad with his unforgettable performances for England, whom he represented 54 times, and played his last international at 42 when his talent was hardly diminished. Always supremely fit and a perfect gentleman on and off the field, he retired from the game after becoming its first knight. Was twice Footballer of the Year, in 1948 and 1963, and European Footballer of the Year in 1956.

When Stanley Matthews was knighted for his services to football, three generations of defenders winced in his honour. For a bow of the head and a dip of the shoulder by Stan had been enough to turn even his sturdiest opponents into gibbering wrecks. In contrast, centre-forwards who had been on his side still smiled in gratitude for the crosses he had sent over; out of reach of both centre-half and 'keeper, and with the lace away from their targets' foreheads.

Matthews had won many matches with his wing wizardy, for Stoke, for Blackpool and for England. There had been internationals in which only his beguiling skill had saved his country; matches in which he had mesmerised the opposition to set up famous victories. But even among this glittering memorabilia there was only one 'Matthews final', in Coronation year when he was 38. At that age, Blackpool's Cup-fighting qualities and his own Peter Pan impressions notwithstanding, it was reckoned to be his last chance of a winners' medal.

'I shall never forget April 1953,' he wrote in his book, *The Stanley Matthews Story*. 'Blackpool were through to the Cup final for the third time in five years and I, at 38, was once again in sight of that elusive winners' medal. My fan mail was fantastic. People who had never seen me play sent me their good wishes. I received hundreds of mascots and thousands of letters. I felt that I had the whole country behind me in my third attempt to win my medal.'

The nation had nothing against Bolton Wanderers, Blackpool's opponents on that memorable day, but sentiment ruled. Matthews was, after all, a national institution, a gentleman and a genius. It somehow did not seem right that a player of his footballing and personal qualities should be denied the ultimate reward. The British sense of fair play decreed that Blackpool should win. There had, however, been drama during Cup final week of which the public were blissfully unaware: Matthews was injured. 'I pulled a muscle in training on the Tuesday and was doubtful,' he says. 'I had to have an injection on the morning of the match and, luckily, I was all right. But I had been very worried about playing as there were no substitutes in those days.'

Even though Matthews had taken the field, it was not looking good for Blackpool as early as the first minute. Bolton's Nat Lofthouse, that great destroyer of reputations, had decided to test the Blackpool 'keeper George Farm early on, and found him wanting. A long-range shot from the right somehow seeped through Farm's nervous clutches and into the net. As Matthews records, 'Blackpool stood spellbound.' Lofthouse almost made it two in the 20th minute, but Matthews maintains he was 'not unduly disturbed' by the loss of that early goal. 'I didn't feel worried because the game had hardly started.' He was right. Bolton's Eric Bell pulled a muscle and became a passenger. Stan Mortenson equalised. Bolton went in front again, but, as Matthews said, the game had hardly started.

At half-time it was still anybody's match. Ten minutes into the second half it was Bolton's. The injured Bell soared to head an heroic third, and Blackpool had the weight of history against them; no club had come back from a two-goal deficit to win a Cup final. As Matthews put it: 'Losing 1–3 with 35 minutes left, it looked as if we needed a miracle.' Mortenson did not quite stretch to that, but his second , from a Matthews cross in the 68th minute, did keep the Tangerines alive. 'It was at this point that I decided the time had come for my all-out effort,' says Matthews. Sensing that Bolton's tiredness may have been tinged with complacency, the 'Wizard of the Dribble' began to weave his magic. 'I pulled out every trick I knew, and after ten minutes I knew they couldn't hold me,' he recalled.

With Ernie Taylor feeding him and poor Ralph Banks, the Bolton left-back, displaying early symptoms of St Vitus's Dance, Matthews started to purr. A dip of the shoulder, a raising of the eyebrow, a feint here, a dart there, and Bolton's defence was in disarray. In a gentle precursor to the Mexican wave, sections of the crowd swayed to the bewildering body-swerves that Matthews inflicted upon the Bolton defenders. As Stan went left, the crowd leaned left; as Stan went right, the crowd leaned right. Wanderers did not know which way to turn, but Blackpool's forwards were wasting his skills. Bolton's defenders were nearing the end of their tether, but so was the match: Blackpool were running out of time.

If will power could have won Matthews a medal, the public would have had it dangling from his neck by half-time. But their hero now knew he would have to do something special even by his extraordinary standards. 'I took a deep breath,' he says, 'and went into battle.' He sent cross after tantalising cross over into the beleaguered Bolton lines, but nobody could get on the end of them. Yet the pressure on Wanderers was such that something had to give. Three minutes remaining, and it was all Matthews. Bolton conceded a free-kick just outside the penalty area. The wall must have seemed like the Maginot Line, but Mortenson saw a loophole and blasted straight through it for the Cup final's first hat-trick. Blackpool were level, the dream still on.

Delirium in the crowd, delirium on the field, delirium across Britain. But on the right wing there was only deadly intent. From the kick-off Blackpool went straight on to the attack and, with just over a minute left, the ball was once again at Matthews's feet. Getting it quickly under control, he went past Banks in the penalty area.

'Morty knew that when I beat a man inside the penalty area,' he says, 'there were three things I could do. First choice was to cut it back inside; second was to send it to the far post; and third was to put it across the goal. When I'd beaten Banks, I waited for Morty but he did something, very unselfishly, that few fans appreciate even now: he ran out of position dragging a defender with him. By doing that he made it possible for us to score as he had created a gap for Bill Perry. The rest is history, but Morty had scored three and made one.' So perhaps the most dramatic Cup final of all had its fairy-tale ending.

Morty's final? That was not the script. As someone once said: 'The last bloke to score a hat-trick in a Cup final was Stan Mortenson. He even had it named after him: the Matthews final.'

Blackpool: Farm, Shimwell, Garrett, Fenton, Johnston, Robinson, Matthews, Taylor, Mortenson, Mudie, Perry.

Scorers: Mortenson 3, Perry.

Bolton Wanderers: Hanson, Ball, Banks, Wheeler, Barrass, Bell, Holden, Moir, Lofthouse, Hassall, Langton.

Scorers: Lofthouse, Langton, Bell.

Bobby Moore

West Ham 2 Munich 1860 0
European Cup-Winners' Cup final, Wembley, 19 May 1965

Born 12 April 1941. A better cricketer than footballer in his schooldays, a county career beckoned until West Ham invited him to join their groundstaff. Progressed rapidly enough to win 18 caps at England youth level and graduated through the Under-23 team to full England honours. Replaced Malcolm Allison in the West Ham side, making his début in 1958, before going on to take Bobby Robson's England shirt. Played 545 League games for the Hammers before ending his career at Fulham. Earned 108 caps for England, leading his country to the 1966 World Cup triumph and his club to the FA Cup in 1964 and European Cup-Winners' Cup in 1965. Always a majestic figure, he led by example and was said by no less a judge than Pele to be 'simply the best defender in the world.'

'If winning the World Cup has to be the pinnacle of my career, the game that gives me most satisfaction at club level was the Cup-Winners' Cup victory over Munich 1860 at Wembley,' says Bobby Moore. 'For this was the best of both worlds: playing with your mates, guys whom you train with week in and week out, and in front of your own fans in a major final on the international stage. Wonderful.'

The seeds of this spectacular Hammers triumph were sown years earlier when Malcolm Allison, the man whom Moore replaced in the famous claret and blue shirt, used to bend the ear of like-minded colleagues such as John Bond and Noel Cantwell in tactical discussions after training. When players at other clubs were wending their way around the golf course or the pool table, animated conversations were held at Upton Park over both the finer points and the fundamentals. Pretty soon, word got out about these think-tanks, and the West Ham 'academy' was instituted. Manager Ron Greenwood was the ideal professor.

Playing cultured football of which thinking men approved, West Ham swept sweetly on in three FA Cup campaigns in the mid-1960s. Lacking the steel with which to maintain a serious assault on the League title, the Hammers nevertheless were a joy to watch, employing tactics ahead of their time while developing the brilliant triumvirate of Moore, Hurst and Peters which was to form the cornerstone of England's 1966 success. With the FA Cup well and truly won in 1964, West Ham launched themselves upon Europe in the Cup-Winners' Cup, confident that they could maintain their roll. Delighting packed houses at Upton Park and cutting a stylish swathe through the meanest of continental defences, Messrs Moore, Peters and Hurst earned a golden chance to add to their silverware; the Cup-Winners' Cup final was at Wembley that year.

'We obviously fancied it,' says Moore, 'because we had happy memories of the Cup final the year before and we knew that all our supporters would be able to make it. Munich were a skilful side and it was always going to be close, but playing at Wembley made us favourites. It was a chance the lads did not want to miss.'

Under Moore's cool but inspirational leadership, West Ham had managed to rise to the big Cup occasions ever since a memorable FA Cup semi-final victory over Manchester United at Hillsborough in 1964. 'It was the United of Law, Best and Charlton,' says Moore, 'and after beating them we felt we could beat anybody.' They had. Now 100,000 people, by far the biggest crowd that most of the team had played before, assembled to see if they could collect a first European crown. The natural buoyancy of the East End supporters was only slightly dented by the

absence of two experienced forwards, England internationals Peter Brabrook and Johnny 'Budgie' Byrne, who
were both injured. Virtual unknowns Alan Sealey and
Brian Dear came in. Few of the watching TV audience had
heard of them, and even Hammers fans were not all that
familiar. But the new boys would not let them down.

'We knew Munich weren't mugs,' says Moore, 'because
they'd beaten Torino, supposedly the top team in the
tournament, in the semis and had come third in the West
German League, a tough competition. They also had four
German internationals and a brilliant Yugoslav 'keeper.'
A win – any sort of win – would have done for most fans,
but not for West Ham's. Having taken the 'academy' to
their hearts they demanded style, and Greenwood knew it.
A scraped 1–0 win in a tight, drab match would not have
done for them, nor for him. 'Be positive and win it in
style,' he told his men.

The tempo was up-beat from the kick-off and the giant
Yugoslav custodian, Radenkovic, was soon displaying his
eccentric brand of defiance, making thrilling saves from
Sealey and Dear, neither of whom was in the least bit
overawed by an electric atmosphere. Galvanised by
Moore's imperious presence and the smooth touches of
Peters, West Ham held the upper hand. But the Germans,
not least their colourful 'keeper, were almost matching
them in both style and substance. It was another Wembley
cracker.

A 0–0 scoreline at the break gave no hint of the feast that
had been served up in the first 45 minutes. Fast, flowing
football, in which all of the great stadium's manicured
hectares had been gloriously utilised, had been punctuated by daring breaks for goal at both ends, and Jim
Standen, between the West Ham posts, had to be at his
best to thwart the dangerous German skipper, Rudi
Brunnenmeier. But just as Munich might have taken
control, John Sissons hit a post and then Sealey, who had
been married only four days earlier, thought he was back

on his honeymoon when he slid home a right-foot shot in the 69th minute.

Ronnie Boyce's willingness to run himself into the ground had set up that one, but West Ham revealed their full repertoire when Moore's pin-point free-kick sought out the lurking Sealey for the clincher less than two minutes later. Said Sealey, whose wife was in the crowd, 'I did a somersault after the first and when the second went in I wanted to jump over the stand.' Greenwood added: 'I would like to be judged by that match; it presented the game in the best possible light.' Indeed, both teams shared an award for fair play and sportsmanship afterwards – from the United Nations, no less.

'It was a tremendous performance on a marvellous occasion,' said Moore, who did not know there were even greater triumphs to come. But that was probably his finest hour at the club where he gave such magnificent and stalwart service. 'We had a very talented side but still lacked the consistency to do it at League level,' he added. 'So it was more important for us to make the most of the Cup occasions.' They did that all right: the 'academy' had graduated with honours.

West Ham: Standen, Kirkup, Burkett, Peters, Brown, Moore, Sealey, Boyce, Hurst, Dear, Sissons.

Scorer: Sealey 2.

Munich 1860: Radenkovic, Wagner, Kohlars, Bena, Reich, Luttrop, Heiss, Kuppers, Brunnenmeier, Grosser, Rebele.

John Motson

Hereford United 2 Newcastle United 1 (aet)
FA Cup third round replay, Edgar Street, 5 February 1972

Len Shackleton said, 'It will be Sotheby's versus Steptoe & Son – a game when class and brass count.' Malcolm McDonald declared, 'I'll smash the Cup scoring record.' Just two reactions when humble Hereford United of the Southern League were drawn to play mighty Newcastle United on Tyneside. McDonald was the Magpies' dynamic centre-forward with the lethal left foot, and perhaps he can be excused a little hyperbole. But 'Shack' should have known better; he had been in the 'Bank of England' Sunderland side that had lost to Yeovil Town twenty-three years earlier, the last time a non-League team had beaten one from the First Division.

After an epic 2–2 draw at St James's Park, both men were understandably more wary. The result had been greeted with disbelief in some quarters, but there had been sufficient interest across the country for the BBC to send a camera crew and a commentator to Edgar Street. John Motson was the man with the mike. 'I was just making my way as a commentator,' he recalls, 'and it was my first season with "Match of the Day". They wanted the game covered, but it was scheduled for a ten-minute slot and the third feature of the programme. We were there for the possibility of an upset, but I think it is safe to say that everyone assumed Newcastle would put Hereford in their place.

'Of all the matches I have since covered, this is the one that stands out, and yet it was not until late in the game that things really happened. Of course, there had been a terrific atmosphere throughout, but no one could believe the events of the last few minutes and extra-time, least of all those who were involved in them.

'One of the reasons the night was so unforgettable is that I actually drove down to Hereford the day before with two of their players. Ricky George had been a lifelong friend, and Billy Meadows was also in the car. They were regaling me with tales of the 2–2 draw on Tyneside. But that was nothing to what they had to say the following night. After arriving in Hereford, I remember meeting the late Jackie Milburn who asked George if he was playing. Ricky replied that he did not know. It was 11:30 p.m., and Milburn remarked that if George had been in his team he would have been in bed by now. We had a good laugh about it, but little did we know.'

Colin Addison, the Hereford player-manager, had not been deluded by the draw at St James's Park, commendable though it had been. 'I knew they would be raring to make us pay for what we had done to them before their own fans,' he said. 'Also, we were now aware of the strength of McDonald and that he had a fearsome left foot. We knew that if we gave him enough room he would murder us, and we knew their other strengths. But if we had dwelt on all that we would have been running scared. Instead, we battled for every blade of grass. We took a battering in the first half, but we survived and no one lost his nerve. As the game wore on, we grew stronger to such a point that I knew we had them.'

That point was after McDonald had put Newcastle in front, whereupon Motson told his bosses back at the Beeb: 'McDonald 1–0 – looks like staying that way.' The view was based more on the way these matches tend to go and the gulf between the two clubs rather than the never-say-die spirit of the non-Leaguers, who, roared on by a still-hopeful crowd, seemed to sense their date with destiny, even if no one else did. Marshalled magnificently by Addison in midfield, and with Fred Potter surpassing himself in goal – 'I knew he was a fine 'keeper,' said

Addison, 'but he astonished me with his sharpness and courage' – Hereford never stopped running and refused to yield this tension-racked tie.

With Dudley Tyler a source of constant torment to United's defence, Mick McLaughlin putting the shackles on McDonald and the whole team battling to achieve League status as well as to stay in the Cup, Hereford desperately sought an equaliser as the minutes ticked away. 'I knew we were as fit as Newcastle,' claimed trainer Peter Isaac, 'so I wasn't worried about extra-time. I knew that they wouldn't give up. We had the same approach as a League team, and after the first game I knew we'd win the replay.' But, for all their pressure, Hereford still needed a goal. Four minutes to go.

Says Ron Radford: 'I got a good look at goal in the first half and missed the chance. I made up my mind that the next time I saw an opening I would take a crack. The trouble was, it just didn't happen until after Newcastle had scored. I played a one-two with Brian Owen and then hit it for all I was worth. I thought it was going too high to begin with, but once it was on its way I knew it was a goal.'

It was a stupendous strike, almost bursting the net from all of thirty yards. Ecstasy was a wholly inadequate word to describe the Edgar Street reaction. 'It was absolutely magnificent,' says Motson, 'and was subsequently voted goal of the season by BBC viewers. It was then that I knew that the match would be getting considerably longer than ten minutes on "Match of the Day". It was now anybody's match, but Hereford would have fancied extra-time more than Newcastle.' The Magpies Irish international 'keeper, Ian McFaul, said of Radford's long-range missile: 'It was the best goal I have had scored against me. I just couldn't believe it as I watched the ball scream into the net.' Said Addison: 'I'll never know how he dragged from his boots the strength to fire that shot.'

Radford was a hero in midfield, too, where he, Addison and the tireless Tony Gough refused to allow Newcastle the space they wanted to exhibit their allegedly superior skills. Hereford had never known a day like it, and Newcastle were rocking soon after extra-time began. But, unbeknown to anyone, least of all to himself, full-back Roger Griffiths was the biggest hero of all.

The 26-year-old canning factory fitter, who had collided with his own 'keeper in the fifth minute of the game, had played 75 excruciating minutes with a broken leg. 'He complained of the pain,' says Addison, 'but made it clear he wanted to carry on. He did magnificently but just had to go off in the end. He was in agony.' Edgar Street gave him a great reception and roared on George, his replacement. They would have roared at anything now; they have seen nothing like it before or since. Motson also knew he was witnessing a major happening: 'The tension was in-credible from some 15,000 people,' he says, 'the game was now poised on a knife-edge and it was rapidly going to the front of the schedule on "Match of the Day".'

'Prior to the goal,' said Newcastle manager Joe Harvey, 'I couldn't see Hereford coming back into the game. But we paid for our mistakes: we had several chances in the first half and after Radford's goal were really struggling. They just never gave up.' With anything now possible and the Southern Leaguers well and truly inhabiting the FA Cup dream, George scored in the 103rd minute. Radford had put Tyler through on the right, and the midfielder then set up the substitute for the winner. 'When I took the pass and turned I couldn't believe my luck,' George said. 'I could see that the far corner of the net was unguarded and shot straight away. It was wonderful when I saw the ball go over the line.'

Says Addison: 'I knew that we'd do it when Radford scored. I knew that he had shot us into football history. George's goal was simply confirmation. When I am an old hand I will still remember the response I got from my lads in that last half-hour. I am so proud. Whatever happens to me in football, I know that nothing will touch me like that 2–1 win.'

Hereford went on to draw at home to West Ham in the fourth round before going down at Upton Park in the replay. But they earned their League status and not a few accolades. The watching Ron Greenwood thought that they were 'an exceptional non-League side,' while a gracious McDonald declared: 'I'll give them ten out of ten for their performance.' Shackleton said: 'Yeovil's win over Sunderland was a fluke, whereas Hereford deserved theirs.' Motson shares this view, adding: 'It ended up being the main feature on "Match of the Day", and I think it was this game that made the BBC feel I could handle a big occasion.' So, too, could Hereford.

Hereford United: Potter, Griffiths, Mallender, Jones, McLaughlin, Addison, Gough, Tyler, Meadows, Owen, Radford.

Sub: George (Griffiths).

Scorers: Radford, George.

Newcastle United: McFaul, Craig, Clark, Nattrass, Howard, Moncur, Busby, Green, McDonald, Tudor, Hibbitt.

Scorer: McDonald.

Phil Neal

Liverpool 3 Borussia Münchengladbach 1
European Cup final, Rome, 25 May 1977

Born 20 February 1951. Spent six years with Northampton
Town before being one of Bob Paisley's first and most important
signings in 1974. Coped admirably with the quantum leap from
Cobblers to boot room, where he assumed the role of penalty-
taker and, eventually, captain. A solid rather than spectacular
right-back, Neal was renowned for his overlapping and posi-
tional play. Earned 50 caps for England and is the only player to
have appeared in all of Liverpool's four European Cup finals.
Made 453 appearances for the Reds. Appointed player-
manager of Bolton Wanderers in 1985.

Deciding the greatest night in the history of Liverpool
Football Club is akin to choosing a World XI to play Mars or
selecting the finest painting in the Louvre: a lot of discussion,
little agreement, but a wonderful excuse to trawl through
priceless treasures. There had been so many triumphs since
the arrival of Bill Shankly: the FA Cup in 1965 after a
seventy-three-year wait, and again in 1974; five League titles
in fourteen years; the UEFA Cup in 1973 and 1976 . . . But
what the Kop really wanted was the European Cup. They
knew Liverpool were the best team in Europe but they
wanted it officially recognised. These other trophies were all
very well, but the Champions' Cup was THE one to win. So
when Borussia Münchengladbach were rolled over on a
steamy night in Rome and the massive trophy was on its way
to Merseyside, it was hard to challenge Bob Paisley's claim
that it was 'the greatest night in the club's history.'

It was certainly THE match of Phil Neal's life, for it saw,
he claims, 'Liverpool at their best. Not just the team

performance, but the team spirit and the rapport with the fans. Above all other games, it showed just what Merseyside football is all about. It demonstrated the special thing we had going there among the players and the supporters. It was unbreakable.'

The change-over from Shankly to Paisley had been accompanied by only the merest blip on the graph of greatness. Liverpool ended as runners-up to Derby in 1974–75 and, in the European Cup-Winners' Cup, went out to old enemies Ferencvaros. Paisley, however, had righted the ship; the League had been won in 1975–76 in some style and so had the UEFA Cup. The 1976–77 season was embarked upon in similar style and the 'impossible' treble of League, FA Cup and European Cup looked a realistic possibility. 'We sewed up the League and then met Man. United in the final at Wembley,' says Neal. 'We were strong favourites, but it just didn't go for us on the day.' United's winning goal was a lucky rebound off Jimmy Greenhoff, and Paisley was swiftly on to the pitch afterwards trying to lift his players. Borussia and an even bigger occasion were waiting.

'We never thought our fans would make the journey,' says Neal, 'as many had used their Giro cheques to get to Wembley, and we felt that we had let them down. It took a while after that to get our spirit back, but I'll never forget walking out on to the pitch with the other lads an hour or two before the kick-off in Rome and being greeted by thousands of Liverpool fans. We couldn't get over it. Later we heard what they'd done to get there, and it was unbelievable. Some had auctioned off personal belongings while others had even sold their cookers. But even before we knew the details we said to ourselves right there and then that we just could not let these people down again.' Suitably fired up, Liverpool launched this final stage of their thirteenth successive European campaign by carrying the fight to their German opponents, whom they had beaten to win the UEFA Cup in 1973. Ignoring

Borussia's reputation for counter-attack, Liverpool tore
into them with a zeal that alarmed their own fans, who
were accustomed to a more patient build-up.

'The Liverpool fans drive you to extremes,' explains
Neal. 'You end up being as committed as they are, and we
were not going to miss out on this one. We played some
good stuff.' Indeed they did, taking a deserved lead in the
27th minute through Terry McDermott. Steve Heighway
supplied the pass, but Kevin Keegan and Ian Callaghan
both played their part, the all-action Keegan taking the
mighty Berti Vogts with him on a decoy run to the left as
McDermott ran through to score like an old-fashioned
inside-right. But Borussia, who had already hit the post,
were dangerous on the break and equalised through Allan
Simonsen in the 51st minute.

Five minutes later Ray Clemence kept them out with a
magnificent save from Uli Stielike and then, just as
Liverpool began to show their Wembley wobble, it was a
case of cometh the hour, cometh the man. A corner by
Heighway was crashed into the net by none other than
Tommy Smith, whose farewell appearance this was
scheduled to be. Headers from the iron man were so rare,
he decided to celebrate by carrying on for another season.
'Worthy of Dixie Dean,' quipped a delirious Smith. 'I
don't think I'll want to wash my head again after that.'

Neal agrees it was the turning point: 'It gave us a
tremendous boost and we were back controlling the game
again afterwards.' But still there was more drama to come.
With an irrepressible Keegan running Vogts ragged,
Liverpool went for the clincher, and it was the Hamburg-
bound Keegan who forced his despairing marker to trip
him as he dashed through for what might have been his
farewell goal seven minutes from time.

'So,' remembers Neal, 'it was left to me to seal it. I had
taken over from Kevin as a penalty-taker and accepted the
situation. But I do remember seeing their 'keeper towering
over Clemmy [Ray Clemence] at the start and thinking

then that if I got a penalty I'd better keep it low. But I'd never been under such pressure. It was definitely the most crucial kick of my career. I knew that if I scored that would be it, but if I missed they could well have been lifted enough to come back at us.

'I'd also taken a penalty in the semi-final and was sure the 'keeper would have seen it on video. I had hit that one to the 'keeper's left so I decided to put this one to the right. But, as I ran up, you could hear a pin drop from our lot in the crowd. Out of the corner of my eye, I caught sight of Ian Callaghan with his hands together in prayer. He had played in all thirteen seasons in Europe, and that's how much it meant to him. I just could not let him or half of Merseyside down. I stepped up and, luckily, I held myself together to hit it firmly. To the 'keeper's right. He dived to his left.'

Liverpool: Clemence, Neal, Jones, Smith, Kennedy, Hughes, Keegan, Case, Heighway, Callaghan, McDermott.

Scorers: McDermott, Smith, Neal (pen).

Borussia Münchengladbach: Kneib, Vogts, Klinkhammer, Wittkamp, Bonhof, Wohlers, Simonsen, Wimmer, Stielike, Scaffer, Heynckes.

Subs: Hannes (Wohlers), Kulik (Wimmer).

Scorer: Simonsen.

Peter Reid

Everton 3 Bayern Munich 1
European Cup-Winners' Cup semi-final, second leg,
Goodison Park, 24 April 1985

Born 20 June 1956. Signed for Bolton at 18 and made over 250 appearances for the Wanderers as a dynamic right-half. Overcame a catalogue of injuries to become the midfield hub, developing passing skills to match his bite in the tackle. Almost joined Everton for £600,000 when Gordon Lee was in charge at Goodison, but the move was halted by a recurrence of leg problems which had included a broken knee-cap in 1978 and a broken leg in 1981. However, Everton maintained their interest, and Howard Kendall snapped him up for £60,000 in 1982. He was to prove one of the bargains of the decade, masterminding Everton to their triumphs of the mid-1980s and winning 13 England caps, turning out in the 1986 World Cup finals in Mexico.

If you discount a slightly laboured 1−0 aggregate win over University College of Dublin, Everton strolled into the semi-finals of the second most important competition in Europe in 1985. The reward was a tie against the redoubtable Bayern Munich, one of the strongest club sides in the world, with, significantly, the away leg first. The reward for a superb 0−0 draw in the Olympic Stadium was a packed Goodison, roaring in anticipation of finishing the job. It had the makings of a memorable evening.

'Without question,' says Peter Reid, 'that was the best night in all my years at Goodison. Unbelievable. Different class. Different class even to the final. You ask any of the lads.' Goodison had, of course, seen some nights. The great ground's excellent acoustics retain the swelling roars which bounce off the double-decker stands and back on to the pitch, 'right down the players' lug-holes', as one ex-Evertonian used to say. Derby matches have a special atmosphere of their own, but European nights were something different again.

It was as if all Evertonians had sensed a change in the famous port's footballing fortunes, as if the Mersey tide was turning from red to blue. Everton were going strongly for a domestic double, but it was in Europe where they really wanted to outshine Liverpool. Evertonians had endured a great deal during Liverpool's halcyon couple of decades. Those who had been weaned on Dave Hickson were grandads by the time Howard Kendall had built the mid-1980s side. But now a unique treble of League, FA Cup and Cup-Winners' Cup loomed, and not even Liverpool had done that.

Even long-time sufferers – and there were some terminal cases – of the Liverpool success had been impressed by the magnificent defensive display in West Germany. Liverpool could not have done it better and now, as Reid puts it, 'all we had to do was win.' Bayern, although disappointed not to have scored in the home leg, were still oozing the class and confidence one would expect from a side stuffed with internationals. Augenthaler, Matthaus and Hoeness were indeed household names outside West Germany, as was Belgium's Jean-Marie Pfaff, and were quite capable of snatching a narrow away win out of this yet.

'They had been favourites to begin with,' says Reid, 'and we were a very strong side. Even so, a lot of our fans felt we'd won the competition when we held them to a draw at their place. But they surprised us by being physical from the off as they tried to stop us getting a rhythm going. Then they cried when we gave it 'em back.'

It was a night to remember, all right. Rugged and passionate from the outset, it was a full-blooded Anglo-German conflict. When Graeme Sharp was fouled by Pflugler, Trevor Steven shot across goal when he might have given Everton the early goal which their supporters craved. With Reid and Steven the perpetual-motion mainstays, there was much to encourage the home fans. Everton's assaults were well-conceived and brilliantly sustained; the pace was frenetic; Gray rampaged, Sharp and Kevin Sheedy threatened . . . and then it got rough. Gray and Pfugler were booked, Sharp also retaliated, and Reid fumed. 'It was all go,' says Reid, 'and we gave 'em a real bombardment.' But it was Bayern who opened the scoring.

Matthaus put Kogl through an Everton defence caught unawares and fatally square and, when Southall came out to block, the 'keeper had the mortification of seeing the ball rebound into the path of Hoeness. The West German star did not miss those, coolly placing his shot past two defenders who had raced back to cover. 'It was a bit of a disaster,' admits Reid, 'because it meant we had to get two.' But three minutes into the second half Pfaff, the Bayern 'keeper, fumbled a long throw by Gary Stevens and Sharp was on hand to knock it in. The ground exploded. Goodison again sensed that victory was possible and, with Gray marauding as never before and Reid now irrepressible, Bayern began to wobble. 'We felt it was ours at that point,' says Reid.

With Goodison vibrating to the sort of Mersey sound on which Liverpool had had a monopoly, Everton tore at their opponents with a fearsome intensity. 'It was tremendous stuff,' says Reid, 'and I don't think the Germans had had a night like that before.' Indeed, they had never encountered anything like Gray, about whom they complained after the match. Well, they would, wouldn't they? He scored the second.

Capping a fiercely competitive performance that evoked memories of both Dixie Dean and Tommy Lawton, Gray smashed one in from close range in the 72nd minute to put the Blues in front. Bedlam broke out all over the ground and, with the crowd now at fever pitch and the previously resolute Germans visibly wilting, Steven ensured that a final place was Everton's by bursting through to score a third with just four minutes left.

'Unbelievable, terrific, magnificent,' says Reid, and that was just the crowd. Not everyone, however, was impressed. 'Gray should play rugby,' said Udo Lattek, the Bayern coach. The Scot had simply not allowed anything or anybody to stand in his way, and not even his first-half caution could slow him down. Soon after his tangle with Pfugler he collided with Eder who came off second best, blood pouring from a head wound. The Germans clearly could not cope with his brimstone brand of aggression, let alone his predatory skills.

Alex Young he was not, but that night Evertonians could not have taken the 'Golden Vision' to their hearts any more than they warmed to the 'Blond Bomber'. 'He had a good 'un,' acknowledges Reid, who had something similar himself. As the late Eddie Waring might have said: 'He ran his little legs off himself.'

Everton: Southall, Stevens, van den Hauwe, Ratcliffe, Mountfield, Reid, Steven, Sharp, Gray, Bracewell, Sheedy.

Scorers: Sharp, Gray, Steven.

Bayern Munich: Pfaff, Dremmler, Willmer, Eder, Augenthaler, Lerby, Pfugler, Matthaus, Hoeness, Nachtweih, Kogl.

Sub: Beierlozer (Willmer).

Scorer: Hoeness.

Bobby Robson

England 1 West Germany 1 (3–4 on penalties)
World Cup semi-final, Turin, 4 July 1990

*Born 18 February 1933. Brought up in the mining community of
Sacriston, County Durham, Robson signed for Fulham in 1951.
He was 'the legs' in a midfield partnership with Johnny Haynes
but did not team up with him in the England team until he was
sold to West Brom for £25,000 in 1956. Scored twice on his
international début in a 4–0 win over France and went on to win
20 caps. Returned to Fulham as a player and then made a false
start to his managerial career with Vancouver Royals who went
bust. Took over at Fulham where he was sacked after seven
months but was hired by Ipswich, a humble fourth choice for
the job. He eventually turned the unfashionable Portman Road
club into one of Europe's top sides. Runners-up in Division One
in 1981 and 1982, they won the FA Cup in 1978 and the UEFA
Cup in 1981. Won 47 of his 95 games as England manager but
had to endure an increasingly acrimonious campaign mounted
by certain sections of the press. Spent much of his eight-year
tenure with an expression one scribe compared to that of 'a man
who fears he might have left the gas on.'*

For a man who once said, 'The first 90 minutes are the
most important,' it must have been particularly poignant
to lose a World Cup semi-final on penalties after his team's
two preceding matches had gone to extra-time. 'The West
Germany clash has to be the match of my life,' he says. 'It
was my second-to-last game in charge of England and
probably the best performance by an England team since
we won it in 1966. There have been many memorable
moments in my career both as a player and a manager, but
you can't beat that game, really, can you? It had every-

thing. It had high-quality football, tension, drama, commitment and it carried the hopes of the country. It had them dancing in the streets, and it had them crying into their beers. It left me scarred, mentally scarred: the disappointment was so acute.'

The country had been amazed that England had reached the semi-final stages of the 1990 World Cup, and if the man in the street had eventually rallied behind the team it had not been without an initial reluctance. Indeed, the large army of invading English hooligans had seemed more likely to make an impact on Italy than Robson's players. As for the press, it had not been long since certain tabloids were screeching 'Plonker' in the direction of the manager. After one poor performance, the *Mirror* had demanded: 'In the name of God, Go!' After a draw in Saudi Arabia, he was urged to leave 'In the name of Allah'. Mercifully, when England then went to Greece, a 2–1 win ensured that Zeus was not called upon.

A seventeen-match unbeaten run, ultimately broken by Uruguay, did not convince the sceptics that England were likely to be a force in Italy, and their worst fears were confirmed by an almost unwatchable 1–1 draw with Jack Charlton's Republic of Ireland in the first group match. One Italian paper was so appalled by that lacklustre display that its headline cried: 'No football please, we're English.' The *Sun* screamed: 'Bring them home.' But in the time-honoured English manner, the team muddled through its qualifying group with a 0–0 draw against Holland and a 1–0 win over Egypt. Performances improved, but Belgium proved a tough nut and it took a moment of sheer magic by David Platt to beat them in the last minute of extra-time. 'We got better as the tournament went on,' claims Robson, but England still had to come from behind to defeat Cameroon 3–2 in a memorable quarter-final. And so to West Germany.

With Franz Beckenbauer's side looking the most formidable outfit in the competition, England appeared to need all the help they could get. Predictably, the tabloids, those same tabloids, thought they could oblige by whipping up jingoistic fervour. Prior to the semi-final, the *Sun* consigned its entire front page to a Union Jack which it implored its readers to stick in their front windows for moral support. It seemed it was now worth keeping our brave boys out there.

Robson, whose team was at no better than stand-off point with the touring press, resisted the temptation to have a copy faxed out to him. He says, 'The players had tremendous will and spirit. They had the country at heart, and I did not have to motivate them for this one. But I did tell them to be positive and to try to dominate the match from the kick-off, for that is what the Germans do. They always play well early on. I told them to give the Germans some of their own medicine and not to wait for them to come at us. I said, "They'll try to knock you over; knock them over instead." They liked that and responded magnificently.'

Unlike the other semi-final between Argentina and Italy, this was a football classic, a rare example in a barren tournament. Neither the 62,628 crowd inside Turin's Stadio Della Alpi nor the thirty million viewers at home, many of whom had left offices and shops early in order to have the take-away ordered before the game, could believe what they were seeing. England, muddling England, were flowing and doing exactly what their manager had told them. With the Geordie trio of Paul Gascoigne, Peter Beardsley and Chris Waddle showing Newcastle United fans just what they had been missing, England rattled the Germans but were unable to take advantage of their clear superiority in the opening half-hour. The Germans came back into the match towards half-time and were dangerous on the break but, at the interval, England looked the more likely winners. A World Cup final against a weakened Argentina was beckoning.

'At the interval,' says Robson, 'I just told 'em to go and do it again. They had proved the point, and I was delighted with the way they had played. Another half like that, and we would have won.' It was in the 59th minute when the goal came, but it was not an England goal. A free-kick by Brehme bounced off Paul Parker and, agonisingly, excruciatingly, it flew up over the wall and just a manicure above Peter Shilton's despairing reach. It was the cruellest of goals. There was only half an hour to go.

England showed what they were made of and, with barely ten minutes remaining, a cross from Parker on the right landed at Gary Lineker's feet in the penalty area. In a trice, the ace striker whipped it low and true into the far corner. It was the tenth World Cup goal of his career and the most crucial. It had given England a lifeline when only a cruel fate looked available. 'I honestly thought we'd do it then,' says Robson. 'I could see the Germans' heads drop a little, and at 1–1 I thought it might not even go to extra-time. We were so fit that we grew stronger as the game wore on, even though we had been through extra-time in our previous two matches and they hadn't.'

A taut, knife-edge half-hour followed with both sides hitting the woodwork, but the dreaded lottery of penalties could not be avoided. But, it seems, England had not dreaded them that much. 'We were very confident about penalties when we went over there,' says Robson, 'but in that semi-final we were without two of our best: Bryan Robson, who had gone home, and John Barnes, who was not in the side. Even so, we had some good kickers and we deliberately chose Stuart Pearce as the fourth man, because that is the most vital kick in the five. And he never missed.' A year later, Robson seemed to gulp as he said it.

'All I said to them before the penalty shoot-out was not to change their minds, to decide on where they were going to put it and stick with that. When it comes to penalties, he who hesitates is lost. I felt a bit like a caddy; you can advise, but it's the player who has to play the shot.' Amid unbearable tension, Lineker kept his legendary composure to put England ahead. He had chosen the correct club, but so had Brehme who clinically equalised. Next it was Beardsley. No trouble, but Matthaus was even more assured. Two-two. Platt did the business for No. 3, but Riedl rifled his home, too. Three-three. England had taken their penalties superbly, but there was a ruthless efficiency about the Germans that was frightening. Shilton had not moved an inch. He couldn't – the ball was past him before he could blink.

And so to Pearce, the Forest left-back with a competitive spirit as ferocious as his left foot. He ran up. He lifted that left tree-trunk of his. Wham! Alas, it was straight at the German 'keeper Illgner's leg. Pearce was distraught. So were thirty million viewers. They knew the Germans would not miss and they were right. When Thon put Germany 4–3 ahead, everything depended on Waddle. With an unbelievable amount of pressure weighing on his shoulders, the Marseilles man opted for power, not precision, and blasted the kick . . . over the bar.

A nation in mourning, a bench in despair, a team in tears. Gascoigne had already shed his at being booked and realising he would miss the final. But now there would be no final, not for England, anyway, and Gazza's tears were the mere source of a mighty river now in flood. But amid the English grief and German jubilation, it was good to see Matthaus attempting to console the weeping Waddle. Pearce had already burst his private banks. A strong man, indeed, but he was not the only one.

'In all my time in football,' says Robson, 'I have never known a dressing-room like it. Such despair, such desolation. It was like death. There was nothing you could do to bring it back. That moment, that wonderful chance to bring the World Cup back to England, had gone for ever. I felt helpless at that point. There was nothing I could say to them. Or them to me.'

England: Shilton, Pearce, Walker, Parker, Wright, Waddle, Butcher, Platt, Gascoigne, Beardsley, Lineker.

Sub: Steven (Butcher).

Scorer: Lineker.

West Germany: Illgner, Brehme, Kohler, Augenthaler, Buchwald, Berthold, Matthaus, Hassler, Thon, Voller, Klinsmann.

Subs: Reuter (Hassler), Riedl (Voller).

Scorer: Brehme.

Don Rogers

Swindon Town 3 Arsenal 1 (aet)
League Cup final, Wembley, 15 March 1969

Born 27 October 1945. A dazzling, goal-scoring winger who found the net 149 times in League matches for Swindon where he began and ended an unfulfilled career. An England youth international, he never won a senior cap and had frustrating spells at Crystal Palace and QPR where he was hampered by injuries. One of the greatest players the West Country has ever produced, he gave Swindon its finest hour with two goals to lift the League Cup, a performance that will never be forgotten.

There was a touch of the bandit about Don Rogers: dark, moustachioed, with disrespectful sideburns and the ability to skin any full-back alive. It was wise to ignore both his Wiltshire burr and Third Division status; the former England youth international was more dashing bomber than country bumpkin. 'You don't tell Goya how to paint or Caruso how to sing,' said Swindon manager Danny Williams. 'And I don't tell Don how to play.' Rogers wouldn't have listened anyway. An old-fashioned, goal-scoring winger whose control could take him through a thicket of defenders, his party-piece was to waltz around the on-rushing 'keeper and plant the ball firmly into the far corner. But could he do it against Arsenal at Wembley?

The portents were good. Two years earlier another Third Division club, Queens Park Rangers, inspired by a similarly cavalier individual in Rodney Marsh, had shown the way with a marvellous come-back to beat West Brom in Wembley's first League Cup final. A year earlier Arsenal had lost 1–0 to Leeds in an altogether different type of match and thought that their niggardly defence was capable of dealing with anything the Third Division could throw at it. But Swindon were riding high in the League and their swashbuckling style had received some rave notices *en route* to the twin towers. So, too, had their resilience. Replays were needed to see off Bradford City, Derby, Coventry and Burnley, which suggests that Williams's yeoman years at Rotherham had rubbed off – opponents discovering steel where they had expected straw.

There had been plenty of that at Wembley only days before – someone unkindly suggested that it was to make Swindon feel at home – as the Horse of the Year Show had churned the hallowed turf into something you would expect at Quorn. Heavy rain had not helped and, by the time the two teams lined up for the kick-off, a small reservoir had been pumped away while the topsoil looked as if it had come straight from the Sahara. Old-timers anticipating a bowling green saw something they might have landed on at Normandy. It put the fear of God into Arsenal. The Londoners had already been laid low by a flu outbreak and, when they trod the sludge-dump before the match, they could have been forgiven for reaching for the antibiotics.

Don Rogers knew that his hour had come. 'We really fancied it,' he insists. 'We knew we were a good side, far better than our status suggested, and we had nothing to worry about in footballing terms. We could mix it with the best of them. What's more, we felt that Arsenal knew we could, so we were certainly not overawed.' Thirty thousand West Country voices, not to mention most neutrals, ensured that they weren't, and a tremendous din greeted the Wiltshire side. 'Swindon just closed down that day,' remembers Rogers. 'It was the first time the club had been to Wembley and the first time is always the best, isn't it?'

Although Arsenal had the better of the early exchanges,

Swindon were never outplayed and the Gunners, for whom Ian Ure, Peter Storey and Frank McLintock provided a touch of iron at the rear, did not possess the artillery capable of breaching a defence as steadfast as the one marshalled by John Trollope. With Peter Downsborough having one of those days between the posts that underdog 'keepers tend to have on big occasions, Arsenal's unease was manifest. As for Rogers? 'I was being marked by Storey, and we were having a good tussle. It was a helluva game.' But there was no hint of the heroics to come.

Unlike QPR, who had come from behind two years earlier, Swindon chose a different route to glory, having the audacity to take the lead just before the interval. 'It was a Charlie Chaplin effort,' Rogers recalls, 'and definitely the funniest goal I've ever seen. I've watched it on video dozens of times and I'm still not exactly sure of the sequence now. But the main thing was, it was us who were laughing at half-time. The ball suddenly seemed to have a will of its own as a back-pass bounced off Bob Wilson's feet on to Peter Noble's chest. He squared it, Simpson missed it and Smart nipped in to score. When something like that happens, it's when you're meant to win. I knew then that fate was on our side.'

It did not look it when Downsborough made his only error of a defiant afternoon and mistimed a run off his line as Arsenal, desperate now, sought an equaliser. 'Even when Bobby Gould managed to level four minutes from time and then cried in relief behind the goal, I did not change my mind,' insisted Rogers. 'We knew we were the fitter side and could cope with extra-time whereas you could see Arsenal didn't want it. They were relieved to have got it, of course, but they had thrown everything at us, and we were still coming. They blamed the flu for their tiredness, but we were just fitter.'

Rogers certainly played as if to run them ragged and, relishing the encore at the game's premier theatre, turned on the style that had left Third Division defenders chasing his shadow. After waiting in the wings, he took centre-stage at a timely moment, a minute before the extra-time break, to put Swindon in front again. The roar could have been heard back in the Cotswolds. Displaying the dash and control that made him a legend in the lower divisions, Rogers whisked his way around three of the League's most resolute defenders to plant a drive past Wilson from eight yards. 'Of my two, that was the better goal,' he says now, but his second, he acknowledges, 'is the one for the archives.'

Receiving the ball inside his own half, Rogers embarked upon a run that has entered Wembley and West Country folklore. With ears pinned back and moustache bristling, he ran straight for Wilson, a 'keeper who knew how to close down an oncoming forward better than most. It was no contest. 'I knew that I could walk it round him,' says Rogers. 'That was my greatest strength.' He did that all right and, as all of Wiltshire held its breath, he rammed the ball home. Arsenal knew that they could not come back from there. 'I can't describe it,' says Rogers. 'We knew that we'd won it then. It was just unbelievable. Our fans were behind that goal; I just could not have scripted it better. The noise level was something else. I couldn't hear a thing anybody said to me.

'Yet if Roger Smart had not hit the post with an earlier header in normal time, we would have won 2–1 and that would have been that. As it was, I got all the glory. Swindon just went mad, and one of the first things I remember was Bob Monkhouse at the do afterwards – absolutely brilliant. Then there was an open-topped bus tour through the town and a civic reception. You just couldn't top it.' Rogers, the country boy, had mugged the city slickers in their own backyard, and had done it in an unforgettable style. Williams was right: you could not teach anybody to play like that. It was sheer, instinctive genius.

Swindon: Downsborough, Thomas, Trollope, Butler, Burrows, Harland, Heath, Smart, Smith, Noble, Rogers.

Scorers: Smart, Rogers 2.

Arsenal: Wilson, Storey, McNab, McLintock, Ure, Simpson, Radford, Sammels, Court, Gould, Armstrong.

Scorer: Gould.

Len Shackleton

Newcastle United 13 Newport County 0
Second Division, St James's Park, 5 October 1946

Born 3 May 1922. Joined Arsenal's groundstaff after being capped by England schoolboys but was released in 1939 because he was 'too frail'. A Bradford City fan, 'Shack' found himself playing for rivals Park Avenue before Newcastle bought him for £13,000 after just seven games. Was sold to neighbours Sunderland for £20,000 only eighteen months later and became a Wearside folk hero, scoring most of his 126 League goals (from 384 matches) for the Roker club. Became known as the 'Clown Prince of Soccer', the title of his famous autobiography in which he left the chapter entitled 'The average director's knowledge of football' completely blank. Paid for his irreverence by being awarded only five England caps, a derisory total for a truly masterful inside forward.

'If I had gone to bed and dreamed about the perfect début for my new club, which had just paid the then third highest fee for me, I would not have come up with scoring six. I may have settled for a hat-trick; just one, but certainly not two,' says Len Shackleton. 'Yet, you know, it was the worst thing that could have happened to me. Scoring five in the next match would still have been failure, wouldn't it? No, there was just no way I could follow that. It was dream stuff but it was also a rod for my own back.'

Shackleton's characteristically forthright assessment was as accurate as his shooting and, sure enough, he was never to settle at St James's Park, moving down the road to Roker the following season. But such was the anticipation on Tyneside that, three days after his transfer from

Bradford, no fewer than 52,137 turned up to watch
Newport in the Second Division. But the Newcastle fans
were not simply flocking to see Shack: they had a useful
forward line even without the new boy. On that day,
though, it read: Milburn, Bentley, Wayman, Shackleton
and Pearson.

But if Newport thought that Charlie Wayman was taking
pity on them when he sent a second-minute penalty wide,
they were soon jolted out of any such reverie by the full
force of the Magpies attack. So, too, was Jackie Milburn,
who said, 'I thought, "Oh, no, it's going to be one of those
days." ' He need not have worried. By half-time Wayman
had made amends with a hat-trick while Shack had scored
four. It was sensational stuff which left even the hyper-
critical St James's Park crowd well and truly sated. But not
Shack, who said: 'We ought to have been shot for not
scoring 20.

'Everything I tried came off; it was just one of those
games. I could have scored with my eyes shut,' he
remembers. Knowing the clowning character he was, it's
a wonder he didn't. That apart, he revealed the full
repertoire of both his sauce and his sorcery: he chipped
over and blasted past a brave Charlie Turner in goal; he
waltzed disdainfully through tackles as if the defenders
weren't there; he turned his markers inside-out; he laid it
on the proverbial plate for his colleagues and threw in a
generous sprig of parsley; and, long before Jim Baxter
thought of it, he sat on the ball. He brought the house
down.

'The only goal of the six I remember was when I
chipped the 'keeper from the corner of the penalty box.
The ball had come back to me and, from that angle, I
flicked it over him with the outside of my right foot. It was
what you'd call a real footballer's goal. Textbook stuff.'
Shack treated the fans to an exhibition, where he made the
ball talk in a West Yorkshire accent and reduced the
Newport defence to something beyond disarray.

'Actually, they weren't that bad,' he recalls generously. With a line he would love to use as a sports-writer once he had hung up his boots, he added: 'but they were lucky to get nil.'

The Welshmen were also fortunate that in Turner they had a brave last line without whom it probably would have been 20. 'It was like facing a firing squad,' claimed the 'keeper. Newport boss Tom Bromilow said: 'They'll need to change the scoreboard at St James's Park to a cricket scoreboard.' Milburn managed to get his name on the existing one with a second-half brace, as did Roy Bentley, but it was Shackleton's show, the débutant taking his tally to six.

'I didn't even get the ball afterwards,' he jokes. 'I should have been given two, but you had to buy your own bootlaces in those days, so I suppose I couldn't expect any different. That night I just got the train home to Bradford as usual. I didn't stick around and celebrate as my wife was expecting our first child. It was all very matter-of-fact and down-to-earth.'

Milburn added: 'I felt sorry for Newport as Shack was just unstoppable that day.' Turner said: 'Newcastle are now certs for promotion. There is not a defence in the League that can contain them if they play like that.' It was left to Bromilow to say: 'The next time we play Newcastle we are going to lock Shackleton in the dressing-room and throw away the key.' Little did they know that the next time the clubs met, Newcastle needed to win to clinch promotion while Newport were already doomed to go down. The dressing-room doors remained open, but Newport won 4−2!

But the last word on the first game must go to Bromilow, who said of Shack's six-shooting debut: 'What's he going to do when he settles into the side . . . ?' There was a poignancy about the remark which Bromilow could not have realised for Shack, of course, never really did settle. 'Newcastle was a Christmas club. There was always in-fighting among the directors as there is now. The fans deserve better. I wanted to leave the club but not the area, as the people are wonderful, and Sunderland suited me fine.' A side he did 'settle' into.

Newcastle United: Garbutt, Cowell, Graham, Harvey, Brennan, Wright, Milburn, Bentley, Wayman, Shackleton, Pearson.

Scorers: Shackleton 6, Wayman 3, Milburn 2, Bentley 2.

Newport County: Turner, Hodge, Oldham, Rawcliffe, Low, Cabrie, Davies, Wookey, Craddock, McNab, Bowen.

Graeme Souness

AS Roma 1 Liverpool 1 (2−4 on penalties)
European Cup final, Rome, 30 May 1984

Born 6 May 1953. Raised in a prefab, he represented Edinburgh Schools before winning Scottish schoolboy honours and starring in an international at White Hart Lane. Signed for Spurs as an apprentice but left, homesick and disillusioned, before playing in the first team. Signed for Middlesbrough in 1973 and, under Jack Charlton, harnessed his aggression, honed his skills and took command of midfield. Crunching in the tackle, precise in the pass, powerful in the shot, Souness became a key man in the rise of Middlesbrough from the Second Division and earned the first of his 54 Scottish caps while at Ayresome Park. Attracted the attention of Liverpool, who paid £350,000 for his considerable presence in 1978. Along with Kenny Dalglish, Souness became the lynch-pin of the great Liverpool side of the late 1970s and early 1980s, collecting five League Championship medals, three European Cup-winners' medals and four League Cups. Sold to Sampdoria for £650,000 in 1984 and won the Italian Cup before becoming player-manager at Rangers in 1986. Piloted the Light Blues to three Scottish League titles before returning to Anfield in 1991 to take the manager's job vacated by Kenny Dalglish.

Graeme Souness was touring Australia, of all places, with Middlesbrough when he became a Liverpool supporter. He describes the occasion thus in his book, *No Half Measures*: 'I watched Liverpool beat Borussia Mönchengladbach 3−1 in Rome on a television in a bar full of German expatriates in a little mining town just outside Sydney. I was proud to be British among the Germans who were so sure that their team were going to knock seven kinds of stuffing out of Kevin Keegan and his boys.'

That was Liverpool's first European Cup triumph in 1977 and, within four months of arriving at Anfield, Souness was in the team that successfully defended the trophy against Bruges. He also played a major role for the Liverpool side that beat Real Madrid in 1981. But his third successful European Cup final, and Liverpool's fourth, against Roma in 1984 was the most memorable, on many counts. It was part of Liverpool's unique treble of League, Milk Cup and European Cup, and meant that only Real Madrid had won the champions' trophy more times; it was against Roma on their own ground; and it was achieved after a dramatic penalty shoot-out in which Souness scored one of the goals with his last kick for Liverpool before signing for Sampdoria.

So, even by the exalted standards of a European Cup final, there was a great deal to play for when Roma entertained Liverpool in their own Stadio Olimpico. The hosts were attempting to win the cup for the first time and, if Liverpool were not a formidable enough hurdle, their own frenzied supporters on their home ground certainly were; and then there were the frantic intrusions of the Italian press. As for Liverpool, they were out to maintain their own and English clubs' hold on Europe's most coveted prize, while manager Joe Fagan was bidding to land three major trophies in his first year in charge and so surpass both Bob Paisley and Bill Shankly in terms of silverware. As for Souness, he writes: 'Speculation grew about my possible transfer abroad, until it was generally agreed that the European Cup final would be my last game for Liverpool – unless I played badly in Rome.' There was not much danger of that.

Even though the Scot claims that the speculation was mainly 'gossip' and that he was 'determined to put it all out of my mind and to concentrate on the job in hand,' he concedes that, 'nagging at the back of my mind was the knowledge that I would be putting myself on show to all the potential buyers against the successful Brazilian combination of Roberto Falcao and Toninho Cerezo.'

But if Souness was in the shop window, Roma were under the most intense surveillance. By the time of the kick-off, the home side would have preferred to have played almost anywhere but their home patch – except Anfield. 'They had been feeling the strain for three weeks,' says Souness.

In contrast, Liverpool had a 'remarkably relaxed' build-up, and Souness vividly remembers Fagan's team talk; there was not much to forget. 'It must have been all of ten seconds,' he says. 'It was at lunch-time on the day of the game and was the first time he had spoken about Roma. He said: "These are obviously a good team you are going to play, but they are not as good as you. Now get to your beds and rest." '

Although Liverpool felt it was not right to play a European final on the home ground of one of the con-testants, Souness acknowledged: 'It created a phenomenal atmosphere.' The Italian capital was awash with Roma's red and gold favours, and the Roman holiday to celebrate the win began before the kick-off. 'We were not con-sidered to have a chance,' remembers Souness. Fagan disagreed. Ripping up a piece of paper with the Roma team written on it, he declared: 'If we play, there is nothing in it for them.' Souness added: 'Come on lads, let's buzz.'

After the cacophony of a full-scale Roman carnival had greeted the two teams, Liverpool did not so much buzz as draw the Italians' sting, passing the ball about crossfield with characteristic precision before grabbing a gift of a goal in the 15th minute. Craig Johnston hoisted a deep cross that Tancredi, the Roma 'keeper, could not hold under Ronnie Whelan's challenge. In an almost comical sequence, Bonetti and Nappi tried desperately to clear, only for the ball to hit the distraught 'keeper and rebound to the feet of Phil Neal. The full-back gratefully prodded it home.

With the Roman legions stunned into silence, Liverpool assumed control, with Souness, fierce in the tackle and crisp in the pass, wielding both bludgeon and rapier to equal effect. As he recorded in his book: 'We all knew the stage suited us. The Olympic Stadium was a perfect setting with a great surface, and we were quite happy to let others tell us that the odds were stacked against us and that we were the underdogs. I also knew that, sitting up in the stands, were the people who were going to help me decide my immediate future and, Brazilians or not, I was going to show them all that Graeme Souness had come a long way from his prefab in Edinburgh.'

Liverpool were shaken two minutes before half-time when Pruzzo looped a header above Bruce Grobbelaar and into the far corner of the net to equalise. Roma dominated for the first 20 minutes after the resumption before Liverpool – and Souness – restored order. But the goal would not come. Tancredi twice made amends for his earlier error with saves from Ian Rush, and the game drifted to the inevitable penalty shoot-out. The portents were not good for Liverpool: not only did Souness lose the toss and find himself asking his team to take the kicks at the end where the hard core of Roman support was assembled, but a rehearsal had gone badly wrong a couple of days before. Kicking against their youth team, Liverpool had lost 2–5 with Messrs Neal, Dalglish and Souness all missing!

When Steve Nicol, who had volunteered to take the first penalty, blasted over the bar, it was easy to sense that this was not to be Liverpool's night. Roma skipper Di Bartolomei, taking the ball off Graziani, put Roma in front from two paces. But Neal, as he had in 1977, kept his nerve and Liverpool's hopes alive. There followed two classic moves in counter-intimidation. Souness first complained that the *paparazzi* behind the goal were using their camera flashes when Liverpool were kicking, but not doing so for Roma, while Grobbelaar, in a masterly piece of lighthearted 'gamesmanship', waggled his knees and behind in simulated nervousness between the posts. It was hardly the sight to soothe jangling Roman nerves and it worked. Bruno Conti, star of the 1982 World Cup, shot weakly over to bring Liverpool back into it. Souness, concentrating as if his life depended on it, made no mistake. But neither did Righetti, to make it 2–2.

After Rush had scored, Graziani stepped up again and this time he was allowed to get on with it. He hit it on to the top of the bar and over. It was 3–2 to Liverpool and, amid tension worthy of the Colosseum and with Graziani looking anxiously for lions, Alan Kennedy stepped up. Souness writes: 'There were a few of the team who didn't fancy his chances.' But they were wrong. He had scored in the final against Real Madrid and he scored again on this occasion. Souness admits: 'I went berserk. For the first time I wept tears of joy.' The iron man weeping? Well, he was only doing what the Romans were doing.

AS Roma: Tancredi, Nappi, Bonetti, Righetti, Nela, Falcao, Di Bartolomei, Cerezo, Conti, Pruzzo, Graziani.

Subs: Strukelj (Cerezo), Chierico (Pruzzo).

Scorer: Pruzzo.

Liverpool: Grobbelaar, Neal, A. Kennedy, Lawrenson, Whelan, Hansen, Dalglish, Lee, Rush, Johnston, Souness.

Subs: Robinson (Dalglish), Nicol (Johnston).

Scorer: Neal.

Bob Stokoe

Sunderland 1 Leeds United 0
FA Cup final, Wembley, 5 May 1973

*Born 21 September 1930. Signed for Newcastle at 17 and made
his début on Christmas Day 1950, scoring in a 2–1 defeat at
Middlesbrough. Spent fourteen years on Tyneside and won an
FA Cup-winners' medal in 1955. Developed into one of the best
centre-halves in the game and represented the Football League,
but could not replace Billy Wright in the England side and was
never capped. Joined Bury in 1961 and helped them to the Third
Division title in his first season, before taking over as player-
manager the following year. Then managed Charlton,
Rochdale, Carlisle, Blackpool and Sunderland, where his FA
Cup win was followed by promotion to the First Division.
Resigned after nine games the following season, and managed
all the same clubs except Charlton again before retiring to
concentrate on scouting.*

Never has a manager owed so much to a goal-keeper in a
Wembley Cup final as Bob Stokoe did to Jim Montgomery
after this momentous upset. The sight of a delirious
Stokoe, in tracksuit, raincoat and trilby, sprinting across
the sodden turf to embrace his 'keeper once the final
whistle had gone will live in the Wembley annals along
with the white horse, Stanley Matthews's final, the
Hungarians of 1953 and Geoff Hurst's third goal against
West Germany. But there was one save above all others
that won this match for Sunderland, a double save so
extraordinary that it appeared to defy the laws of physics,
let alone physiology. From that moment, one sensed that
Leeds, as superstitious as they were innately superior,
knew that this was not their day.

Certainly, it was then that Stokoe had 'a little bit of a feeling' that it might be his. But then Sunderland's latest 'messiah' had always thought that arguably the biggest upset of FA Cup final history was a realistic possibility. However, all but one-eyed Wearsiders were sure that Sunderland needed a miracle. Leeds were at the awesome peak of their powers, impregnable at the back, dynamic in midfield and lethal up front. It was perhaps Don Revie's most complete team and, although the League had slipped away, the Yorkshiremen were on course for a Cup double, AC Milan being their European Cup-Winners' Cup final opponents in ten days' time. Sunderland were, of course, in the Second Division and, although on something of a roll, were not expected to live with the merciless men in all-white. Indeed, before Stokoe's arrival in December, the Wearsiders were second to the bottom of the division and, even in their remarkable Cup run, had struggled against some mediocre sides.

'We lost my first game as manager,' recalls Stokoe, 'and, before I had been there very long, found ourselves losing 0–1 at Notts. County in the Cup. In the second half, they had a chance to wrap it up and Jimmy [Montgomery] made a save that was almost as good as the one against Leeds. Two-nil would have been goodnight, but we changed the formation a bit and snatched a late equaliser. Then we beat them at Roker. We also needed a replay to get rid of Reading, but in the next round, after a tremendous 2–2 draw at Maine Road, we produced one of the finest performances seen by a Sunderland side since the war to beat the Manchester City team of Franny Lee, Mike Summerbee and Colin Bell.

'We got past Luton but then needed another bit of Monty magic to see off Arsenal in the semi-final at Hillsborough. I can see it now: a tremendous save from a deflection at the near post. I don't know how he got to it, but it put us in the final. Sunderland had only won the Cup once in their history, so we were determined to make the most of our visit, staying down south for a few days before and even going to a sports-writers' do. That was frowned upon by some people, but it was our way of enjoying the build-up and gaining a bit of confidence. Not that we needed much as we had risen to sixth in the League.

'I certainly wasn't knocking on players' doors at night or anything like that, and I remember playing golf with Jackie Milburn and Len Shackleton during the week. We did not even have a team meeting until the Friday and then we allowed the ITV cameras on the coach. I wanted the lads to take it all in as I had been to Wembley as a player and I knew what it meant.' One can only wonder how this must have contrasted with the customarily fraught goings-on at Leeds for whom complacency would have been a welcome respite. But Sunderland were a team to be reckoned with, and Stokoe's laid-back approach cleverly concealed their considerable potential.

Somehow it seemed as if the Wearsiders were going to Wembley simply to savour the rarefied atmosphere. But Stokoe, a hero in Newcastle's 1955 Cup triumph, was well aware that in Dave Watson he had the best young central defender in the country, in Billy Hughes and Dennis Tueart two strikers of rare talent, and elsewhere a judicious blend of youth and experience. Of course, he also had Montgomery.

'We felt that we would do ourselves justice, having beaten Arsenal and Manchester City, who had knocked out Liverpool,' Stokoe says. 'We did not need to go into too much detail at the team talk. We knew that Bremner and Johnny Giles were the engine room, and if you denied them space you had a chance. We also decided to keep them as far out as we could and prevent the supply of usual balls to Allan Clarke and company. It all worked unbelievably well.' Inspired by the passionate exhortations of their fans, Sunderland were anything but over-awed, and Leeds were soon made aware of the Second Division threat – even if it had been 1931 since a team from there had walked off with the trophy. Watson was an early pillar, Bobby Kerr a rousing captain, and Leeds's frustrations were soon evident.

'Bremner became niggly and Giles was cut off,' says Stokoe, 'so I was quite happy with the way it was going.' But after 32 minutes he was even happier. Ian Porterfield, who possessed a lovely left foot but not much of a right, forced home a knock-down from the dangerous Vic Halom – with his right! 'It's only used for standing on,' quipped the Scot. But it did not give Leeds 'keeper Harvey a chance. The favourites found more urgency now and, with the elegant promptings of Paul Madeley, created an opening or two. But for once Clarke was slow to react and then Peter Lorimer blasted straight at Montgomery's up-stretched palms.

Early in the second half there was one of those decisions on which the destiny of such trophies hang. Watson lunged at Bremner's legs and the Leeds skipper went down inside the area. It could have been a penalty, but referee Burns brushed the appeals aside. If Leeds had felt that it was not going quite right, their furrows lengthened perceptibly after that. Although Bremner and Giles were getting more space as Wearside limbs wearied, incisive tackling led by the magnificent Watson kept them at bay. An hour had passed and the much-anticipated massacre had not materialised.

'The night before the match,' says Stokoe, 'the team stayed up to watch the preview on TV, and we got murdered by the panel. In fact, the best result we could get was a 0–3 defeat. It was said that Eddie Gray would roast Malone, so one of the best moments for me was when Gray was substituted after Malone had had a blinder.' But it was not the best moment. Not by a mile.

With Leeds upping the tempo, Mick Jones played a ball back from the edge of the box to Paul Reaney who chipped toward the far post. Trevor Cherry threw himself at the ball and met it firmly with his head. Montgomery stretched for it and, with his left hand, pushed the ball out. It was an incredible piece of athleticism, but there was no time to appreciate it, and the effort looked wasted anyway. The ball went straight to Lorimer. Without hesitation and from six yards, one of the most powerful strikers of a ball in the modern game took careful aim. There was nothing to stop him. The goal was empty. Wembley and half of the north of England were resigned to 1–1. So was the commentary box. Lorimer let fly. Wearsiders dare not look. He struck it cleanly. 'Goa . . .': the commentary stopped. So did tens of thousands of hearts.

Montgomery, from the other side of the goal, leapt and got a hand to it. He pushed it on to the bar. Disbelief settled over the great stadium and resignation overcame Leeds. To this day, Elland Road die-hards believe fate and not Montgomery saved Lorimer's shot. 'Rubbish,' said one Wearsider, 'fate could not have reached it . . .'

'When I die,' said Montgomery, 'I shall have my left hand embalmed. I have never been more proud of a save than that one. I don't think Peter could believe it. I'm not sure I could, either.' But he had not finished yet. Although Leeds now believed that it was really not going for them, they did not stop trying. Indeed, it was all Leeds from that moment on. Terry Yorath, who had replaced the ineffectual Gray, was sent through by Madeley and appeared to have equalised, his shot seemingly passing beneath Montgomery's body. But the indefatigable 'keeper somehow snatched it back from behind him. When he was beaten by Madeley shortly afterwards, Pitt cleared off the line.

It was not to be for Leeds, and Sunderland almost notched a second, Harvey doing well to deny Halom at the death. Enter that man in a trilby. 'If you thought I had gone mad,' he says, 'you should have seen it when we got home. Sunderland simply went mad. Why, even the cows in the fields outside the town were wearing red and white . . .'

Leeds United: Harvey, Reaney, Cherry, Bremner, Madeley, Hunter, Lorimer, Clarke, Jones, Giles, Gray.

Sub: Yorath (Gray).

Sunderland: Montgomery, Malone, Guthrie, Horswill, Watson, Pitt, Kerr, Hughes, Halom, Porterfield, Tueart.

Scorer: Porterfield.

Gordon Strachan

Leeds United 2 Leicester City 1
Second Division, Elland Road, 28 April 1990

Born 9 February 1957. Learned his football at Craigroyston School in Edinburgh and went on to represent Scotland at schoolboy, youth, Under-21 and senior levels. Joined the Dundee groundstaff and became captain at 19, before being snapped up by Billy McNeill at Aberdeen for £50,000 in 1977. Only 5ft 6in and just over 10 stones, Strachan developed into one of Scotland's modern dynamos, whether in midfield or on the wing, winning the first of his 40-plus caps against Northern Ireland in 1980. Appeared in the final stages of two World Cups and collected two Scottish League Championships, three Scottish Cups and the European Cup-Winners' Cup in just four years with Aberdeen. Was voted Scottish Player of the Year in 1980 and scored 55 goals in 183 League games before Ron Atkinson paid £500,000 to take him to Old Trafford in 1984. His buzzing presence helped Manchester United win the FA Cup in 1985 but, after four largely unfulfilled seasons, he was sold by former boss Alex Ferguson to Leeds for £300,000. Won promotion from Division Two in 1990 and earned a recall to his country's colours at the ripe old age of 33.

Alex Ferguson knew Gordon Strachan better than most football managers did, for the irrepressible little red-head had run his big heart out for him enough times when the two were at Aberdeen. So the Manchester United boss might have known that Strachan would want to show him there was still plenty of life left in the ageing terrier when he decided to unload him to Leeds. But Fergie, under pressure from the increasingly impatient Old Trafford faithful, was refashioning his midfield with some expensive, younger blood and, on the face of it, £300,000 was not bad money for a 31-year-old. Equally, it was a good chance for the wee man to see out his career at a progressive, albeit Second Division, club. Altogether, it did not seem a bad bit of business.

By Strachan's standards, his stay in Manchester had not been as rewarding as his time at Pittodrie. An FA Cup-winners' medal apart, the Brasso tin was unused whereas he had had to buy the stuff wholesale in Aberdeen. No one doubted Strachan's class, but when he went to Elland Road, he did so with something to prove.

Leeds United had lingered long enough in the lower reaches of Division Two. The Don Revie era of dominance seemed like a figment of elderly imaginations to younger Yorkshire fans; Bremner, Hunter, Giles & Co. were ghosts of a bygone age. But, under Howard Wilkinson and an ambitious board, Leeds were beginning to stir once again. Young players were coming through, exciting recruits were being captured, and crowds were rising. All the club needed was a spark to set the team alight.

'The club had been down in the dumps for too long,' says Strachan, 'and I sensed that they'd had enough of it as soon as I walked through the door. The place was steeped in tradition and now it was burning with ambition. And they had had a near-miss the season before. They were not prepared to spend much longer outside the top flight.' At Leeds, however, they have long memories of missing out at the death – Revie's sides actually had it down to a fine art – so there was an element of nervousness, not to say desperation, about the place late in the 1989–90 season. 'They had to go up that season,' says Strachan. 'They had just spent so much money, and the fans couldn't have handled it if they'd missed out.'

For much of the campaign it had looked as if Leeds were going to gain an automatic promotion place, but the Second Division is seldom a stroll, and Leeds had slipped up at Barnsley of all places as the finishing tape was in sight. 'The Leicester match was the vital one,' recalls Strachan. 'It was the key to it all. If we had lost that, then we would probably have been looking at the play-offs as our only means of promotion. After what we'd been through, well, we didn't want to have face that.

'It was the second-to-last match of the season, and Leicester had nothing to play for. We should not have had any worries, really, but then you can never tell. Losing to Barnsley hadn't helped, and the tension was unbeliev-able. If Newcastle did not beat West Ham we were up anyway, but we weren't taking anything for granted. In my whole career I can honestly say that I have never known such tension.'

Old Leeds hands agreed. Don Warters wrote in the *Yorkshire Post*: 'I have sat through many vital matches involving United over the years and experienced much tension, but I simply cannot recall a previous game where there was as much of it in the air as there was for this crucial contest.' Not even Mel Sterland's powerful low drive in the 13th minute which gave the home side an early lead could lift it, and a combination of defiant goal-keeping by Martin Hodge, commendable spirit by Leicester and the anxiety of Leeds ensured that it did not.

'The ground erupted all right,' remembers Strachan, 'but still we could not relax. I have never played in a team that had worked as hard as this Leeds side, especially that day. They played till they dropped, so it was a real blow when Leicester equalised.' Strachan omits to mention that no one worked harder than he did; toiling in defence, trying to get his forwards going, running ceaselessly, rebuking, cajoling and, in most people's minds, virtually carrying the side.

He had a bit of that to do when Gary McAllister, who later joined Leeds, levelled with a cracking shot that went in off a post. Only a brilliant save by Mervyn Day prevented the Scot from putting Leicester ahead, while Lee Chapman, Imre Varadi and Bobby Davison spurned glorious opportunities at the other end. Undaunted, Strachan drove Leeds on, ferreting all over the field, buzzing, creating; Leicester never knew where he would pop up next. But there were times when it looked as if even these beyond-the-call-of-duty exploits would be denied, especially when Varadi hit a post from three yards. That was bad in itself, but it came after Strachan had set it up for him following another magnificent run past half the visitors' defence.

As the clock ticked on, the tension could not have been more electric had a couple of pylons draped live wires across the stands. Six minutes to go, and, racked with pain, anxiety and exhaustion, Strachan dredged up one last droplet of energy. When Gary Speed tapped a short ball back to him, he rammed home a left-foot drive from the edge of the penalty area. 'I don't know where I got the strength from,' he recalls, 'but when Gary knocked it back I just strained every muscle before hitting it, and it went in. The feeling was relief more than joy, just an unbelievable sense of relief. And disbelief: I had hit it with my left foot!'

The tension had now gone, having exploded at the sight of the bulging net. Leicester finally looked beaten, but it was not the end of the drama. A rumour, somehow started by Vinnie Jones, that Newcastle had lost spread around the ground. If true it meant United were up. But it wasn't. Leeds had their destiny in their own hands when they went to Bournemouth the following Saturday. That was when the fans gave a passable impression of the Mongol hordes in celebration of a 1–0 win. It was a shame for Strachan to have his promotion soured in that way, but he can rightly remember Leicester as his most memorable match. Even though, he says, 'I was too tired even to celebrate.'

Leeds United: Day, Sterland, Beglin, Jones, Fairclough, Haddock, Strachan, Kamara, Chapman, Davison, Speed.

Subs: Varadi (Davison), Batty (Jones).

Scorers: Sterland, Strachan.

Leicester City: Hodge, Mauchlen, Paris, Ramsey, Walsh, James, Reid, North, Kelly, McAllister, Wright.

Subs: Oldfield (North), Mills (Wright).

Scorer: McAllister.

Jack Taylor

West Germany 2 Holland 1
World Cup final, Munich, 7 July 1974

'You are an Englishman,' blurted out Franz Beckenbauer to Jack Taylor. It was the Munich Olympic Stadium in the summer of 1974, and the World Cup final between West Germany and Holland was a minute old. The hosts had yet to touch the ball and referee Taylor, who had been an Englishman for forty-four years, had awarded a penalty against them. Taylor knew that Beckenbauer was not being complimentary. 'He was cold, clinical, and he meant that our countries were old enemies,' says the former master butcher from Wolverhampton. 'We are friends now and I respect Franz a lot, but I'll never forget that comment. Not least because it was uncharacteristic. He WAS a gentleman on the field but, obviously, it was not any old game, not any old set of circumstances.'

Indeed, it was not. The classic all-European World Cup final was a bit special. The two nations playing in it were old enemies, too, and there was still no love lost between their footballers or their fans. Munich was a magnificent venue and Holland, certainly, had a magnificent team with one player, Johan Cruyff, among the all-time greats.

England had, of course, failed to qualify for the finals but, through Taylor, were always in with a chance of having a hand in the final. Taylor and Scotland's Bobby Davidson were both candidates for the supreme honour and, as Taylor points out, it is a rather exclusive club. In the history of football, the number of people who have refereed a World Cup final is just fourteen. Taylor was well-respected and fearless, a good communicator whose decisive actions ensured that both players and fans knew exactly where they stood. Not a homer, not a prima donna, not a man to throw cards around like confetti: Taylor was an ideal choice who would not bottle it.

But even Taylor, who can lay convincing claim to having seen everything in football, had never witnessed a start like it. Holland, the favourites and thrilling exponents of total football surpassed themselves from the kick-off. Before a crowd of 77,833 and some one billion around the globe, they proceeded to string together a move of sixteen passes. At first, the Dutch masters switched the ball about in their own half to derisive whistles from the Bavarian crowd who thought it negative. When it continued, the decibels increased, annoyance being the prevailing sentiment from the screeching klaxons. This was no longer negative, they felt, but a mickey-take. Then the ball was in the German half. Still no home player had got near the thing. Then a lightning thrust, and the ball was deep in home territory. Cruyff was in possession and Berti Vogts was bearing down on the maestro.

'I knew Vogts would mark Cruyff,' says Taylor. 'I'd reffed them enough times.' But it was not Vogts who brought the Dutchman down. He could not get near enough to him to do that. In one coruscating flash of genius, Cruyff was past the lumbering German, and it was Uli Hoeness who sent him tumbling. In the penalty area. There was no doubt on the television. There was none on the terraces, either, apart from those who were accustomed to referees of a weaker will. Taylor immediately put them right on that one: without hesitation, he pointed to the spot.

When the shrieks of protest had died down – and after Beckenbauer had had his little chat – Johan Neeskens calmly placed the ball beyond Sepp Maier's reach. One-nil to Holland. The time: 90 seconds. It was the first time a penalty had been converted in a World Cup final, and the first one awarded before one side had touched the ball. It was not, however, the first big decision Taylor had had to take.

'I was just about to kick off, the whistle was in my mouth, both teams were lined up and the world waited,' remembers Taylor. 'Then I remembered the habit of a lifetime and checked for the corner flags. They weren't there! I held the game up while a little man sprinted round the field sticking in the missing flags. It caused great embarrassment to the West German FA, who, like most of the country's organisations, prided themselves on their efficiency. But, in view of what was about to happen, I shall be eternally grateful I held up play. I still have nightmares about the repercussions there might have been over the penalty then. Technically, the match would have been incorrectly started, and who knows what would have happened then?'

Taylor had clinched his honour with his sound handling of the potentially explosive clash between Bulgaria and Uruguay in Group 3, but had been homing in on the ultimate whistling job since giving up playing at 17. 'I started reffing as soon as I realised that I was not good enough to make it as a player,' he remembers. 'I have been around the world with a whistle, visiting about sixty countries. A previous highlight was becoming the youngest post-war referee at an FA Cup final: Everton v Sheffield Wednesday, when I was 35. I had built up relationships with a lot of the modern greats, as I began my career at the same time as them.' But none of this prepared him for the next 24 minutes in Munich.

Holland continued to stroke the ball around almost arrogantly. But instead of trying to wrap the game up with a second goal, they lapsed into the laid-back habits of the training ground. Gradually the Germans, who were anything but laid-back, got back into the match and, playing with the efficiency that makes Volkswagens start in the morning, they capitalised on the Dutch complacency. In the 26th minute, they, too, had a penalty. Beckenbauer had slipped them into a higher gear without the Dutch noticing and, when Wolfgang Overath throaded through a lovely ball for Bernd Holzenbeim, the German forward went down under a challenge from Jansen.

Taylor admits: 'There was more of a furore about whether the second was a penalty than the first.' He does not, however, bother to add what he thought about it, except that he was 'on the lookout for wingers who dived.' Suffice to say that Paul Breitner did not miss from the spot. With Bonhof ably supporting Beckenbauer, West Germany continued to press. Then, two minutes before the break, Gerd Muller turned in a Bonhof cross, a typical effort on the turn, for his 14th goal of the championship, which surpassed Juste Fontaine's record for France in 1958.

Holland were understandably chastened, and Taylor had to deal with Cruyff's demand for greater protection from Vogts as the teams walked off at half-time. 'It was sheer frustration,' reckons the Englishman. 'He was normally an excellent character but I had to do something about it. Referees have to make sure that players do not dictate, and this was the World Cup final. There was a lot at stake. The behaviour was not surprising in the circumstances and given the characters involved, but I was in charge and I had to remind them of that – whether their name was Cruyff or Beckenbauer.'

Holland were all over Germany after the interval but were already beginning to rue a first-half miss by Johnny Rep. Cruyff had inveigled his way past Beckenbauer to set up Rep, who hesitated fatally and the chance was lost, Maier diving at his feet to foil him. Maier then stopped a fierce drive from Neeskens. How they could have done with a Muller!

The 'Bomber' almost notched his 69th goal for his country but for a marginal off-side decision – Taylor's mettle was certainly tested – although Holland continued to play the Germans off the park. However, Beckenbauer, performing like an athletic Herbert von Karajan, was just about keeping Cruyff's Rembrandt at bay. A desperate second half unfolded, Taylor remembers, 'with plenty of whistle. A lot happened, but it went very quickly as I was so involved.' The Dutch cause was hardly helped by the injuries to Rensenbrink and Rijsbergen and, as the game wore on, Dutch pressure notwithstanding, most neutrals felt that the Germans would hold out. Their organisation was admirable, but once again one of the great sides left the ultimate arena empty-handed.

Helmut Schoen, the West German manager, said: 'We could have been unsettled by that early penalty, and it was a brave decision by the referee.' Beckenbauer added: 'In a strange way, conceding that early goal worked to our advantage. It brought defeat into focus and, once we had weathered that opening burst, we knew that we had lived with their best efforts.'

For England, there was the not inconsiderable consolation of Taylor's performance. Many West German observers showered him with praise for his courageous decision. 'But I don't kid myself,' he says. 'I get invited back and was given some good press at the time, but I know that if West Germany had not won I wouldn't have been nearly as popular.'

West Germany: Maier, Vogts, Schwarzenbeck, Beckenbauer, Breitner, Bonhof, Hoeness, Overath, Grabowski, Muller, Holzenbeim.

Scorers: Breitner (pen), Muller.

Holland: Jongbloed, Suurbier, Rijsbergen, Haan, Krol, Jansen, van Hanagem, Neeskens, Rep, Cruyff, Rensenbrink.

Substitutes: R. van der Kerkhof (Rensenbrink), de Jong (Rijsbergen).

Scorer: Neeskens (pen).

Danny Wallace

Southampton 8 Coventry City 2
First Division, The Dell, 28 April 1984

Born 21 January 1964. A London boy, Danny joined the Bob Higgins Soccer Academy at 12 and trained there until he was 16. He signed schoolboy forms with Southampton at 14 and became an apprentice at 16, making his first-team début nine months later at Old Trafford. A fast, goal-scoring winger, he was capped at Under-21 level and earned a full England cap against Egypt in 1986, scoring in a 4–0 win in Cairo. His skills attracted numerous scouts to the Dell before Alex Ferguson paid £1.2 million to take him to Manchester United on 16 September 1989. Won FA Cup-winners' medal in 1990.

'It was one of those days,' beams Danny Wallace, 'when everything you touch turns to . . . goals. Coventry were not that bad a side, but we just murdered 'em in the end, although they played some nice stuff before and between all our goals. Like I said, it was just one of those days. You wish you knew what the secret was, so you could bottle it up and get it out again for every game. There are so many games when you try everything and run your legs off, yet never look like scoring. Then you have a day like this, for no real reason. OK, we played really well but we've played better and not scored one, never mind eight.'

It was end-of-season fare. Southampton had nothing to play for but pride as they were in mid-table and had been knocked out of the FA Cup by Everton in a semi-final replay at Highbury. Saints had just about got that out of their system with a win over West Ham the previous

Saturday and a draw at Watford in midweek. The great Frank Worthington came back into the side as did Mick Mills, who replaced Mark Dennis. For Coventry, a name to conjure with is that of Stuart Pearce, at left-back.

As a crowd of 16,746 sun-baked souls wondered what sort of afternoon they were about to experience, Saints soon gave notice that they were taking it seriously. Attacking from the outset, they surged at the Sky Blues with Wallace heavily involved. 'I remember getting an early touch,' he says, 'and from then on it never seemed to leave my feet.' But he could not quite reach a David Armstrong free-kick in the opening minutes, and Perry Suckling punched clear. Then Wallace crossed, but Suckling held it safely. 'I thought their 'keeper was going to have a good game at that point,' says Wallace. After Peter Shilton had been brought into the game, it was Suckling who once again distinguished himself to rob Steve Moran. Saints were sending in cross after cross, but Wallace remembers that 'no one could get on the end of them, and neither team created a decent chance for quite a while. But the closest Saints came to scoring was when Ivan Golac crashed a twenty-five-yarder just past the post. Twenty minutes, 0–0, and no hint of what was to come.

Then it was Coventry's turn, Shilton having to make three saves before the deadlock was broken in the 28th minute. 'I got in another cross from the left,' says Wallace 'and there was Armstrong to nod home.' Coventry immediately strove for an equaliser but it would not come, and eight minutes later they found themselves 0–2 down. 'Mark Whitlock found me with a long ball, and I got my head to it,' says Wallace. 'A rare header. Yes, I was really chuffed to get that one. It meant more than a few with my feet.'

With Suckling wearing a cap to shield his eyes, Coventry were indeed being dazzled but it was Wallace and not the sun that they were finding hard to contain. But they held on until half-time and obviously thought that they were still in the game. Indeed, it was the visitors who took the match to Saints after the resumption, and Shilton had to be alert to stop Ashley Grimes from pulling a goal back in the opening moments of the half. However, Saints weathered the Midlanders' storm and effectively clinched the 3 points with a third after 57 minutes.

Steve Moran rose to head firmly past Suckling from Golac's superbly-weighted free-kick from the right, before Shilton had to rush off his line to thwart Daly. But after 64 minutes it began to look like a romp home when Wallace notched his second. 'This was a good one,' he says. 'I took a long ball from Mick Mills and, with my back to the goal, I turned, went past a man – I think it was Pearce – and curled it in with my right foot. Very pleasing, very pleasing. I was established in the side by then, but was trying to make a name for myself, and two good goals didn't do me any harm.'

But Coventry, as befits a side managed by Bobby Gould, would not give in, and two minutes later Grimes had spoiled Shilton's day by sending a speculative shot soaring into the roof of the net out of nothing. But the fans didn't worry too much as they could see that Wallace was in irresistible form. He found Moran in space, but Suckling dived to save, and moments later Wallace centred for Worthington to notch Saints' fifth – and their fourth header – in the 69th minute. Moran soon poked in his second of the game after Suckling had been unable to hold his initial shot. The cross had come from Wallace; who else?

'Everything I did came off,' he says, 'and the team just clicked. But we hadn't finished yet; nowhere near.' Another Wallace cross, another Moran goal, his hat-trick and 22nd of the season, after 82 minutes. 'By now the crowd were in ecstasy; they were loving it and they wanted more. And I wanted a hat-trick.' Substitute Dave Puckett obliged by sending over an inviting cross with five minutes left. Wallace, now relishing his newly-discovered knack in the air, soared to make it eight, and three for himself. It was an end-of-season carnival, and no one had enjoyed it more than Wallace. Not even Moran. Yet, amazingly, there was still time for Coventry to snatch a second through Micky Gynn. And that, gentlemen, concluded the business for the day.

'The crowd gave us a standing ovation,' says Wallace, and it was the greatest feeling, walking off after scoring a hat-trick and having had a hand in a few others. But it had been easy. We had a good side with Dave Armstrong and Steve Williams running everything in midfield and Frank Worthington showing some great touches. What a player!' But Worthington was not the name on everyone's lips as they left the Dell that afternoon. It really was one of those days for Danny Wallace.

Southampton: Shilton, Mills, Golac, Curtis, Whitlock, Wright, Holmes, Moran, Worthington, Armstrong, D. Wallace.

Sub: Puckett (Curtis).

Scorers: Armstrong, D. Wallace 3, Moran 3, Worthington.

Coventry City: Suckling, Butterworth, Pearce, Daly, McGrath, Jacobs, Gibson, Grimes, Ferguson, Gynn, Platnauer.

Scorers: Grimes, Gynn.

Ray Wallace

Norwich City 4 Southampton 4
First Division, Carrow Road, 9 September 1989

Born 2 October 1969. Twin of Rod and younger brother of Danny. Learned his skills at the Bob Higgins Soccer Academy from the age of 11 until the age of 16. The Wallaces were the first brothers to play together in the First Division and the first to become £1 million players. Danny went from Southampton to Manchester United in 1989, and Ray and Rod joined Leeds in May 1991.

'The most attractive and exciting game I've ever been involved in was this early-season match at Carrow Road,' says Ray Wallace. 'We'd only played three games apiece and, on paper, it was never going to amount to much. But what a game! It had everything: goals, drama, a fight-back, and free-flowing football. And all three of us [brothers] played in it for Saints before we started moving anywhere.

'We really should have won it but we let them off the hook at the end. That, though, made it all the more amazing – we were 3–1 and 4–2 up and should never have let them get back from there. So, for us, it was a disappointing result to a great game. I didn't score, but I remember it vividly. Rodney got two goals and all three of us played well. The crowd loved it and they cheered both teams off the pitch at the end.'

The tone was set by the home side who opened briskly and immediately threatened Southampton's goal, only to be caught off-side. It took Southampton four minutes to mount a worthwhile attack, and then Paul Rideout, who had done well to gain possession on the left flank, pushed forward before driving in a thirty-yarder that 'keeper Bryan Gunn was glad to get round the post. Although the corner was initially cleared, the ball came back and Neil Ruddock got in a glancing header that just went wide.

'Right from the kick-off it was lively stuff,' confirms Ray, 'but we held the upper hand for most of it and were very confident early on as we felt we were the better side. But they had plenty of confidence, too, as they'd just beaten Manchester United at Old Trafford.' It took Saints only six minutes to go in front, following a free-kick awarded when Barry Horne was fouled by Ian Butterworth. Horne required treatment but so did Norwich, Rideout rising to head home Jimmy Case's kick for his first goal of the season.

The Wallace brothers were all playing leading roles but when Danny, about whom transfer rumours were spreading, tried to put Rod through, Gunn came swiftly off his line to gather. The pace was frenetic, the tackling fierce and free-kicks the only interruptions in a football feast. Ruddock nodded wide from Danny Wallace after another Case free-kick had been turned out to the wing. Both trainers were kept busy as Kevin Moore and then Tim Sherwood needed attention for robust challenges, Glenn Cockerill being cautioned for the tackle that caused Sherwood to be helped off for further attention.

Perhaps Southampton relaxed against the ten men; perhaps it would have come anyway. But Norwich were soon on terms, and even Ray admits: 'It was a brilliant goal, in keeping with the match. Robert Rosario just spun round and hit a left-foot volley from twenty yards. It was a real stunner, sailing into the top corner, and Tim Flowers had no chance. It shook us, and they pegged us back a bit after that. But not for too long.'

Sherwood limped back to join the Norwich celebrations, but Rod Wallace soon brought a fine save from Gunn – another sharp reminder that this was fundamentally an end-to-end affair. Rosario, it seemed, was well aware of that and twice went close before Southampton restored their lead in the 38th minute. 'A brilliant break-away goal,' says Ray. 'Norwich were attacking, but Micky Adams got it away and Jimmy Case carried it on upfield. Danny latched on to it and sent a superb ball through with the outside of his foot to Rod, who finished it in style from about fifteen yards. Another cracking goal.'

Saints almost added a third just before the whistle when Danny Wallace, no doubt impressing his suitors, put Horne through, but the shot was scrambled on to a post by the heroic Gunn. Less impressive was when Danny turned Norwich defender as he tried to flick a Ruddock header over the line; to his dismay, he only succeeded in clearing it. 'We were pretty pleased at half time,' says Ray, 'and definitely felt the match was there to be won. We were a bit upset that we'd allowed them to get a goal and were determined to show 'em that we were in charge as soon as we got back out there. It didn't take us long.

'This one was really down to Rod who picked up a long ball out of defence, beat Andy Linighan and cut inside to shoot past Gunn. At that point we felt we had not only won the match but could keep scoring all day long.' Unfortunately for Southampton, Norwich harboured similar thoughts and gleefully cashed in on Saints' visible relaxation. Sherwood, basking in a lot of space, headed Dale Gordon's centre past the diving Flowers to delight the home crowd. 'They just kept coming back at us,' says Ray. 'It was annoying, really, as we were playing so well.' He might have added, 'in attack'.

Saints' irritation showed immediately when they went straight down to the other end and scored the third goal of an amazing three-minute spell. Rideout picked up a loose ball and sent a fierce drive screeching past Gunn from twenty yards. 'Unstoppable,' says Ray, 'and we thought that must be it. We were playing some good stuff and created one or two more chances. For a few minutes they looked beaten.' But Saints spurned those chances and Norwich weren't beaten.

Rosario, who had been a constant menace, shook Southampton with two goals in the last 13 minutes to complete his hat-trick and pinch a point from a match which Saints always thought was theirs. 'It was very disappointing,' says Ray, 'and we blamed ourselves for letting 'em come back. But they never stopped trying no matter how far behind they were. It must have been terrific for the fans.

'I had another reason to remember the match for I volleyed the ball away and hit Andy Townsend in the face. It laid him out, and he swallowed his tongue. I must admit that it shook me for a while, but the physio saved him and he soon recovered. I 'phoned him up afterwards to find out if he was all right, and he appreciated that. Phew, I'm just glad I can remember a terrific match for the right reasons. To pick one we didn't win tells you how good it was.'

Norwich City: Gunn, Sherwood, Bowen, Butterworth, Linighan, Townsend, Gordon, Fleck, Rosario, Crook, Phillips.

Sub: Cook (Sherwood).

Scorers: Rosario 3, Sherwood.

Southampton: Flowers, Ray Wallace, Adams, Case, Ruddock, Moore, Rod Wallace, Cockerill, Rideout, Horne, D. Wallace.

Sub: Osman (Moore).

Scorers: Rideout 2, Rod Wallace 2.

Rod Wallace

Southampton 4 Liverpool 1
First Division, The Dell, 21 October 1989

Born 2 October 1969. Twin of Ray and younger brother of Danny. Like his brothers, Rod was a member of the Bob Higgins Soccer Academy before joining Southampton as a junior. A winger of great pace and skill with a knack of scoring brilliant goals, he has already won England Under-21 honours and, along with Ray, was transferred to Leeds United in May 1991.

It was the sort of day Southampton love. Early season, firm pitch, hopes high, and the Saints were on a bit of a roll. With Liverpool the visitors, there was a big crowd bringing a big-time atmosphere to the Dell. 'Liverpool don't like coming to the Dell,' reckoned Rod Wallace. 'We have found a way of beating them,' claimed manager Chris Nicholl. Unbeaten in seven matches and fresh from a 4−1 win at Queen's Park Rangers, Southampton were almost bullish before their clash with the all-conquering visitors.

'We really fancied it,' confirmed Wallace, whose performances were beginning to alter terrace thinking on the respective merits of his illustrious clan. Danny had gone and was badly missed, but his kid brother could play all right. Then there was twin brother Ray. 'Any more where this lot came from?' wondered south-coast supporters.

Knocking it around with almost Liverpudlian precision, Southampton began as if their manager knew there was a chink in the Anfield armour but wasn't quite sure of its precise location. Wallace and Matthew Le Tissier probed down the wings, and Jimmy Case and Glenn Cockerill

commandeered midfield. Playing a cavalier 4–2–4 formation, Saints refused to allow Liverpool to settle. 'The
crowd were a bit quiet to begin with,' remembers Wallace,
'but once they got behind us they stayed behind us.'

They found their voices in the 15th minute when, after
Cockerill had dispossessed Steve McMahon in midfield,
Paul Rideout smacked the bar with a thunderous thirty-
yarder that had 'keeper Grobbelaar beaten. The ball was
somehow scrambled to safety, but it had given Saints the
scent. Neil Ruddock, who had passed a fitness test on a
troublesome knee before being presented with the Barclays
Young Eagle of the Month award for the South-East,
snatched at a good chance in the 24th minute, but the home
side's pressure was soon rewarded. With the full house now
roaring them on, Saints took the lead with a superb header
from Paul Rideout, his first goal at the Dell in fourteen
months and his first against Liverpool in eight attempts.
'Jason Dodd [who was making his début] crossed, Paul got
in a diving header and in it went,' recalls Wallace.

Liverpool, seeking a swift equaliser, almost got one when
Beardsley beat the off-side trap and sent in a low shot that
looked goal-bound, but Tim Flowers dived to his left and
saved well. John Barnes then beat Dodd down the wing, but
Ronnie Whelan wasted his pass by blasting wide. Saints
were soon back on the attack. 'We were still high from the
win at QPR,' says Wallace. 'But at 1–0 against Liverpool, we
were flying.' They were, too, and, whenever they surged at
Bruce Grobbelaar's goal, Liverpool's defence, normally so
niggardly and resolute, looked as if the QE2 could have
breached it at any moment, let alone the torpedo boats of
Wallace and Le Tissier.

Somehow Liverpool weathered subsequent Southampton forays and, with half-time approaching, their bewildered defence must have been looking forward to a
respite, if not the inevitable tongue-lashing from Kenny
Dalglish. But on 38 minutes, with the crowd baying for a
second, Wallace seized upon a wayward header by Glenn

Hysen to send Le Tissier on a run. 'He beat one or two players in a great dribble and crossed to me on the edge of the box,' recalls Wallace. 'I got past Barry Venison with a few touches and, from about fifteen yards, hit a pretty powerful shot past Bruce Grobbelaar. The crowd loved it.

'As you'd expect, Liverpool came out looking more determined in the second half. They knew that they had a real battle on their hands and might have taken us a bit lightly before the break. In one attack Tim Flowers made a good save from Ronnie Whelan, otherwise things might have turned out differently. But then again, I don't think so; we were just too good on the day.' Unbeaten in the League, Liverpool replaced full-back Barry Venison with Ray Houghton at the start of the second half and soon made their intentions clear. Nicol switched to left-back but pressed forward in now urgent raids, and Flowers had to save from Whelan, Houghton and Rush. But Saints stormed back.

'What did them and made it for us was the third goal,' says Wallace. 'Dodd played it out wide for Le Tissier who went down the line and crossed to me. I was on the right side and slid it through Grobbelaar's legs. The crowd loved that, too, and so did I. We didn't think they'd come back from that, but you never know with Liverpool and when Jimmy [Case] brought [David] Burrows down just inside the area, Peter Beardsley scored easily from the spot.'

With half an hour to go Liverpool still had a chance but, against buoyant opponents, a blustery wind, and tigerish tackling from Russell Osman who marshalled his young defence superbly, Beardsley, Barnes and company could not get a look in. Wallace had a chance to set up Alan Shearer for a fourth but put his cross just too far in front of the midfielder.

'They still kept coming at us,' says Wallace, 'and Tim [Flowers] had to be on his mettle, saving from Nicol, and McMahon and Rush missed chances.' At the other end, Rideout hit a post – he and Neil Ruddock had earlier rattled the woodwork – and Beardsley of all people headed a Ruddock effort off the line. But the crowning moment came from Le Tissier with just six minutes of a marvellous afternoon left to savour.

'It began with Rideout going past Steve Nicol and sending a cross into the middle of the area. When Burrows jumped, Matt leapt up to nod past the 'keeper. Liverpool would have been proud of it,' says Wallace. 'The crowd were really roaring us on, and I honestly don't think that they'd seen us play like that for years. Coming off having murdered the mighty Liverpool was some feeling. I had a good match myself and scored two goals, but what I remember most was the team performance. It was tremendous, and one they still talk about at the Dell.'

'Give Southampton credit for this one,' insisted McMahon. 'Whenever we get beat people are quick to knock us, but they worked hard and took their chances superbly.' Kenny Dalglish was less gracious: 'We began badly and got progressively worse,' was his assessment. But even the laconic Scot would have been impressed by Southampton's unwavering commitment in midfield and marvellously-sustained cohesion in attack. Case was magisterial against his old cronies but could not steal the show from Wallace, whose wizardry on the flanks and ruthlessness in front of goal confirmed his class at the highest level. 'My best yet,' he smiles. But better check stop press.

Southampton: Flowers, Dodd, Benali, Case, Ruddock, Osman, Rod Wallace, Cockerill, Shearer, Rideout, Le Tissier.

Scorers: Rideout, Rod Wallace 2, Le Tissier.

Liverpool:Grobbelaar, Hysen, Burrows, Nicol, Whelan, Hansen, Beardsley, Venison, Rush, Barnes, McMahon.

Sub: Houghton (Venison).

Scorer: Beardsley.

Kenneth Wolstenholme

Real Madrid 7 Eintracht Frankfurt 3
European Cup final, Hampden Park, 18 May 1960

'They said you couldn't play football at Hampden,' remembers Kenneth Wolstenholme. 'Prior to this match, Scotland had drawn with England and lost to Poland, and everyone was talking of the swirl, the bumpy pitch and the ball going out of shape. Thankfully, Real Madrid were not listening.' They came to Glasgow as the undisputed masters of European football, being the only club to have won the coveted champions' trophy in the four years of its existence. With the footballing cream of South America and Europe in their ranks, they had such a cosmopolitan flavour that they could have passed as a World XI, and their strength can be gauged by the presence of the fabulous Brazilian, Didi, in their reserves.

The star of a glittering cast was Alfredo di Stefano, a balding 33-year-old impresario of a centre-forward who ran the show while managing to score in every final so far. Alongside him was another ageless legend in the Hungarian exile, Ferenc Puskas. Even in his twilight years Puskas could still uproot goal-posts with his left foot and make the sturdiest 'keepers tremble. On the left wing was Paco Gento, a Spanish international whose speed had left a continent's full-backs trailing in his slipstream, while daintily, delectably linking this lot together was another Spanish star, Luis Del Sol who, it was said, could dribble his way out of gaol.

Completing this galactic forward line was Brazil's brilliant right-winger, Canario, but in assembling their team Real had certainly not neglected their defence. Commanding that like a field marshal was the magnificent

Uruguayan, Santamaria, while the Argentine 'keeper Dominguez was an acrobatic, if sometimes under-employed, custodian. It was a team of all the talents, the like of which has not been seen since.

Ranged against them were the West German champions, Eintracht, who had had the temerity to suggest that they might prove a little troublesome by the brusque manner of their semi-final dismissal of Rangers. A 12–4 aggregate win which included an unpalatable 6–3 annihilation at Ibrox had brought the Scots in their droves to the final to witness what some felt could be the end of Real's reign. Only 27,000 had witnessed Scotland's recent defeat by Poland, yet Hampden was heaving with a capacity crowd eager to see for themselves what these so-called maestros were made of. The fascination stretched from the West of Scotland to Eastern Europe. Over to Kenneth Wolstenholme.

'Although people always associate me with the 1966 World Cup final,' says this doyen of commentators, 'the most memorable match for me was this one. I plump for it without hesitation.' Wolstenholme introduced Real as the champions of champions, and they did not let him down. 'Everything about them was big,' he recalls, 'and they had such style, off the field as well as on it. They would lay on sumptuous banquets, hand out Monte Cristo cigars with the Real band over the top; they would give gold watches, also wrapped in the Real logo. I still have a tie clip with the Real crest on it . . . and on the field they were even better.'

The sense of anticipation from the massed terraces of Hampden was almost tangible, and there were roars in the first minute at the withering sight of Gento. But if the crowd were already overawed Eintracht were not, and a cross from the left landed on the Real bar. It had the makings of quite a match. 'An interesting contrast in styles,' remarked Wolstenholme as the teams went through the motions in those early tension-racked minutes. Pretty fascinating motions. Real stroked the ball, whereas Eintracht's players appeared to use little back-lift when they kicked it. But there were mistakes on both sides, and di Stefano got a derisive cheer when, with extravagant use of the outside of his foot, he passed straight to a German. Del Sol's dexterity and Gento's dangling of his left foot over the stationary ball were the only real hints of what was to come.

Commendably undaunted by Real's towering reputation, the West Germans took the lead after 18 minutes when Kress converted a cross from Stein. Wolstenholme observed: 'Real are not looking too confident in defence.' He had already said: 'So far we have not seen much of the Real Madrid magic.' So far, we hadn't. 'It was only years later that I found out that four minutes of the broadcast were lost because of a power failure,' he chuckles, 'but, mercifully, we did not miss a goal.' When Real scored, they wanted it seen all over Europe; and sure enough, soon after the power came back, Real turned on the style.

With those dulcet decibels of Wolstenholme's rising, the ball was switched bewilderingly about the Frankfurt half: 'di Stefano . . . to Del Sol . . . Gento . . . Puskas . . .' Down the right it came and, when Canario crossed, an unmarked di Stefano turned it in to keep his fantastic record of having scored in every final to date. 'Whatever they pay Alfredo di Stefano, they don't pay him enough,' said Wolstenholme. A fumble by the Eintracht 'keeper Loy let in the maestro for a poacher's second three minutes later, and our commentator informed us: 'Real Madrid have now taken the early sting out of Eintracht.'

Up to now Puskas had been keeping a low profile. But when the Eintracht defence failed to clear another Real raid just before the break, the Hungarian suddenly swooped to pinch the ball off an Eintracht toe and, with the sting of a cobra, whipped an unstoppable shot into the roof of the net from a wide angle. It was frightening, but di Stefano was laughing. Wolstenholme then told us: 'Real have the wind in their favour in the second half.'

It was not now going to be Eintracht's night. The harshest of penalties for an alleged push on Gento allowed Puskas to smack in No.4 after the Germans had looked dangerous, and an unfortunate rebound let in Del Sol who then fed Gento. After a searing greyhound dash, the little winger crossed for Puskas to complete his hat-trick. 'You have to feel sorry for Eintracht,' says Wolstenholme. 'They, too, played their part in this extravaganza.' For that's what it was.

Madrid now indulged in the exhibition stuff. The ball was never kicked; it was either caressed, juggled, stroked, plucked or flicked and, occasionally, launched like a mortar bomb. The crowd loved it. Di Stefano revelled in it, arms waving, perfectly balanced, flitting gracefully over the surface, dancing, darting, a genius at work; like a great conductor at last satisfied that all the sections of the orchestra are in harmony and loving the sound. Meanwhile, Puskas was lurking and lashed in Real's sixth and his fourth. Still the Germans came back, and Stein scored a fine second. But it was the signal for di Stefano to up the tempo and, according to Wolstenholme, 'spreading terror wherever he moves', the great man tore through the heart of the Eintracht defence.

Appearing to release the ball to a colleague only on the condition that it was returned immediately, he picked his spot for another salvo deep into the Hampden netting. 'There is just nothing you can do about Real Madrid when they're in this form,' said Wolstenholme. 'It is bewildering stuff.' Eintracht were indeed unfortunate that they had met the magnificent Madrilenos on this night of nights, when their silky skills elevated the game to new levels of rapture. But, with the occasional hunting horn urging them on and receiving sympathetic applause from the crowd, Eintracht still had enough character to steal a third goal through the ever-alert Stein after a poor back-pass by Vidal. Rangers fans had at least found consolation in that their team had been beaten by a cracking side. But it was not on the same planet as Real's.

For them the ball was a thing of beauty, an instrument of pleasure, a vehicle of delight to be passed around at will, slowly, backwards even, until the goal was in view. Then, switching from a languid, lovely build-up, they would pounce like tigers. It was Swan Lake on turf. Such was the mesmeric quality of play that, when mistakes were made, Wolstenholme would simply say: 'Now that didn't work out, did it?' But, judging by the reception the 127,000 fans gave them, it was not a bad way to spend an evening. 'The crowd would not let them go without parading the cup around the ground,' he recalls. 'And then the Germans formed a guard of honour. I'm sure they'll never forget it. Nor will I.'

Real Madrid: Dominguez, Marquitos, Pachin, Vidal, Santamaria, Zarraga, Canario, Del Sol, di Stefano, Puskas, Gento.

Scorers: di Stefano 3, Puskas 4.

Eintracht Frankfurt: Loy, Lutz, Hoefer, Wellbaecher, Eigenbrodt, Stinka, Kress, Lindner, Stein, Pfaff, Meier.

Scorers: Kress, Stein 2.

Billy Wright

England 3 Hungary 6
Wembley, 25 November 1953

Born 6 February 1924. Once turned away from Molineux for being too small, Wright earned a reprieve for the thorough way he swept the dressing-rooms. Tears turned to triumph as the ironworker's son became a legend, making 490 League appearances for Wolves and 105 for England. An inside forward who switched to wing-half and then to pivot, the Shropshire lad had been an Arsenal fan but became one of Wolves' greatest servants. Took over as captain from Stan Cullis in 1947 and lifted the FA Cup in 1949. Footballer of the Year in 1952, Wright, who was never cautioned, was the supreme exponent of the 'firm but fair' onfield philosophy and won three Championship medals before taking over as manager of Arsenal in 1962. Left in 1966 to become head of sport at ITV until his retirement in 1989.

Billy Wright can still remember their names and rattle them off as if it were yesterday, not a misty November nightmare in 1953. His Hungarian pronunciation is pretty good, too, but then you suspect that he has had a lot of practice. 'Grosics, Buzansky, Lantos . . .' When he gets to 'Hidegkuti', there is a tremor in his voice even now. 'Puskas . . .' and by the time he completes the team with 'Czibor', he's out of breath but full of admiration. Like he was in 1953.

England had never been beaten by overseas opposition at home. There had been a defeat by Eire at Everton in 1949, but that was somehow brushed aside, the Irish Sea being conveniently deemed some sort of British lake. Although England had yet to win the World Cup – indeed, it had been beneath the FA's dignity to enter what was perceived a second-rate competition until 1950 – most citizens believed that Brittania still ruled football's waves. There had been a few ripples of consternation when the United States managed to beat England 1–0 in the 1950 World Cup, but Belo Horizonte was hot and sticky, had a bumpy pitch, a biased ref, and our lads probably ate some of the awful local food the night before. That, too, didn't count.

With players of the calibre of Wright, Stanley Matthews and Stan Mortenson, England were entitled to a little self-confidence. Where they went wrong was in not doing their homework or heeding the warnings. Besides the recent evidence of their own fallibility, the opposition in November 1953 were not the usual mugs. Hungary were Olympic champions and had not lost for twenty-nine matches. 'We just didn't watch our opponents or talk tactics in those days like we do today,' says Wright. 'Walter Winterbottom [England's manager] had seen them wallop France 10–1 and said they were a good side. But this was Wembley, and England had Matthews and Mortenson. You didn't tell players like that how they should play the game. You just let 'em get on with it.'

In contrast, Hungary had the collective discipline that you would expect from an official army side, especially one whose weaponry consisted of ball skills and whose battleground was the enemy penalty area. Under the 'Galloping Major', Ferenc Puskas, manoeuvres were quite simple: keep possession and make opponents chase until they dropped. With his own lethal left foot as the heavy artillery, Puskas had his men honing their techniques until they wore the title 'Magical Magyars' with as much pride as their distinctive blood-red shirts. All this, however, was a mystery to England and the 100,000 fans who filled Wembley on that fateful November afternoon.

It took only a minute for Nandor Hidegkuti, latching on to a pass from Puskas, to shoot Hungary in front. The crowd then watched mesmerised as England were given the runaround, Puskas orchestrating the show and Hidegkuti causing chaos in a normally imperturbable home rearguard. 'The trouble was,' says Wright, 'we had never seen a deep-lying centre-forward before and just did not know how to deal with him. Hidegkuti pulled Harry Johnston out of position and, when he was picked up, it meant greater freedom for the others. They didn't need much space anyway, they were so good on the ball.'

After the initial blow, the Hungarians had the decency to let the crowd recover its composure and did not put the ball in the net again until the 14th minute. It was another Hidegkuti special following phenomenal play by Puskas and Czibor. But, mercifully for England, it was disallowed for off-side, and within a minute Jackie Sewell had equalised. If England felt relieved they had seen nothing yet. 'They came at us and attacked,' says Wright, 'something teams did not do to England at Wembley. It was a shock, all right, to find ourselves running around on our home ground chasing after players we had never heard of.' Thirteen minutes later, these unknown warriors were revered around the football world.

Hidegkuti, who had the unfortunate Johnston blowing like a vacant deckchair on Blackpool beach, made it two before Puskas, with a sleight of foot worthy of Nureyev, had the normally rock-like Wright tackling his shadow before slotting the third. 'Probably the best goal I saw in all my games for England,' the skipper recollects. For good measure, Puskas disdainfully back-heeled a fourth three minutes later which had *Football Monthly* founder Charlie Buchan writing: 'England were outplayed, outgeneralled, outpaced and outshot.' Apart from that, they held their own.

'My feelings at that point,' remembers Wright, 'were to say to the lads that, whatever the lesson we were getting, we were still in there and had to keep going. My attitude is that you don't give in until the 90 minutes are up, and the others felt the same.' The late and great Mortenson certainly did, keeping England just about in touch with a typically bold solo blast just before the half-time whistle. The trouble was, and the fans knew it more than the players, that the home side were flattered by the two-goal margin.

'My job in the dressing-room was to keep up the morale,' says Wright, 'and it was not as difficult as you might imagine. Although we were getting a pasting, the Hungarians had shown that they were vulnerable, as we had scored two goals. Walter Winterbottom had actually seen them practising before the match and said, "If they can shoot like that, we could be in for a hiding." ' But, at the break, Wright, Mortenson and company felt they could get back into it. Ten minutes into the second half everyone knew they could do no such thing.

Bozsik blasted the fifth and Hidegkuti completed his hat-trick, and the rout, after another mesmeric piece of Magyar play. The crowd, which had earlier been aghast at the prospect of England's humiliation, now stood awestruck by the majesty of the Hungarian performance. 'I think they realised that they were watching something that only happens once in a lifetime.' says Wright. Built on a ball control that is seemingly beyond Anglo-Saxons, the Hungarian style was as beautiful as it was bewildering. Puskas's men caressed and cajoled the ball, swept it around like the Harlem Globetrotters without hands; short, slick passes interspersed by occasional long, penetrating ones which were invariably capped by a fierce, devastating shot.

'They were not just a cut above us, they were miles above us,' admits Wright. 'I'll never forget it. We were devastated by a truly great side. We did our best and worked hard, but they were fabulous that day. I honestly think that is when they peaked, and it was a privilege to play against them.' Alf Ramsey coolly slotted home a consolation third from the penalty spot, but it was exhibition stuff at the end and the crowd knew it. But as they trooped into the tube station that night, they at least had the considerable consolation of having witnessed one of the finest performances in the history of the game.

'We could have had ten,' said a jubilant Puskas, 'and yet we had been in awe of the masters of the game.' 'It was a dream come true,' claimed midfielder Jozef Bozsik. Nor was it a fluke: Hungary thrashed England again 7–1 at the end of the season in Budapest. 'We were not at our best that day,' says Wright, 'as we had gone straight there after a very tiring season. But neither time were we disgraced. We should have treated it as a valuable lesson from which we could learn.' Sadly, it seems, we never have.

England: Merrick, Ramsey, Eckersley, Wright, Johnston, Dickinson, Matthews, Taylor, Mortenson, Sewell, Robb.

Scorers: Sewell, Mortenson, Ramsey (pen).

Hungary: Grosics, Buzansky, Lantos, Bozsik, Lorant, Zakarias, Budai, Kocsis, Hidegkuti, Puskas, Czibor.

Scorers: Hidegkuti 3, Puskas 2, Bozsik.

Terry Yorath

Wales 1 Germany 0
European Championship qualifying match, Cardiff, 5 June
1991

*Born 27 March 1950. Won a schoolboy soccer cap for Wales
while at grammar school in Cardiff and could probably have
done likewise at rugby – he was an accomplished scrum-half –
had his father not pushed him into the round-ball game. An
aggressive midfielder, Yorath earned 59 full caps for his
country during a distinguished career that began at Leeds under
Don Revie. Made 143 League appearances for the Elland Road
club before moving to Coventry and then Spurs. Went west to
Vancouver Whitecaps but returned to Yorkshire to play for and
manage Bradford City and then Swansea. Appointed Welsh
national manager in 1989.*

'Germany always qualify, Wales never do,' said Terry
Yorath on the eve of the biggest match of his managership.
'But things can change and I have a feeling that we'll win
by 1–0.' Such a forecast against the unbeaten world
champions was not as outrageous as it might have
appeared; things WERE changing. Wales had already
dealt impressively with Belgium 3–1 in their previous
qualifier and were buoyed by the presence of their
£11million strike force of Ian Rush, Mark Hughes and
Dean Saunders. They were also beginning to benefit from
playing at Cardiff Arms Park and the *hwyl* that goes along
with the famous ground.

Hwyl is that special brand of Welsh passion that is
normally confined to the rugger field but which Yorath
always tried to bring into soccer wherever he played. As
the manager of the national team, he wants it from his

players, the supporters and the whole country. 'There is plenty of room for both sports in Wales,' he insists, 'even at Cardiff Arms Park.'

Yorath, who spent much of his first year in charge of Wales commuting between his Leeds home and Swansea, where he also managed City for a spell, knows just what it has meant to Welsh football to be shunted around, not having a proper home for the national team. He is also fed up with gallant failures. 'That's why our win over Germany, with some great players in the Welsh side, before a good crowd and in a terrific atmosphere at the Arms Park, meant more to me than anything I've done as a player,' he insists. 'It might even change the ways of Welsh football.'

Shortly after being appointed Wales manager as successor to Mike England, Yorath said: 'I've never accepted that soccer should be a second-class sport behind rugby in Wales. After all, John Charles is probably the best known Welsh sportsman, internationally, of the modern era.' Yorath is well aware of the great soccer tradition in South Wales, particularly in the Swansea area, and knows that a return to those standards is long overdue. 'Beating Belgium was a step in that direction and beating Germany an even bigger one. Both wins gave me a terrific amount of satisfaction as manager,' he says. 'To hear a thirty-odd thousand crowd roaring Wales on to victory over the World Cup-holders . . . Yet to be fair to the Welsh public, they have not had a lot to shout about over the years, but these were two of of Wales's best performances since the days of John Charles and Ivor Allchurch.'

Yorath does not need reminding that the last time Wales qualified for the final stages of a major championship was in 1958 when Charles and Allchurch were playing, as were Jack Kelsey, Terry Medwin and Cliff Jones. It was quite a side, but thirty-three years is a long time not to make an impact, a long time to have to live on memories. 'We have some very good players in our side now, and I am determined that they won't go through their careers without featuring in a major championship and getting some glory at international level,' he adds. 'People like Neville Southall, Ian Rush, and now Mark Hughes have won plenty at club level but they've missed out internationally, having to sit at home in front of the telly when the World Cup was on. I hope they watched it thinking: "I'd like a bit of that myself." '

The way Wales set about the seemingly invincible Germans suggested that they had. Taking their manager's assertion that victory was 'up for grabs', Wales's less experienced players such as Paul Bodin, Mark Aizlewood and Andy Melville grew in confidence against those highly-paid mercenaries of the Italian League, Matthaus, Voller and Klinsmann. When Barry Horne grazed the crossbar in an indistinguished first half, it was enough to have the first rendering of *Land of my Fathers* ringing round the ground. But nearby residents might have thought the All Blacks had been beaten when Rush raced through in the 66th minute to produce the kind of finish he normally reserves for the Anfield Kop.

The Germans were not quite their organised selves as Matthaus, worried about a thigh injury, had not come out for the second half and Berthold had been sent off for kicking Kevin Ratcliffe; but it was still a fine goal. Latching on to a long punt from Bodin, the Liverpool ace outpaced Buchwald and aimed a fierce shot past the advancing Illgner for his 19th and most vital strike in 51 games for his country. 'Pulling on a red Wales shirt means a lot to me,' Rush has always said, and there has never been any reason to doubt it, even if he has found goals much harder to come by at international level. After that it was a case of hanging on and leaving it to that other Welsh 'Scouse' hero, 'keeper Neville Southall, who defied an increasingly desperate German attack with some fine saves.

'I looked at this as any other game,' said Yorath. 'But this is the first time in nine matches that we have beaten the Germans, and that makes me proud. There was a feeling all over Wales that we would win. We've got our tactics right, playing with a sweeper, and those lads up front worked very hard for us.'

If the win was not the perfect illustration that Yorath's highly-rated trio of Rush, Hughes and Saunders can function as an effective unit, it showed that Rush can be lethal in his other red shirt and that Hughes can play just behind the front pair. There had been times when playing just Rush and Hughes up front had seemed a bit like donning diamonds to do the washing-up, such was the poverty in the midfield workhouse. When the pair failed to produce their customary quota of goals, there had been pressure on Yorath to jettison the partnership. But, after five goalless games in the World Cup qualifying group, Rush had pleaded: 'Don't split us up. I know we have not scored but we honestly have not had the chances. You could count the number we've had in the five games on one hand. Whenever the team has played well in other matches, it's been either Mark or myself who has scored. It's rubbish to say that we don't complement each other.'

Yorath, whose urbane managerial manner belies his 'hard man' reputation as a player, agreed. He is also shrewd enough to know that, if Wales are going to get anywhere, they do not possess the depth of talent to dispense with even one of their few world-class players. Indeed, the scale of the achievement is truly monumental, for Germany included twelve of their World Cup-winning squad while Yorath had to scour such unfashionable places as Oxford, Norwich and Bristol City to rustle up his eleven. 'I only really have about thirty-five players to choose from anyway,' he says. There are just 51,500 players registered in Wales against 5.3 million in the new Germany. The rewards are commensurate: Yorath was hired on a part-time basis and paid £15,000 a year; his opposite number, Berti Vogts, earns £175,000.

Welsh soccer has endured much torment at both club

and national level since the gentle giant, John Charles, and the golden skills of Ivor Allchurch departed the scene. At club level, only John Toshack's remarkable tenure at Swansea produced success, but that was to be so brief that it was almost an illusion. But with a strike force of Rush, Saunders, Hughes and that new acquisition, *hwyl*, Yorath is hoping that the current revival will be the start of something permanent.

Wales: Southall, Phillips, Bodin, Aizlewood, Melville, Ratcliffe, Nicholas, Saunders, Rush, Hughes, Horne.

Sub: Speed (Saunders).

Scorer: Rush.

Germany: Illgner, Reuter, Brehme, Kohler, Berthold, Buchwald, Helmer, Sammer, Voller, Matthaus, Klinsmann.

Sub: Doll (Matthaus).

Alex Young

Everton 3 Sheffield Wednesday 2
FA Cup final, Wembley, 14 May 1966

Born 3 February 1937. A graceful centre-forward who found his way to Hearts via Broughton Star, Musselburgh Union and Newtongrange Star. Won a Scottish Cup-winners' medal at Tynecastle in 1956 and League Championships in 1958 and 1960, when he also collected the Scottish League Cup, before arriving at Goodison Park for £40,000. In 1962–63 he was an ever-present in the first Everton team to win the Championship since 1939. Added an FA Cup-winners' medal in 1966, but gained a niggardly eight Scottish caps, besides six at Under-23 level and two Scottish League appearances. Left Goodison after seven years and 77 goals in 228 First Division matches. Such was the depth of feeling when he was replaced by Joe Royle that manager Harry Catterick was assaulted by a gang in the car park. Young finished his days at Stockport after a brief spell as player-manager of Glentoran.

It is somehow typical of Alex Young to select a game in which his own performance was overshadowed by a team-mate whom he hardly knew, whose name no one could pronounce and with whom he had virtually no understanding. 'Aye, but winning the FA Cup has to beat just about anything,' he reasons. 'Especially when you experience all the emotions – favourites, flops and finally winners in the 90 minutes.'

Everton were the first club in sixty-three years to reach Wembley without conceding a goal and were overwhelming favourites to beat Wednesday, who had battled long and hard to arrive at their fifth final without having been drawn at home. Sheffield had the spirit, it was

reckoned, but Everton had the class, none more so than the
'Golden Vision'. Only 5ft 8in, Young was not in the
traditional mould of Goodison centre-forwards and relied
on a masterly ability that was more Ivor Allchurch than
Dixie Dean or Tommy Lawton. But Young always seemed to
have more room and more time than mere also-rans, and his
general onfield demeanour led Evertonians to worship him.
'Wembley,' they said, 'would be his perfect stage.'

Young had formed a partnership with the rugged Fred
Pickering, and the pair were the perfect foils for each
other, 'Young oozing class with every blink of the eyelids,'
according to some of his more devoted followers, and
Pickering a more forceful presence in the old-fashioned
manner. The only trouble was, Pickering had been
injured. Although fit again, he had yet to hint at his
previous sharpness, and manager Harry Catterick, taking
his courage into his hands, elected to play Mike Trebilcock, a £20,000 signing from Plymouth who was unheard
of by most viewers and only just known to his team-mates.

'It was one of the great Cup final selection gambles,'
says Young, 'and to be honest, Mike hardly looked as if he
should have been out there for the first 45 minutes. I don't
think he touched the ball before half-time. But it didn't
bother me because I was just doing my own thing while he
got on with his. I felt a wee bit sorry for him at one stage
but was soon feeling even sorrier for myself when we went
0–1 down.' After just four minutes, a Jim McCalliog shot
hit Ray Wilson and sped past Gordon West. 'They were
playing very well and we were hardly playing at all.'

Wednesday pounded the Merseyside defence, but in the
19th minute Everton broke away. It was a characteristic
piece of Young sleight of foot which had taken him
through with only Springett to beat, but the goalie brought
him down. 'Penalty,' roared 30,000 Merseysiders, but the
referee would have none of it.

'I thought the ref was a bit too far behind play to make
the decision,' says Young, 'and I felt aggrieved. What's

more, I allowed it to affect me. So, I think, did the rest of the team. In fact, there was a feeling that it was slipping away from us quite early on. Wednesday were shaping really well, but we just hadn't fired and it wasn't a very good game. At half-time, we decided we had better do something pretty quick or we'd lose, and I went through again only to see Springett make a marvellous one-handed save. Not what we needed four minutes into the half. As we got frustrated, Wednesday became more confident, and they scored again.'

Eight minutes after the Springett save, Johnny Fantham made a run, beat a statuesque Everton defence and fired a powerful drive which West could not hold; Ford slammed in the rebound. Worry turned to despair for the Merseyside masses, and hundreds began to head for the turnstiles. Young admits: 'At that point we really thought it was just not going to be our day.' But from nowhere, out of nothing, Trebilcock of all people pounced. A moment's sloppiness in the Sheffield defence, and the man from the West Country unleashed a shot that sailed past Springett to breathe new life into the favourites. 'It was all we needed,' says Young.

Everton belatedly discovered their form. Young was popping up in places where Wednesday's rugged defence didn't want him, while Derek Temple's darting runs suddenly contained more menace. The terraces were a sea of blue, and the shimmering skills of Young began to shine. The 'Golden Vision' had already won a Scottish Cup-winners' medal; now he wanted the FA Cup to go along with it.

It was only six minutes later that Alex Scott's free-kick was not properly cleared and, amid a mounting crescendo, Trebilcock ensured his place in the annals with a second goal. 'There is nothing quite like coming back from the dead,' says Young, 'and I'll never forget the relief we all felt – and the crowd. Oh, that day the Everton fans were fantastic.' Yet minutes before, some had been leaving. Fantastic but fickle.

'Now we felt it WAS going to be our day,' chuckled Young, who admits, 'I don't think I played that well, but you forget your own performance at times like that. Now we were going for the kill.' There were ten minutes of an already dramatic final left, and the ball was with West who hit a long punt upfield. Gerry Young was underneath it, but the Sheffield defender failed to control it and the ball bounced away from him. There was a surge of expectancy about the Blues fans as they scented blood, and Temple raced on to the loose ball like a terrier. The winger controlled the ball and advanced on the Wednesday goal. There was only Springett to beat. 'No side had come from 0–2 down in the FA Cup final to win at Wembley; that was the stuff of fantasy,' says Young. 'Yet here we were on the edge of doing it in 15 minutes. We hardly dared to look.'

Temple kept on and calmly rounded Springett to slot the ball into an empty net. He had rounded off Wembley's biggest ever turnaround. There was pandemonium on the terraces and something similar on the pitch. 'We just couldn't take it in,' says Young. 'It was unbelievable.' Wednesday were understandably distraught, Everton simply delirious. After the final whistle, people came on to the pitch. Catterick, previously castigated, was chaired on supporters' shoulders, and Trebilcock treated like royalty. Young, as ever, was worshipped by his Goodison flock. The 'Golden Vision' had seen the light at the Wembley tunnel.

Everton: West, Wright, Wilson, Gabriel, Labone, Harris, Scott, Trebilcock, A. Young, Harvey, Temple.

Scorers: Trebilcock 2, Temple.

Sheffield Wednesday: Springett, Smith, Megson, Eustace, Ellis, G. Young, Pugh, Fantham, McCalliog, Ford, Quinn.

Scorers: McCalliog, Ford.

ARMS Therapy Centres and Support Groups

ARMS
Action and Research
for Multiple Sclerosis

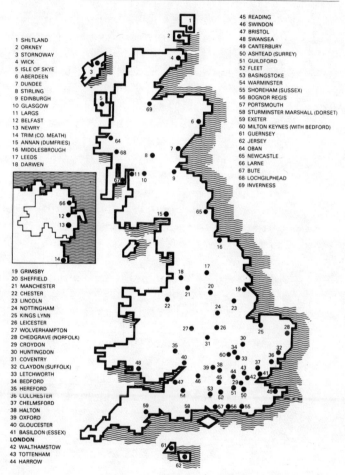

1 SHETLAND
2 ORKNEY
3 STORNOWAY
4 WICK
5 ISLE OF SKYE
6 ABERDEEN
7 DUNDEE
8 STIRLING
9 EDINBURGH
10 GLASGOW
11 LARGS
12 BELFAST
13 NEWRY
14 TRIM (CO. MEATH)
15 ANNAN (DUMFRIES)
16 MIDDLESBROUGH
17 LEEDS
18 DARWEN

19 GRIMSBY
20 SHEFFIELD
21 MANCHESTER
22 CHESTER
23 LINCOLN
24 NOTTINGHAM
25 KINGS LYNN
26 LEICESTER
27 WOLVERHAMPTON
28 CHEDGRAVE (NORFOLK)
29 CROYDON
30 HUNTINGDON
31 COVENTRY
32 CLAYDON (SUFFOLK)
33 LETCHWORTH
34 BEDFORD
35 HEREFORD
36 COLCHESTER
37 CHELMSFORD
38 HALTON
39 OXFORD
40 GLOUCESTER
41 BASILDON (ESSEX)
LONDON
42 WALTHAMSTOW
43 TOTTENHAM
44 HARROW

45 READING
46 SWINDON
47 BRISTOL
48 SWANSEA
49 CANTERBURY
50 ASHTEAD (SURREY)
51 GUILDFORD
52 FLEET
53 BASINGSTOKE
54 WARMINSTER
55 SHOREHAM (SUSSEX)
56 BOGNOR REGIS
57 PORTSMOUTH
58 STURMINSTER MARSHALL (DORSET)
59 EXETER
60 MILTON KEYNES (WITH BEDFORD)
61 GUERNSEY
62 JERSEY
64 OBAN
65 NEWCASTLE
66 LARNE
67 BUTE
68 LOCHGILPHEAD
69 INVERNESS

For more information, contact: ARMS, 4a Chapel Hill, Stansted, Essex CM24 8AG. Tel 0279 815553